GANN MASTERS II

HALLIKER'S INC.

Parts of this book were reprinted from the copyrighted Ganntrader Software manual with permission of Peter Pich of the Gannsoft Publishing Company. Without Peter this book would not have been possible. The Ganntrader software program is unique and is made possible through the long hours of work from Peter.

Copyright © 2001 Halliker's, Inc.

Parts of this book were reprinted from the Ganntrader Software manual with permission of Peter Pich of the Gannsoft Publishing Company.

Published by Halliker's, Inc.

No part of this publication may be reproduced, stored in a retrieval system or transmitted in any form or by any means, electronic, mechanical, photocopying, recording, scanning or otherwise, except as permitted under Sections 107 or 108 of the 1976 United Stated Copyright Act, without either the prior written permission of the Publisher, or authorization through payment of the appropriate per-copy fee to the Copyright Clearance Center, 222 Rosewood Drive, Danvers, MA 01923, (978) 750-8400, fax (978) 750-4744. Requests to the Publisher for permission should be addressed to the Permissions Department, Halliker's, Inc. 2508 W. Grayrock St, Springfield, MO 65810. Phone (417) 882-9697, Fax (417) 886-5180. E-Mail: publisher@tradersworld.com

This publication is written to provide accurate information in regard to the subject matter covered. It is sold with the understanding that the publisher is not engaged in rendering professional services. If professional advice or other expert assistance is required, the services of a competent professional person should be sought.

CAVEAT: It should be noted that all commodity trades, patterns, charts, systems, etc., discussed in this book are for illustrative purposes only and are not to be considered as specific advisory recommendations. Further note that no method of trading or investing is foolproof or without difficulty, and past performance is no guarantee of future performance. All ideas and material presented are entirely those of the author and do not reflect those of the publisher or bookseller.

Ganntrader is a trademark of Gannsoft Publishing Company. Quicktrieve is a trademark of Commodity Systems Inc. IBM is a trademark of the IBM Corporation. Computrac is a trademark of The Technical Analysis Group, Division of Telerate, MetaStock is a trademark of Equis.

Library of Congress Cataloging-in-Publication Data:

ISBN-13: 978-1494711153

Printed in the United States of America

This book is dedicated to W.D. Gann, Peter Pich and all the Gann students in the world who have spend endless hours doing the study and research necessary to understand the mathematics behind the financial markets.

Table of Contents

Introduction 7
Holidays and Weekends 8
Printer Chart Setup 13
Density 14
Adding Blank Space 15
Chart Scale 16
Volume and Open Interest 17
Close Only Charts 19
Grid on the Screen 21
The Tool Bar 22
Invert Price 23
Inverted Dec British Pound Chart 23
Printing Charts 24
Time Span 25
Special Charts 29
Rescaling Charts 30
Printer and Screen Differences 31
Swing Chart (Standard) 32
How to Use the SW and MT Swing Chart 34
Swing Chart (Enhanced) 35
Angles 37
Selected Angles 38
Other Selected Angles 40
Intersecting Angles 42
Two Different Angles 43
True Trend Line 44
Swing Angles 47
Dimension Lines 48
The 1x1 Angle 50
Setting the 1x1 Angle 52
Values for the 1x1 Angle 53
The Live 1x1 Angle 55
Mirror Image Foldbacks 57
Zero Angles 60
Sizes Labels and Markers 62
Squares 64
Natural Squares 66
Temporary Squares Made Permanent 69
Squares of Highs and Lows 70
Modifying an Existing Square 72
Division of the Range 73
Price Targets Using Ranges 74
Price Targets Using 7 Times the Base 75

Squaring a Range with the Mouse	76
Squaring Time with the Mouse	78
Temporary Squares Made Permanent	80
Deleting a Square	80
Temporary Squares:	80
Permanent Squares:	80
Square of 9	81
Square of 9 Time Divisions	84
Square of 9 Price Divisions	85
Other Price and Time Divisions	86
Increment Value	87
Square of 9 Circle Price Lines	88
Square of 9 from a High or Low	90
Other Square of 9 Circle Sizes	91
Time Cycles	92
What is Astrology?	93
Geocentric Planets	94
F1 = Mercury	95
F2 = Venus	96
F3 = Sun or Earth	96
F4 = Mars	97
F5 = Jupiter	97
F6 = Saturn	98
F7 = Uranus	98
F8 = Neptune	99
F9 = Pluto	99
F10 = Signs of the Zodiac	100
F11 = Moon	100
F12 = Moon's Node	101
Heliocentric Planets	102
F1 = Mercury	103
F2 = Venus	103
F3 = Sun or Earth	104
F4 = Mars	104
F5 = Jupiter	105
F6 = Saturn	105
F7 = Uranus	106
F8 = Neptune	106
F9 = Pluto	107
F10 = Signs of the Zodiac	107
F11 = Moon	108
F12 = Moon's Node	108
Planet Angle	109
Time Cycles as Support and Resistance	110
Time Cycles and Time Measurement	113
Transits or Time by Degrees	115

- Averages of the Planets 117
  - Average of 5 117
  - MOf, Mean of 5 118
  - Average of 6 118
  - CE, Circle of 8 119
  - Jupiter through Pluto 120
  - Mars through Pluto 121
  - All except Sun in Geocentric 121
  - All except Earth in Heliocentric 122
  - All planets and the Sun/Earth 122
- Latitude and Declination 123
- Parallels and Contra-Parallels 125
- Dimension 127
- Squaring a Circle 129
- Basic Arcs and Circles 134
- Using Arcs and Circles to Project Price 138
- Vertical Points in Arcs Project Reactions 139
- Expansions of Arcs and Circles 141
- Square Root Expansions 142
- Inside Radii Contractions – Chart #12 143
- Square Root of 3 – Chart #13, Chart #14 144
- Third Dimension Factor – Chart #15, Chart #16, Chart #17 145
- Miscellaneous Expansions 146
- Odd & Even Squares – Chart #18 147
- Odd & Even Square Time Expansions – Chart #19, Chart 20 148
  - Fibonacci Expansions 148
- Modify an Existing Setup 152
- Batch Mode 153
- Default File Setup 154
- Batch Files 155
  - New Name 156
  - Include Set-Up 156
  - Delete 156
  - Show Contents 156
  - Show Chart 156
  - Include Set-Up 156
  - Delete 157
  - Show Chart 157
  - Print List 157
  - Parameters Saved in a Set-Up 158
  - Some Limitations 158
- Putting It All Together 160
- Appendix A 163
- Degree Assignments for Zodiac Signs 163
- Planetary Cycles 164
- Appendix B 165

May Coffee Santos D	166
March Coffee	167
Heliocentric Saturn	168
Heliocentric Planets	169
Important Dates Each Month	170
Heliocentric and Geocentric Aspects	171
Geocentric Maps Movement	172
Soybean Price Resistance Levels	173
Active Angles and Degrees	175
24 Revolutions of Time and Price	176
24 Cent Moves or More	177
Appendix C	178
View Menu	179
Setup Menu	180
Time Cycle Menu	182
Third Dimension Menu	183
Options Menu	184
Tool Bar	185
Appendix D	187
SVGA Video Configuration	187
Authorization Manager	187
Remaining Installations	187
Ganntrader Program Folder	187
Norton Utilities Error [301.2]	188
Error [001.2]	188
Gannsoft Publishing Co. License Agreement	214
Configuration	215
Install the Program	216
Selecting an Item	218
Configure System	219
Holiday Date List	222
Miscellaneous Button	224
Printer Preferences	225
Screen Preferences	226
New Chart Preferences	229
Discount Coupon for Purchase of Ganntrader 3.0 Software	231

Introduction

For those traders who have read Gann's books or studied his Trading Courses the name of W.D. Gann and his accomplishments are well known. For the others, a brief outline of his record should prove interesting. Gann is considered to be one of the most successful commodity traders in history. In a career that spanned over 50 years, he is supposed to have taken 50 million dollars out of the stock and commodity markets. The accuracy of these figures cannot be verified but it is known that Mr. Gann lived quite well for his time.

There were several magazine and newspaper articles that described his accomplishments. One observer watched Gann make 286 stock transactions during the month of October 1909. Of those trades, 264 or 92% were profitable. On another occasion, he turned a $130 account into $12,000 in less than a month. He had the ability to call a market turn within one day and highs and lows to an eighth of a point. All of these claims are a matter of public record.

Gann's trading philosophy can be described in his own words:
Through the law of vibration every stock and commodity in the marketplace moves in its own distinctive sphere of activities, as to intensity, volume and direction; all the essential qualities of its evolution is characterized in its own rate of vibration. Stocks and commodities, like atoms, are really centers of energies, therefore they are controlled mathematically. They create their own field of action and power; power to attract and repel, which explains why certain stocks and commodities at times lead the market and turn dead at other times. Thus to speculate scientifically it is absolutely necessary to obey natural law. Vibration is fundamental; nothing is exempt from this law; it is universal, therefore applicable to every class of phenomena on the globe. Thus, I affirm, every class of phenomena, whether in nature or in the market, must be subject to the universal laws of causation, harmony and vibration.

The purpose of this book is to show you what can be done forecasting the markets via Gann methods through the use of the unique Ganntrader 3.0 program produced by Peter Pich. Gann discovered some valuable but often unbelievable laws that govern the markets. The primary purpose of Ganntrader is to allow you an efficient way to test Gann's discoveries in order to confidently integrate them into your own trading system. The following will go through actual software program setup so you understand the basics of the entire process.

Holidays and Weekends

There are two ways to plot charts. One way is to have trading days plotted on the chart without weekends and holidays. The other way is to have trading days plotted on the chart with spaces for the weekends and holidays.

Which way is better? Probably plotting the trading days with spaces for the weekends and holidays is better. Time is continuous. It does not stop because the trading day stops.

In the end both methods do come out about the same.

There are 52 weeks in a year and 6 holidays.

Trading days are 52 x 5 less 6 holidays, which equals 254 days.

254 trading days divided by 365 equals 69.5%.

Take a timing cycle of 144 days times 69.5% and you get 101 days.

101 X 1.382 (Fibonacci number) equals 139 days.

With Ganntrader set the type of daily trading chart by clicking the type of trading day you desire. You can plot a regular 5 Trading Day Chart, a 6 Trading Day Chart, a 7 Day Chart or a 5 Day Chart.

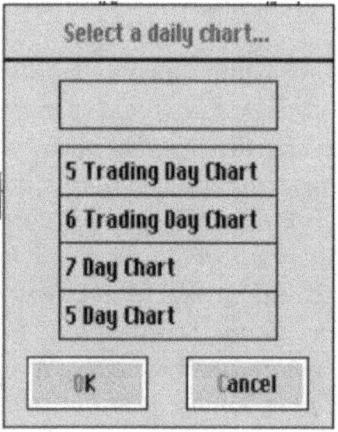

Daily Chart Type

If you take out the weekend, then you must also take out holidays to be consistent. Ganntrader does allow you to do this. Look at figure 2. On the second row of buttons there is Holidays, which allows for the entry of those future holidays that fall on a weekday. When printing a trading day chart these days will not be printed in the extra blank grid lines at the end of the chart. It only affects trading day charts and only those holidays that occur on Monday through Friday that might otherwise be printed in the extra blank grids at the end of the chart.

For example, Independence Day 1999 falls on a Sunday but the following Monday, July 5 will be a trading holiday in most markets. If you were making a trading day chart that had extra blank grid lines that included July 5 no blank bar would be excluded in the chart. A calendar day chart includes weekends as well as holidays so this feature is not used for them. Once a holiday date is surrounded by valid data that holiday can be removed or replaced with a later holiday date. Holidays contained within the date range of the data file are marked as such and can easily be skipped by the program when necessary but there must be a way to tell the program about holidays out into the future. Future year's holidays should be entered here as necessary. Your broker should be able to supply you with market holiday closing dates at least a year in advance.

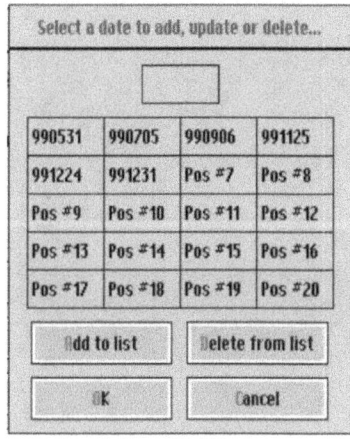
Select Holidays

The following is an example of a 5-Day Chart. Just trading days are plotted. There are no gaps in the prices. Most traders prefer this type of plot, even through it may not be the best.

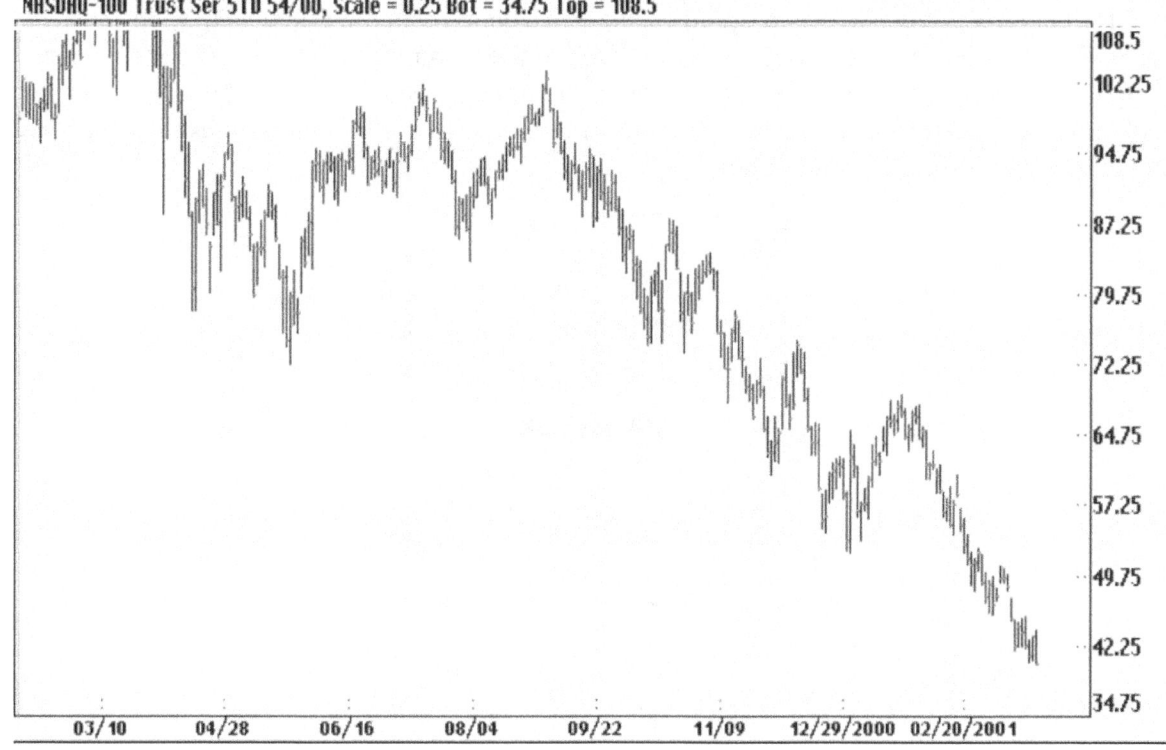

The following is an example of a 7-Day Chart. See the gaps in the chart. This type of chart is called a calendar day type. It is probably the best mathematically correct chart.

Which is the best time span of chart to chart. Gann supposedly used daily, weekly and monthly charts for his forecasting. A good program will allow you to maintain all these time formats and more with just a click of your mouse program. One of the Gann theories is that if a method of trading is valid then it must work the same way will all time frames, (minute, hourly, daily, weekly monthly, quarterly, yearly etc.). If it doesn't work with all the time frames the same way then the method of trading is not valid.

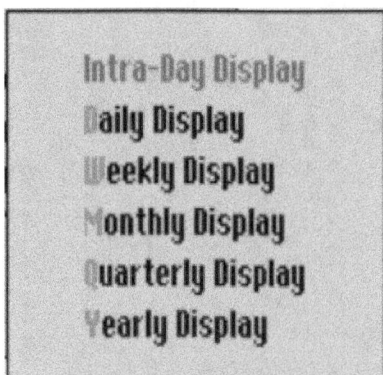

Time Span of Chart

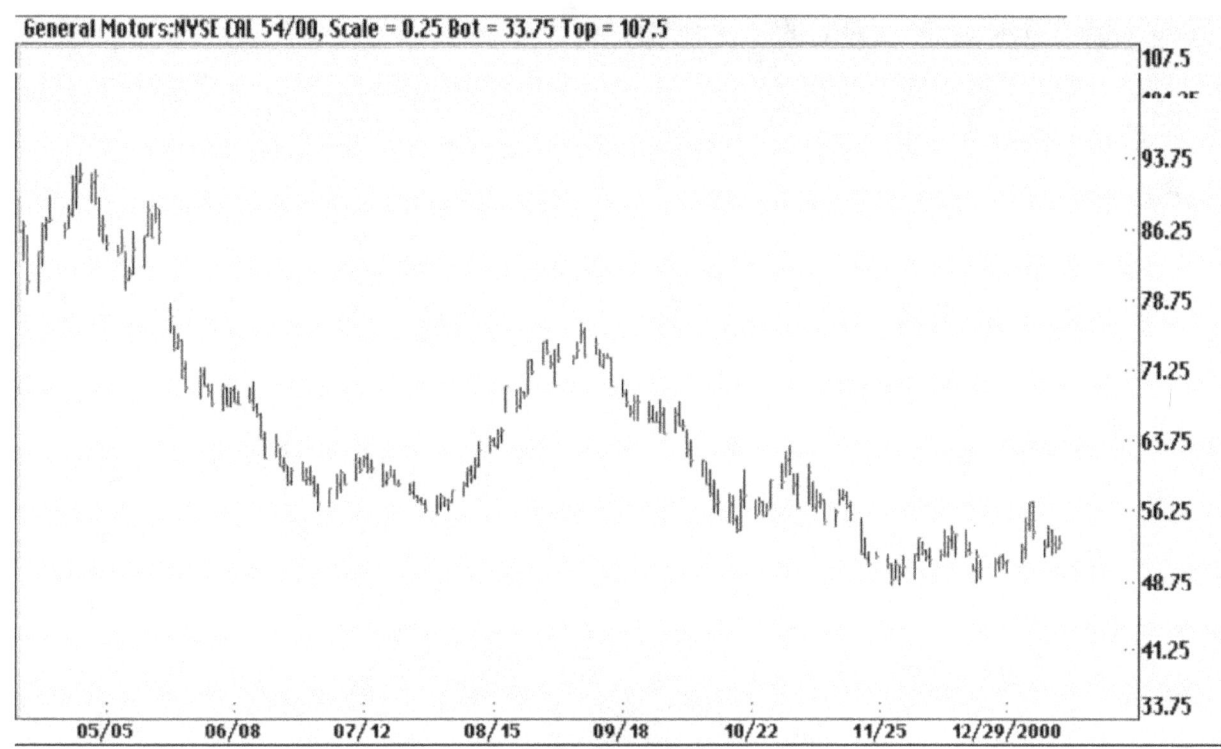
Daily Chart of GM

Weekly Chart of GM

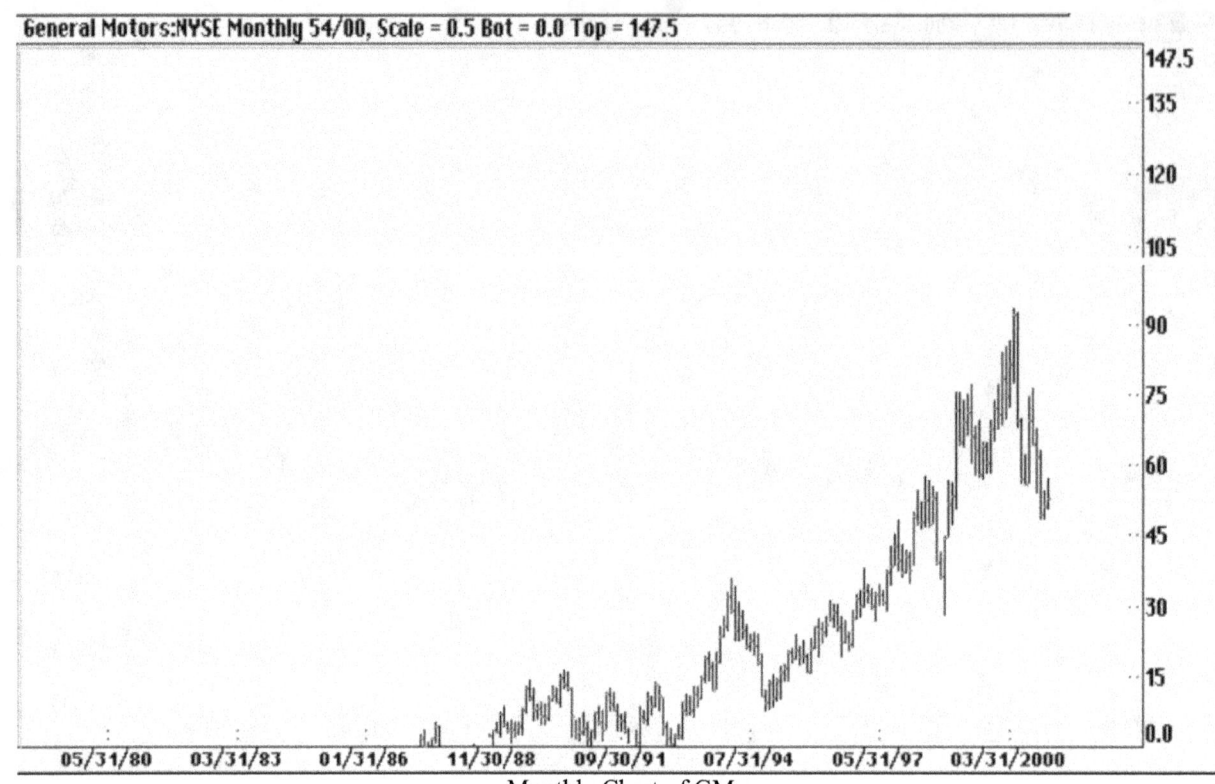

Monthly Chart of GM

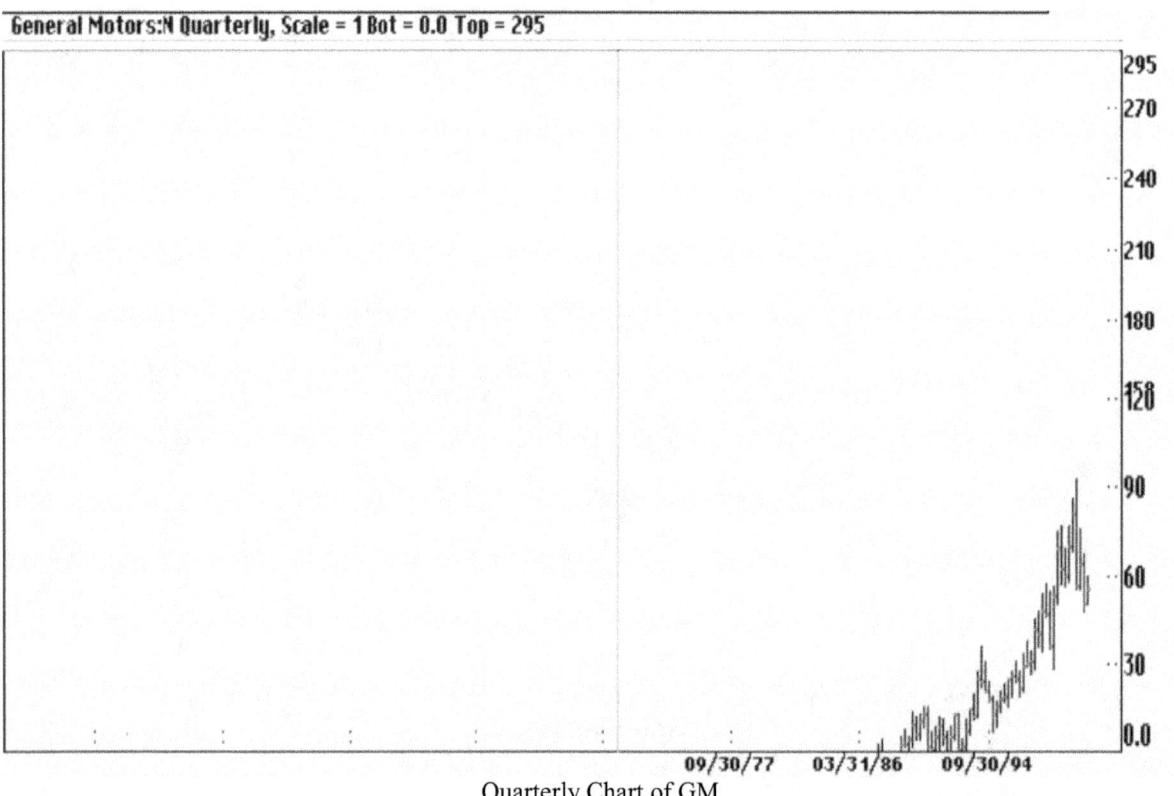

Quarterly Chart of GM

Printer Chart Setup

Many times it is necessary for you to print out a chart to have the perspective to trade like Gann did. You must be able to see the beginnings of trends many years back. With Ganntrader you can print out almost any chart you need for this purpose. The best printer to use is a continuous dot matrix type by Epson. The 15" wide carriage is preferable to the narrow type. You can buy a case of continuous 15" wide paper for around $20.00, which will last you a long time. Grid refers to the dark grid line pattern (8x8, 8x10 or 10x10) or the line that is emphasized when printing. The 10x10 mode is useful for markets that trade in tenths and the 8x10 is better for markets such as T-bonds that trade in multiples of 8. For example, a scale of .125 or 4-32 per grid line would create a full point difference at each emphasized grid line on the chart. The 8x8 pattern matches standard chart paper that you may be using.

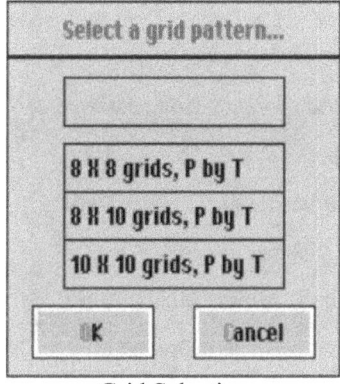
Grid Selection

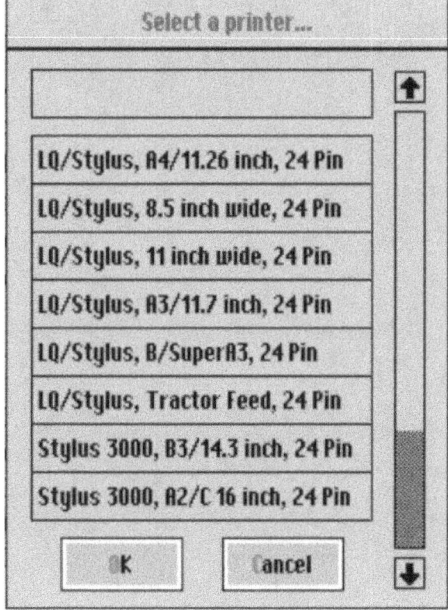
Select a Printer

Density

Refers to grid lines per inch. This is how dark you chart prints. LQ printers offer densities of 8, 10, 12, 15, 18, 20, 22 ½, 30 and 36 grids per inch. Grid lines of 8, 12, 18, 24 per inch are available on the 9 pin printers. Twelve per inch is a good place to start. The light or heavy pattern refers to the number of dots that are used to draw each grid line. The light pattern has a dot at the intersection of the vertical and horizontal lines. The heavy pattern has several dots instead. Most users prefer the light pattern because it makes a chart that is less busy looking and is thus easier to see the other lines that are being plotted. The smaller the grids the more grids you can have on a chart but at the expense of readability. The smaller girds print more than one grid each time the print head moves across the page so the denser grids will print faster.

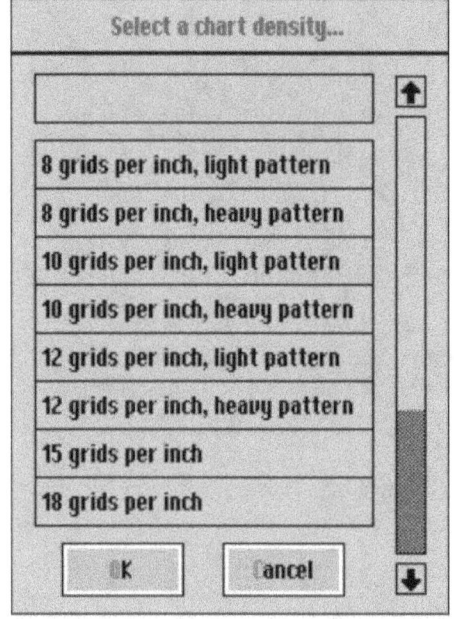

Chart Density

Adding Blank Space

You need room at the end of your chart to plot squares, angle lines and timing cycles. Some programs do not allow you to do this. If you have one of these programs, you probably need to get rid of it and switch to Ganntrader which allows it. Is is absolutely necessary to have this feature for any serious Gann studend. In the Ganntrader program can add extra blank grids to the end of the chart by simply hitting the <+> and <-> keys on the keyboard or the numeric keypad. Each keystroke will add or remove 20 grids to the end of the chart. The default setting for the blank grids is usually 20 but you can enter any desired value under Options: Configure System: Miscellaneous: Extra Grids. The blank space feature is important for longer term forecasting. You will want enough space to all you to determine future turning points. Your Gann angles, squares and timing points will converse out in the future. You should use the Gann Squares, Angles and Cycles to forecast future turning points in both time and price.

Adding Blank Space

Chart Scale

You need to set your chart scale for the prices you are working with. In Ganntrader when a data file is loaded for the first time it will be scaled by the program so that the price bars will fill the screen or will be scaled so that the price bars will fill a printed chart. This is determined by the status of Options: Scale Screen. If this feature is active it will have a check or tick mark in front of it. Scale Screen, when active, will attempt to fill the screen with that portion of the data that is on the screen, rescaling as necessary. When not active the program selects a chart scaling that would guarantee that the entire file would require no more than one sheet of paper to print the price dimension of the chart. As a matter of fact the program automatically reverts to file scaling when you select File: Print Chart regardless of the Scale Screen setting.

The status of Scale Screen can be saved by selecting Options: Configure System and click the Save button. Once a chart is on the screen you can change the scale in quick increments by using the <Ctrl><Page Up> or <Ctrl><Page Down> keys on the keyboard. These key combinations will double or half the current scale settings. Hit the <Home> key to return to the current price bar and automatically rescale the screen. A related item under the Options menu is Auto Center. With this option active the program will attempt to re-center the price bars on the screen as you use the <Ctrl><PageUp> or <Ctrl><Page Down> keys. It can generally be left active and its status will be saved by selecting Options: Configure System and dick the Save button.

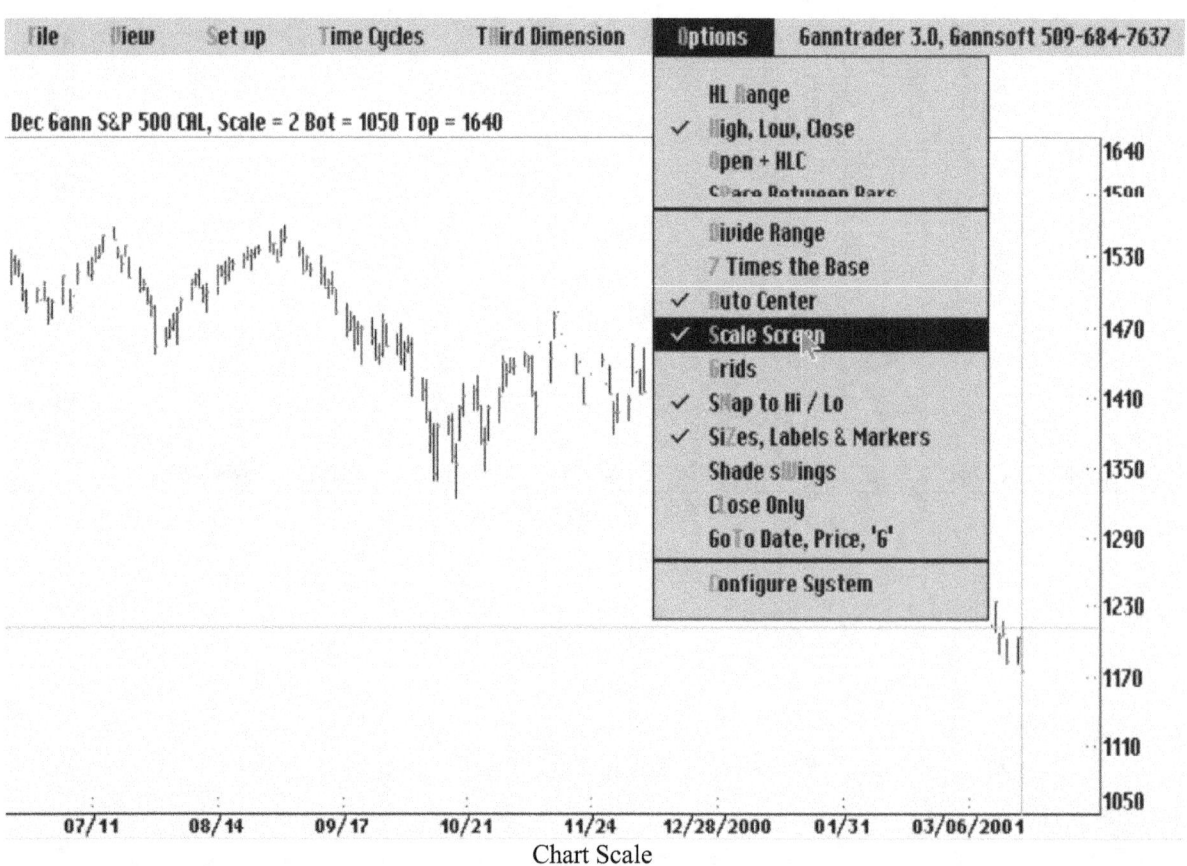

Chart Scale

Volume and Open Interest

Volume and Open Interest is absolutely necessary. These need to be monitored constantly. Ganntrader can display total volume; total open interest or contract volume and contract open interest depending on the type of data loaded. Not all futures contracts contain both total and contract volume and open interest. Stocks will only have total volume. Select Volume and Open Interest under the View menu.

You can change the default scaling for the Volume and Open Interest window by clicking the Left and Right mouse buttons inside the window.

For an up trend to be considered valid the volume must increase and for a downtrend the volume to be considered valid the volume must also increase. Counter trend movements must show a decrease in volume. Open interest should increase in an up trend and the same way as volume increase in a down trend for the trend to be valid. Increasing open interest means that positions are being added.

It is necessary to watch both volume and open interest to know the trend of the market. This gives you a picture of the underlying trend of the market. See the first chart below showing both open interest and volume.

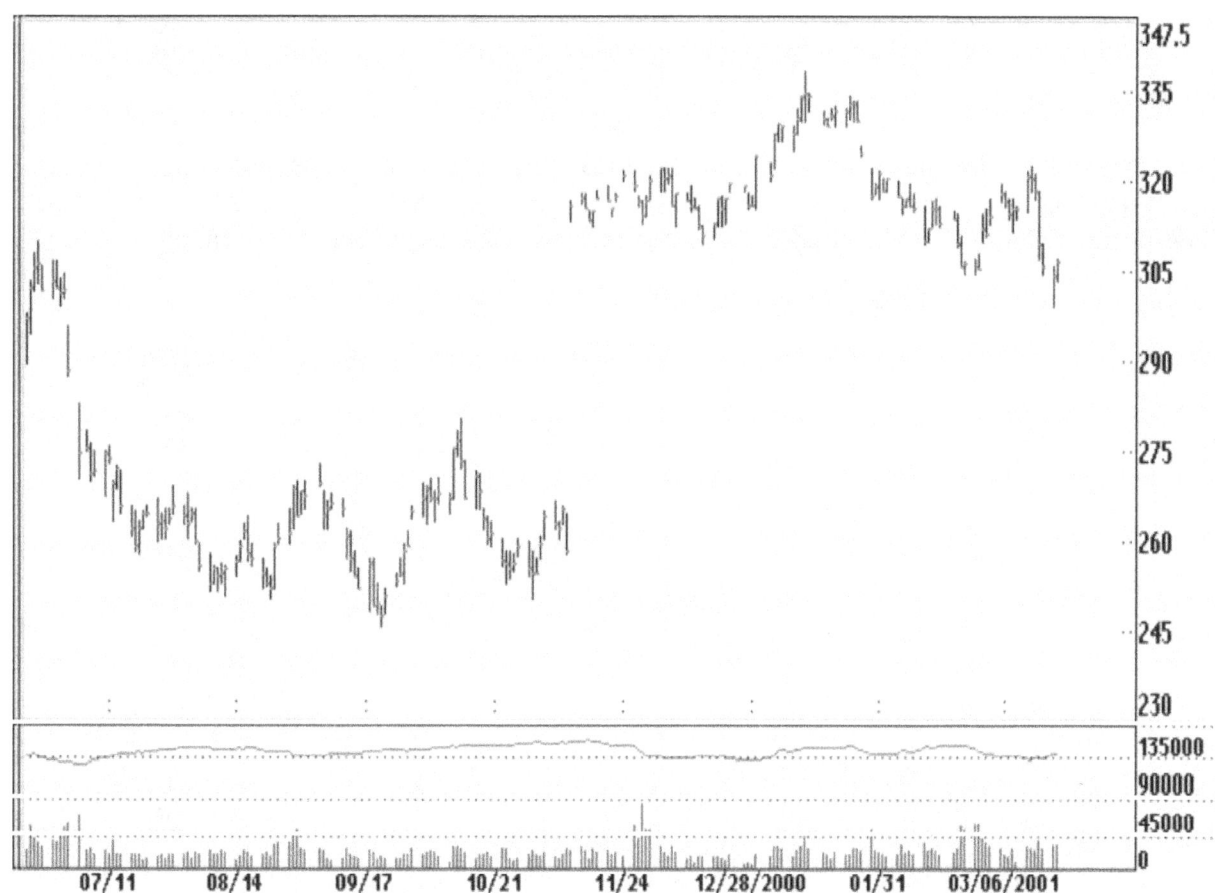

In this chart only volume and prices are displayed to clearly indicate the principals. If you look at A you will see volume increasing with an upward trend in price and volume decreasing with a downturn in price. See however at B with an up trend in price volume no longer increases indicating that the trend is no longer upward. At C you see volume increasing with the downward move and decreasing with the upward move to D which is now very bearish.

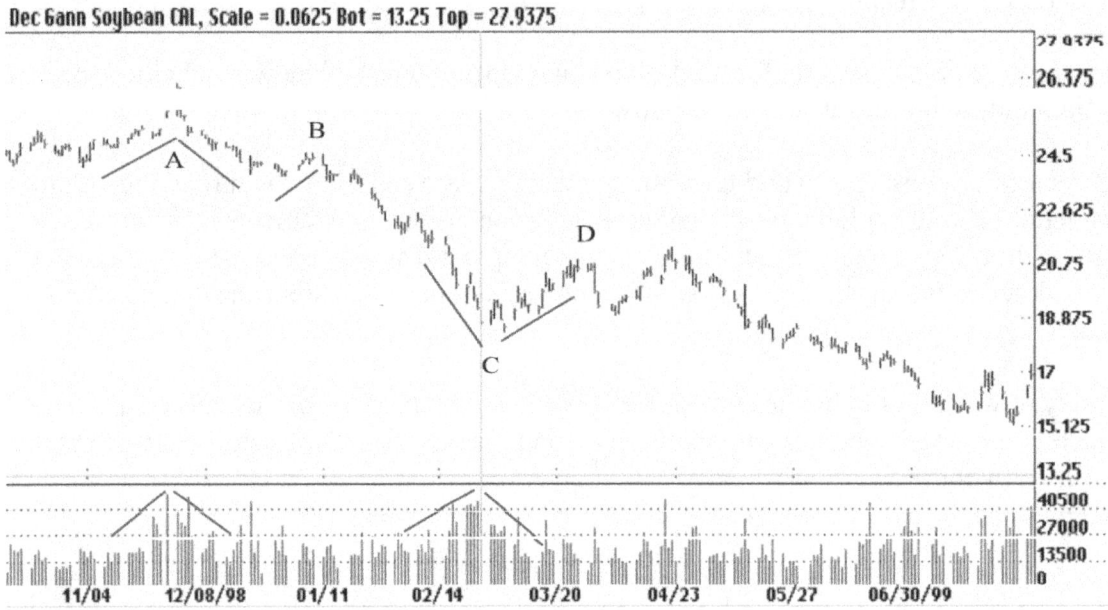

Now look at the following chart. From point A to B open interest increases indicating shorts are increasing their position. From point B to C open interest stays the same. Shorts have maintained their position. From C on the price continues to then fall indicating shorts were right.

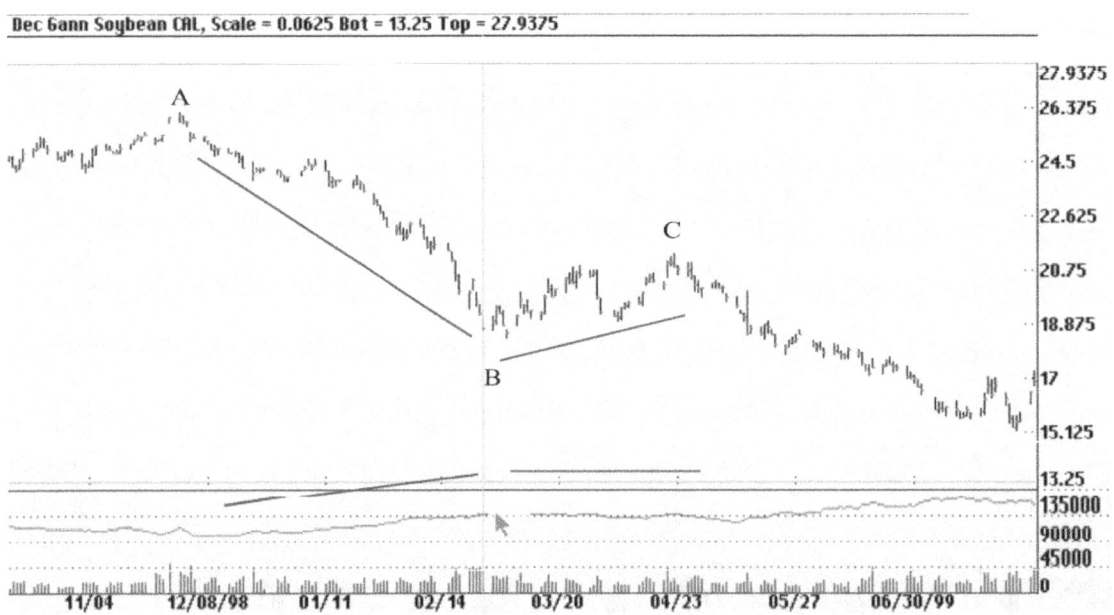

18

Close Only Charts

Many traders prefer to have a Close Only Chart to monitor. It is an important chart to monitor. In Ganntrader select Options: Close Only to display the following type of chart.

Selecting Options can save the status of Close Only bars: Configure System and click the Save button. This option affects the screen display, not the printed charts.

This type of chart is especially value if you want to see the simple price trend of closes, deemed to be the most important part of the trading range. It is said the many large successful traders take their long-term positions near the close of the day. Therefore the close is the most important part of the day. If you see two to three closed below a major angle line, then there usually is an important change of trend.

It is also easier to see the waves using close only charts. Gann did his Wave Analysis on charts to determine where he was in the overall picture of the market. He used a simplified version of the Elliott Wave Theory. Gann's Time and Price Forecasting tells told Gann when and where the price trend would end. Gann's Wave Analysis give him an idea of where he was on the road map before he got to the end of the journey.

You can use the Gann Angles with close only charts very effectively. Look at the following chart using the 1x1 and 1x2 angles.

Close only charts can also be used to determine when counter trend are over. Gann always said to go with the main trend of the market and enter it after the correction of the market was over.

Grid on the Screen

It is very desirable to have grid on your charts whether you are looking at a screen or your chart paper. With Ganntrader you can select Options: Grids if you prefer to see price grids on the screen. Most examples in this manual have the grids turned off for clarity.

Having grids on your screen or chart paper does also help you to have a better perspective when you view the overall long-term trend. Many artists use similar grid patterns when they do their artwork. Your eyes can play tricks on you if you don't have grid lines. You might see two tops as the same price range when in reality they are not.

The status of Grids can be saved by selecting Options: Configure System and click the Save button.

To see the various grid patterns for printed charts, go back to Appendix D to Chart 1. There are many different grids available through this program. Gann used the 8x8 to the inch grid. Many astrological traders prefer the 8x8 to the inch.

You will find that some grids work better with grains like the 8x8 to the inch and others work better with the financials like the 10x10 to the inch.

The Tool Bar

For a trader to be successful he must have a software program, which is easy to use. Menus are very popular in most software programs using the Microsoft windows programs. Ganntrader has the Tool Bar across the top of the chart gives you a way to access the program's most common features. For the most part they duplicate a keyboard or menu item. When an equivalent tool bar function is available we will display its icon to the left of the text. So here's the first tool bar icon for a function that doesn't fit well into any other part of this manual.

The Tool Bar gives you the ability to use the simplicity of the mouse for quick and easy chart applications.

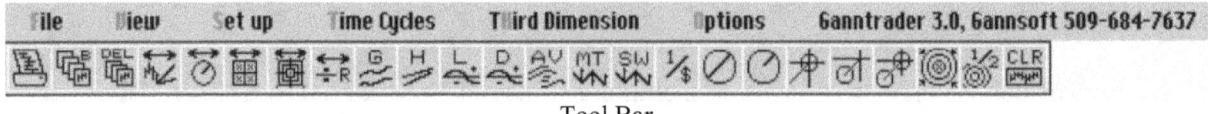

Tool Bar

The Ganntrader 3.0 program also allows you to use the easy keyboard shortcuts using a simple template that you place on top of the F keys at the top of you keyboard. Almost every function of the program can be imputed with just a simple keystroke. See the following template. (This is supplied to purchasers of the software).

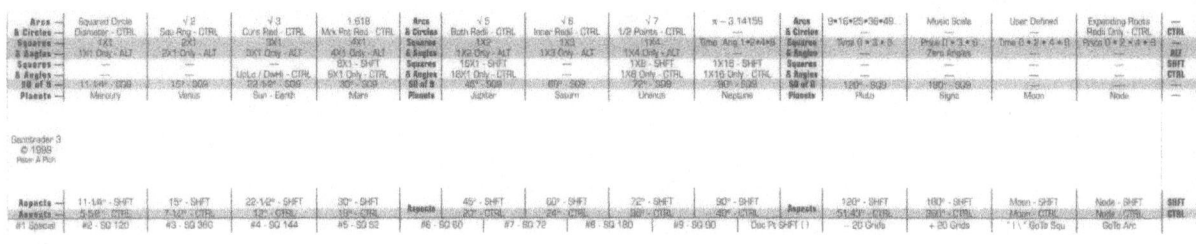

Template for on Top of your Keyboard

Invert Price

There are times you may want to display the inverted price or 1\$. Its most useful purpose would be for currencies. For example, if your data displays British Pounds as £ *1* $ you can invert the display to *$1* £ with this function in the Ganntrader program. The keyboard command for this is <Shift> 6, the <A> character, or use the Tool Bar icon. After inverting the price you may want to shift the decimal point left or right to better present the prices. Use the <Shift> key to do this.

Another reason to invert price is that human nature is naturally bullish. One always wants a stock or commodity to go up. This is a bullish bias that can hurt your trading in a bear market. Sometimes it is advantageous to invert price to change you psychological state of mind.

Inverted Dec British Pound Chart

Printing Charts

If you are a serious Ganntrader, you will need to print out charts to give you the big perspective. Many traders feel that you can't get the same feel of the market looking at a computer screen as you can with real charts on paper. Some traders say that the computer screen fools your eyes. The curves computer screens do not give you the true chart picture. In Ganntrader to print a chart select File: Print Chart or click on the Tool Bar icon. This will open up the following dialog box.

Along the top half of the box a description of what is about to be printed will be shown. In this example we are about to print a calendar day chart with every tenth line emphasized. The chart will not include volume or open interest. The default date range for a chart is the entire data file. A scale is determined that will allow the chart to be printed on a single piece of paper in the price dimension. The number of price by time sheets of paper and the estimated printing time is also displayed. In this example the chart will require 109 sheets of paper (over 99 feet) in length and a print time of almost 4 hours! We may want to specify a shorter chart since this is a daily chart back to 1960.

The print time calculation is based on the value entered under Options: Configure System: Miscellaneous: Grid Speed. For the most accurate calculation print a chart and measure with a stopwatch the number of seconds the print head takes to print 20 passes and enter the average time per pass. The default entry is 1 second per pass and is fairly close for newer printers.

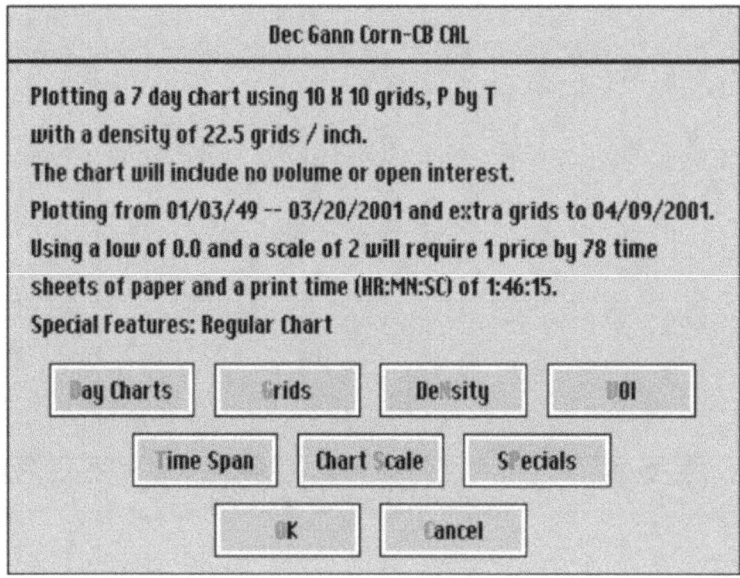

Time Span

As a trader you need to print out time spans of prices on your charts. In the Ganntrader you can do this by clicking the Time Span button you can specific a starting and ending date as well as the number of blank grid lines at the end of the chart. The default setting of 20 will produce at least that many blank grids after the last price bar. The program may print a few extra blanks to end the chart on the next emphasized grid line.

Many traders also find that using the Ehrlich Cycle Finder with long term printed charts is a valuable technique. This is a plastic tool that looks like a coat hanger with 10 points on each side. It can be expanded and contracted to find cycles in the market. For more information on this tool, contact Traders World.

Some users like to print several inches of blank grids at the end of the chart and then hand update the charts. On the third line enter any ending date for the chart you desire and the program will print blank grids until the date is reached. If you will be printing a large number of blank grids at the end of the chart and you are printing trading day charts make sure you keep the Holiday Date List current. See the System Configuration chapter for more details on the Holiday Date List.

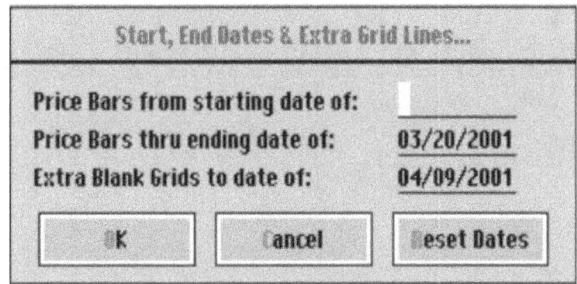

To get a true trend picture of a stock or commodity, it many times is necessary to print the chart back to the beginning. Gann used daily, weekly and monthly charts the most. Pattern recognition is important. You should scan the chart back to the beginning to determine if similar patterns exist in its price structure. You will find that the markets move in 10-year time periods. For example go back 10, 20, 30, 40, 50 and 60 years and compare the price patterns. You will find that the trend might be up in the same month in the different 10-year time spans for 5 out of the 6 time spans. If it is true, then there is a good chance it will again happen this year. The probabilities greatly favor it. You can also print out these charts and overlay the 10-year time segments on top of each other for a direct pattern analysis.

Here is an example of December Corn taking the point August 15 and checking out what the market did in the past time periods such as 2000 versus 1990, 1980, 1970, 1960 and 1950. Notice that August 15 is a key to the market. When the price breaks that point the entire market reverses to the downside or upside. Also notice how similar the patterns for this time period of the year. You can invert the chart in many cases and get an exact duplication of the trend of the market.

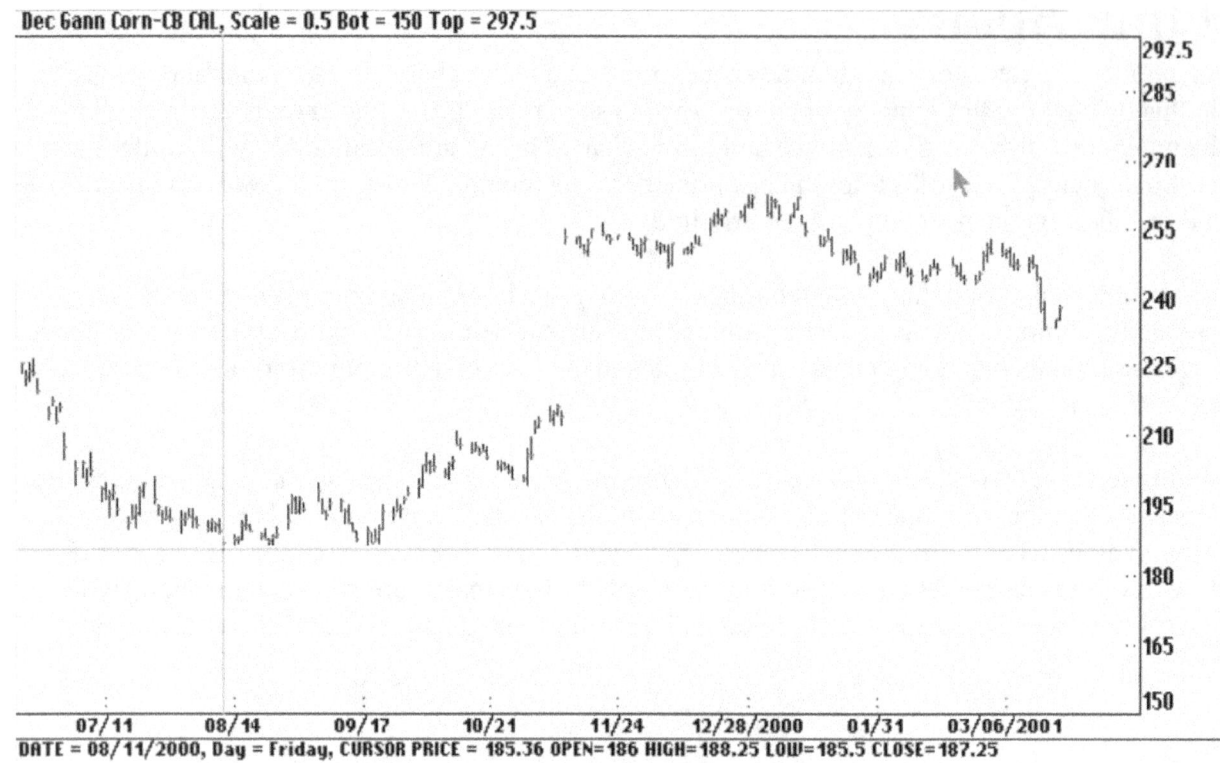
December Corn – 2000 Up Trend

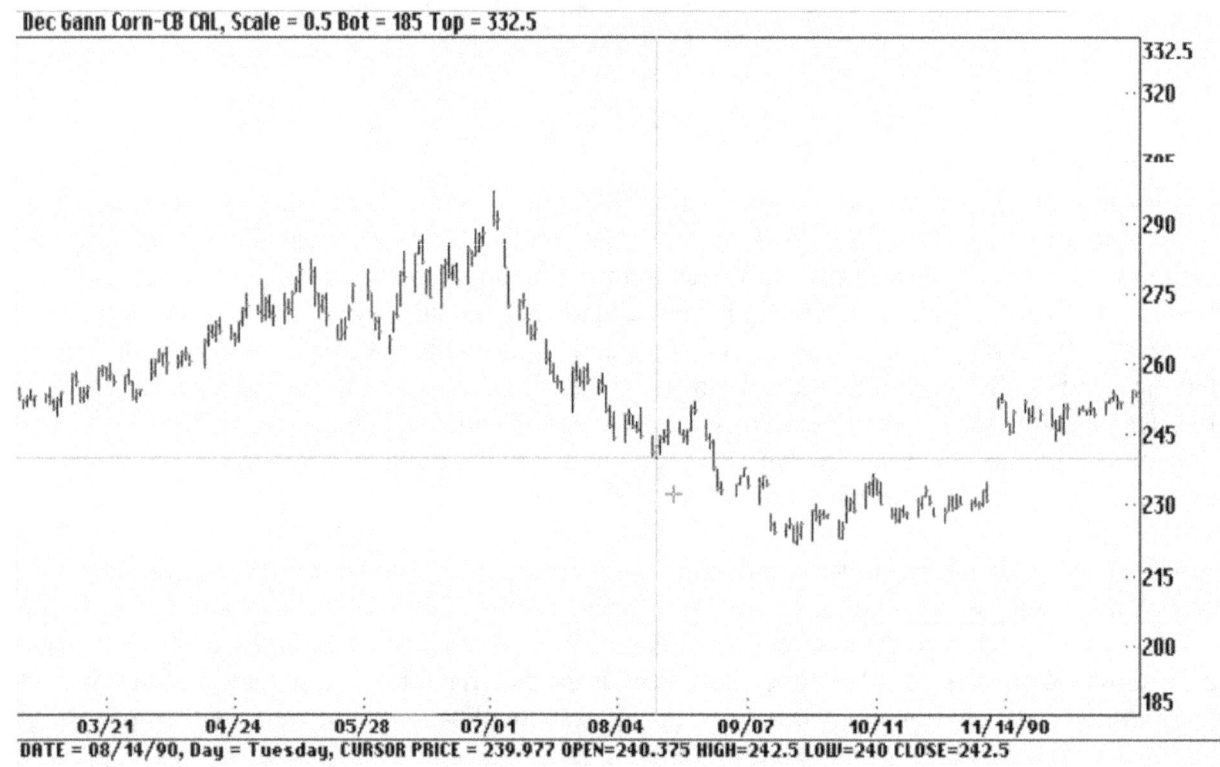
December Corn – 1990 Down Trend

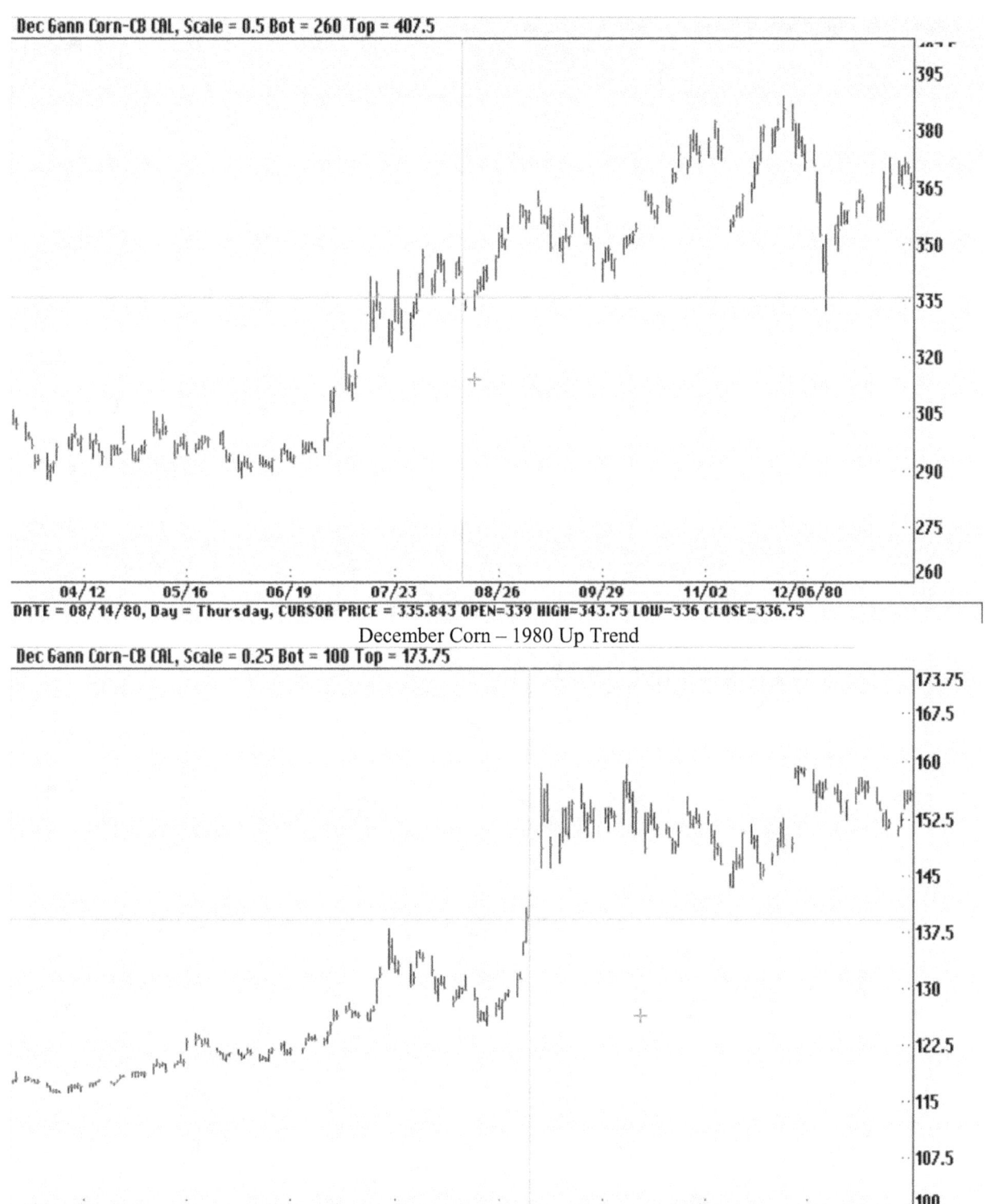

December Corn – 1980 Up Trend

December Corn – 1970 Up Trend

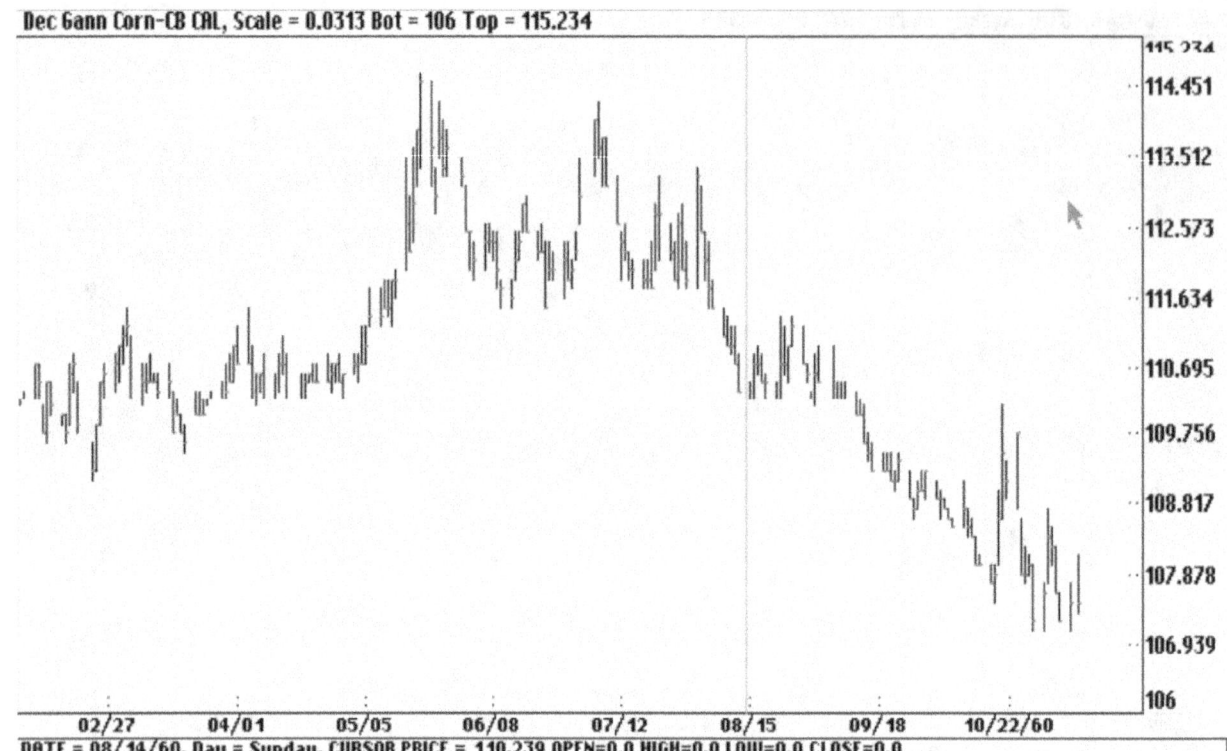
December Corn – 1960 Down Trend

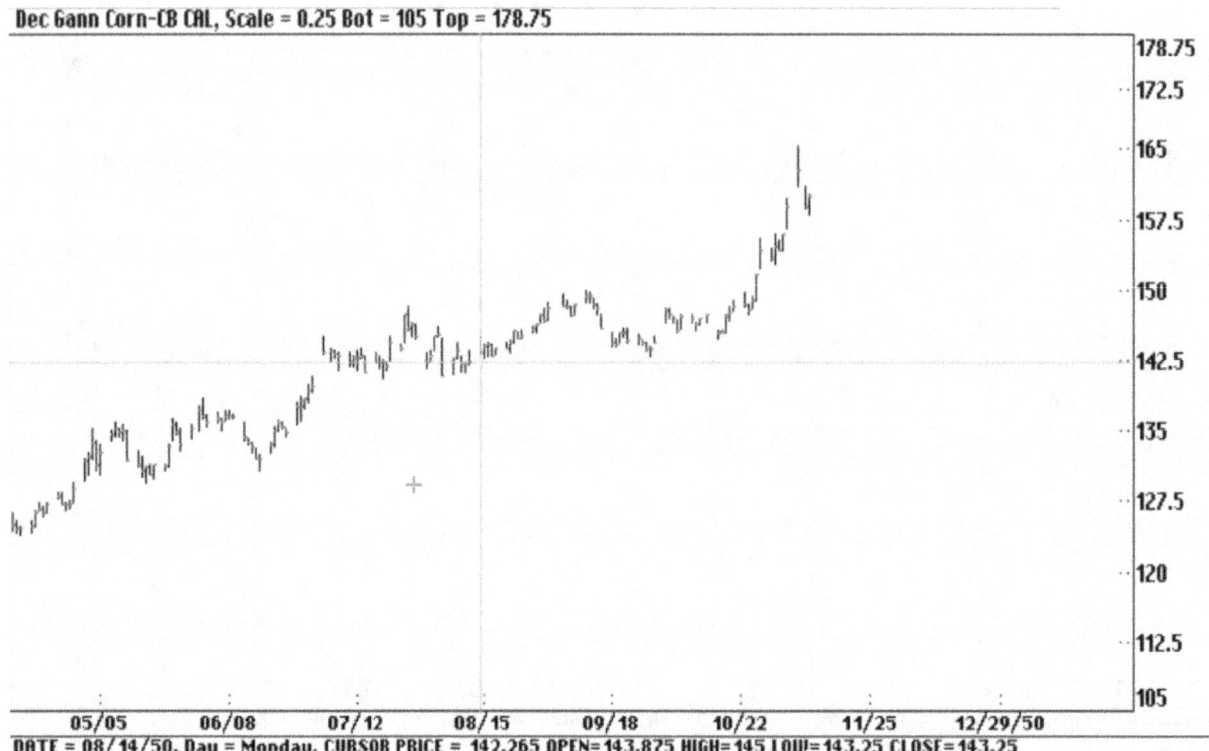
December Corn – 1960 Up Trend

Special Charts

Doing your research into trading, there may be times when you will want to leave off part of the printed portions of a chart. For example, Overlay on Blank Paper and Overlay with Dates would print a square or planet plot only with no prices, grids or labels. You could then reproduce these on clear plastic to produce your own overlays. The next three Blank Chart options are in the Ganntrader program and are a handy way to make some blank chart paper for hand charting purposes. Load any file that covers the time span desired and leave off any elements you don't need. The last selection, Chart, No Background Grids works well when you want to FAX a copy of a chart or reproduce it in a book or newsletter. The background grids often produce too much clutter when reproduced.

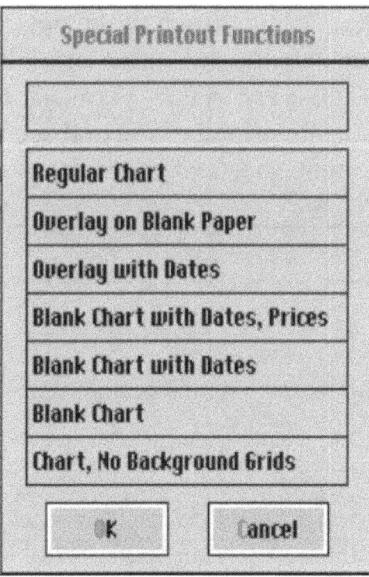

Rescaling Charts

Whenever you make a change to a chart setting that would affect the chart's scale many times you need to rescale the chart. Some software trading programs do not allow you to rescale the chart. In the Ganntrader you can easily rescale the charts. With Ganntrader this box will appear so you can easily do this. For example, changing the time span to be printed might eliminate a very low price from the early part of a chart and require a different scale per grid line. Adding volume to a chart would reduce the number of grid lines available for the price bars and require a new scale. By clicking OK a new chart bottom and scale will be calculated based on the new reality. You can also click on the Chart Scale button and set any values desired. Notice the 2 buttons, File and Screen. File scaling will be the default setting and reflects the highest high and lowest low for the time span entered. You can enter a different chart bottom and or scale but notice that the "top of the first page…" will change as the new values are entered. If this value is less than the highest high in the chart's range then the chart will need to be printed with 2 passes, a lower and an upper, for later past up. It is certainly permissible to do this and is sometimes necessary. Ganntrader will automatically print the first and second pass. This print dialog box will reflect the number of price and time sheets of paper necessary to print the chart.

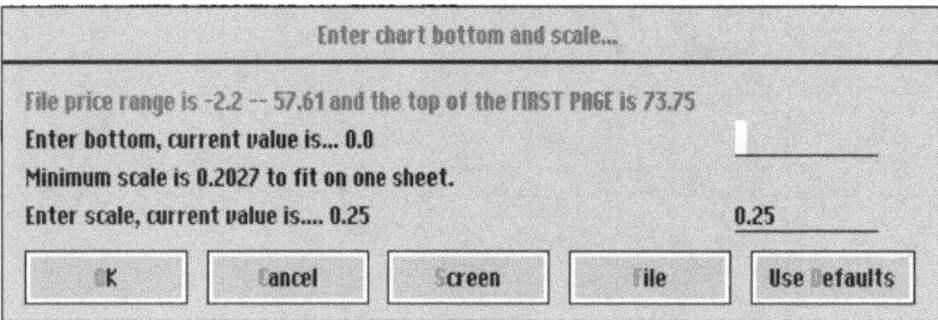

Printer and Screen Differences

As a trader you need to know that what you see on your computer screen is the same thing you see on your charts. There are very few trading programs that allow you to do this. In the Ganntrader, for the most part, the program operates on a "What You See is What You Get" basis meaning if it is on the screen it will print on the printer. A few exceptions follow:

Angles are identified on the screen by their colors. The printed charts label the angles with '1x1', '2x1' etc.

Planets are identified on the screen by their colors. The printed charts use the astro symbols as shown in Appendix A.

The selected angles on screen include a dimension display showing the time and price difference from the angle's origin and the current cursor's position. The printed chart displays a time count every 8 or 10 lines from the angle's origin.

The price and time divisions of a printed square are labeled with their fractional parts.
On screen they are identified by color.

The price labels on the printed chart are redone every 16 inches. The screen is priced on the far right of the screen only.

The price bars on the printed chart may or may not have the 'hats' marking the high and low of each price bar. The screen's price bars are always a single line for the price bar's range. The 'Mirror Image Foldbacks' feature used with Selected Angles works only on the screen.

You can now click the OK button to print the current chart. As we go through the rest of the features of the program you can print a chart by following these procedures again.

Swing Chart (Standard)

Gann developed two different swing charts, the Standard Swing Chart and the Main Trend Swing Chart. In the Ganntrader the Main Trend draws a line up or down if the price bars make higher highs or lower lows for at least 3 days in the same direction. Inside days are ignored. The Trend Line or Swing Chart is drawn up or down depending on whether the price penetrates the previous swing by a certain number of points. Gann used 3 days, sometimes 2, days for the Main Trend and 1/4 point for soybeans. His descriptions for them leave a number of unanswered questions. They are simply a trend following system. If a market is making higher highs the trend is up. If a counter-trend move exceeds the previous counter-trend move the trend may be about to change. The MT and SW indicator can be selected under the View menu or by clicking on the MT or SW Tool Bar icon.

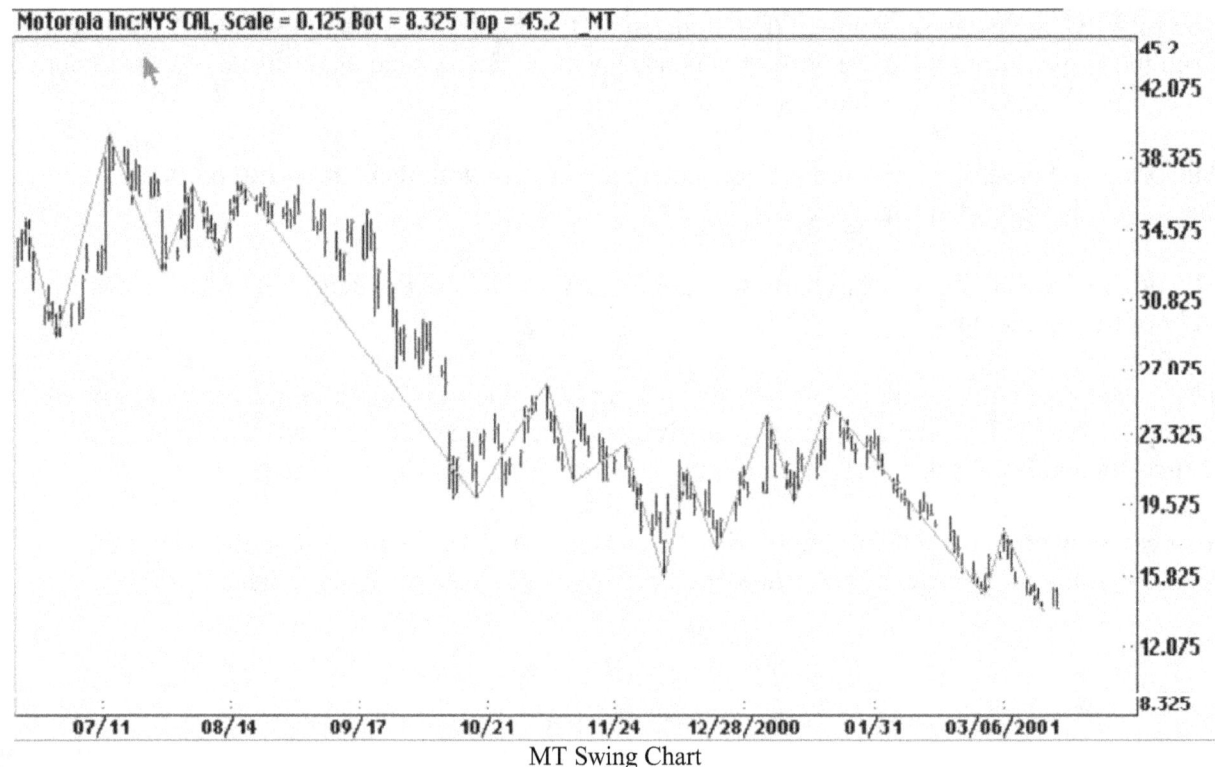

MT Swing Chart

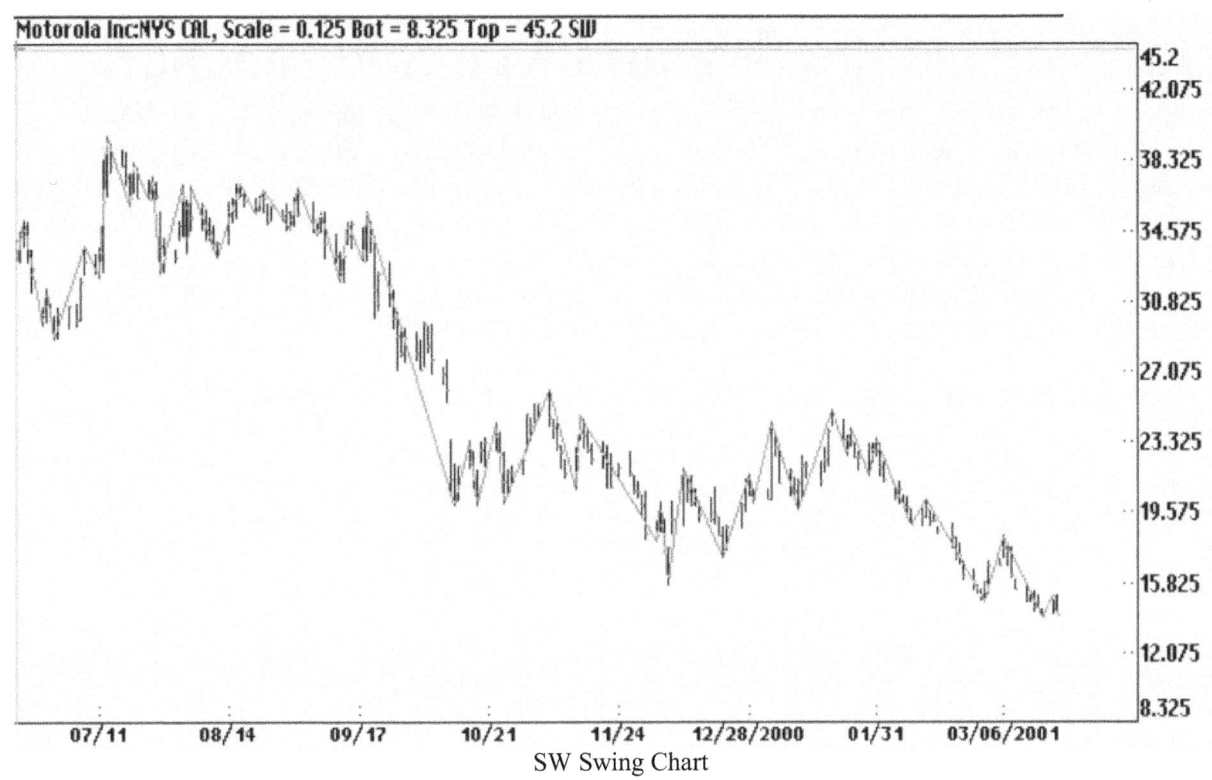
SW Swing Chart

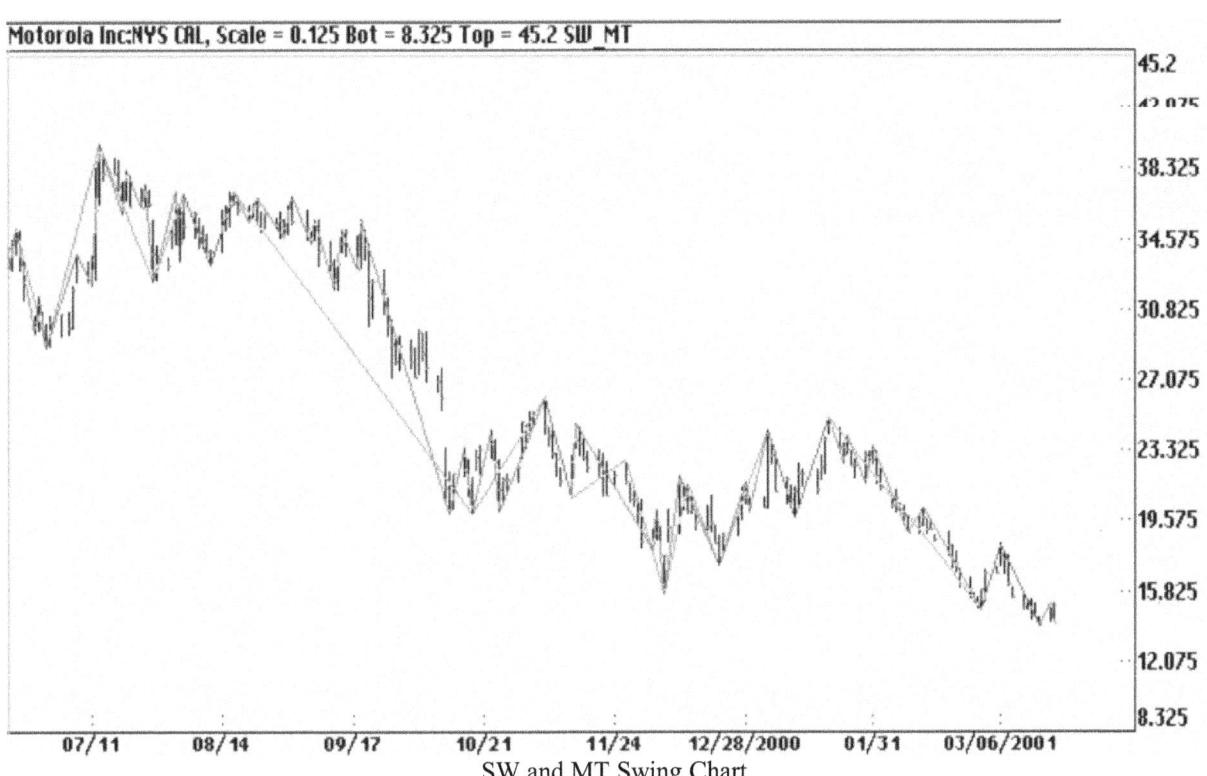
SW and MT Swing Chart

How to Use the SW and MT Swing Chart

For one to make money in the markets, it's usually best to trade with the main trend of the market. In the Ganntrader using the SW and MT Swing Charts this is easy to do. You should follow the main trend of the market first using the MT Swing Chart. If the MT Swing Chart is down, then wait for the market to reverse (make a higher high) on the swing. Then use the SW Swing Chart to go long with when it reverses and makes a higher high when it is in a downtrend. If you look at the following chart of Apple Computer you will notice that both the MT and SW Swing charts both went long on 4/24/99 and the market took off.

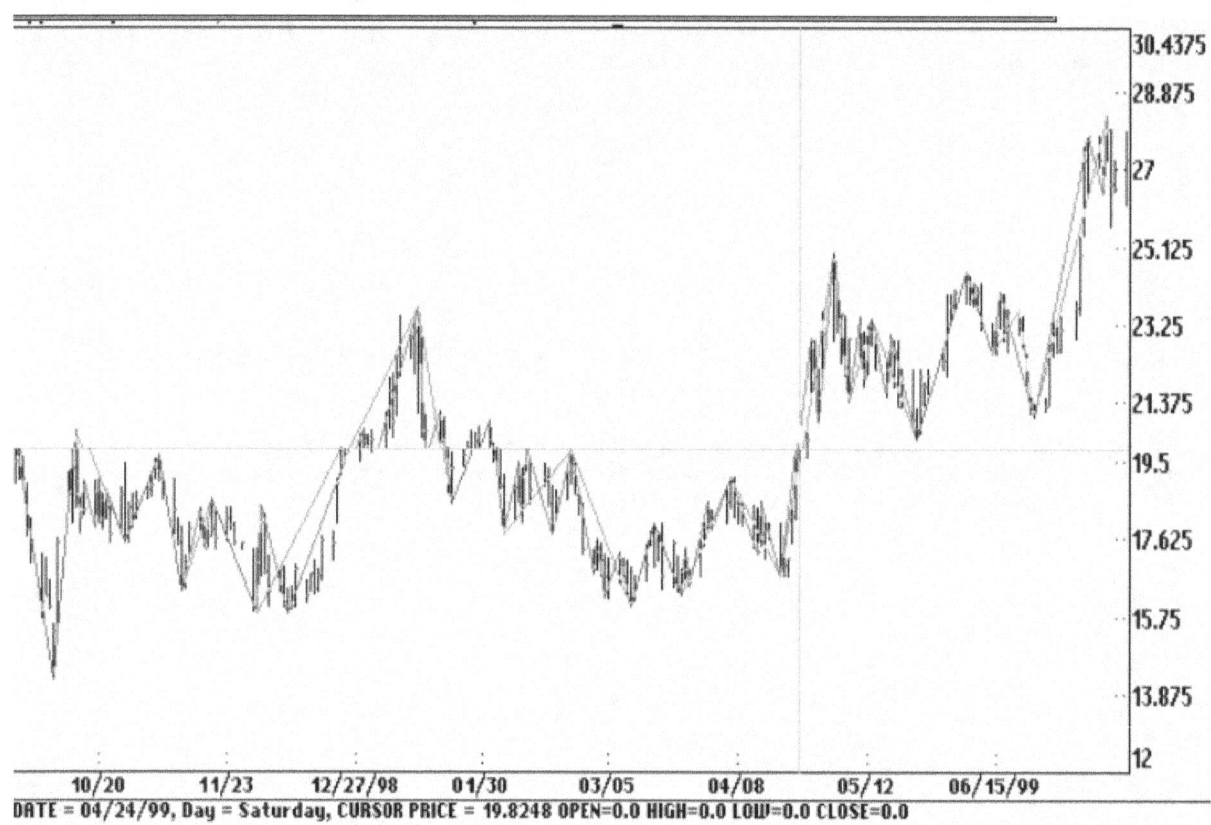

Swing Chart (Enhanced)

Gann Trader adds an enhancement to help you spot the changes in the size of the countertrends by shading the swings. It is selected under Options Shade Swings.

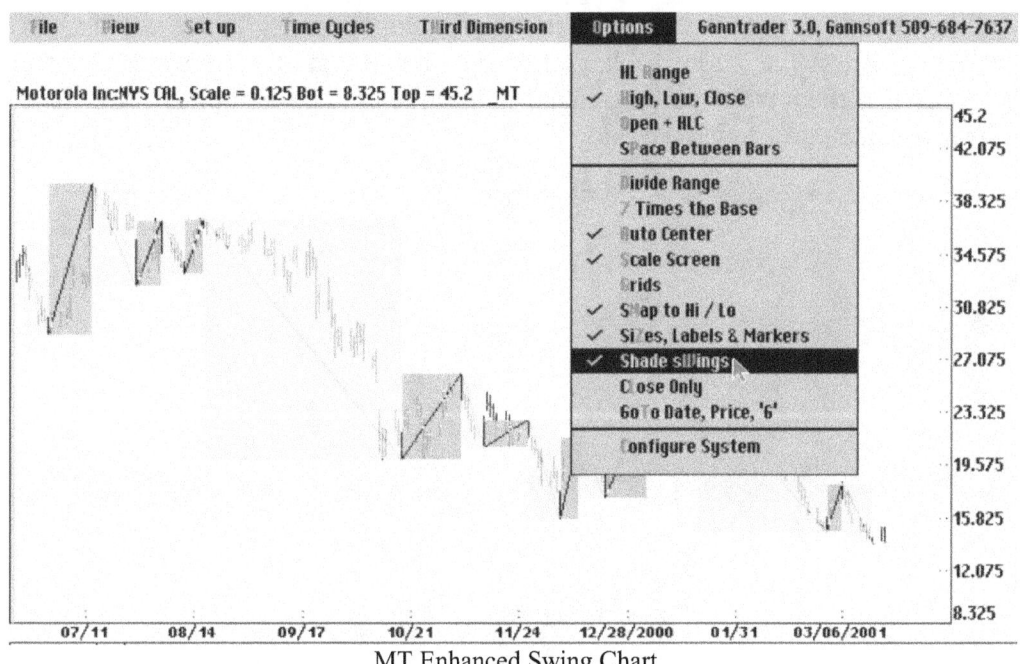

MT Enhanced Swing Chart

SW Enhanced Swing Chart

Notice the width as well as the height of the swings is shown with the shaded areas. Gann said that when the price range of a counter-trend exceeded the previous range the price was overbalanced and a change in trend was possible. He put more emphasis on the overbalance of time when the number of time periods in a counter-trend move exceeded the previous move. You can display both the Swings and the Main Trend indicator. The Swings will be the more sensitive of the two indicators. When shading is active the colors mix on the screen in such a way that the overlapping swings are green when both indicators are moving together, both up or both down, and dark blue when they are not moving together. Therefore it is obvious that you trade with the direction of the market when both indicators are moving together or green in color. Looking at the Motorola chart below the market took a large drop in late July. The indicators were green indicating the both of them were working together. A large amount of money could have been made on the short side into late November.

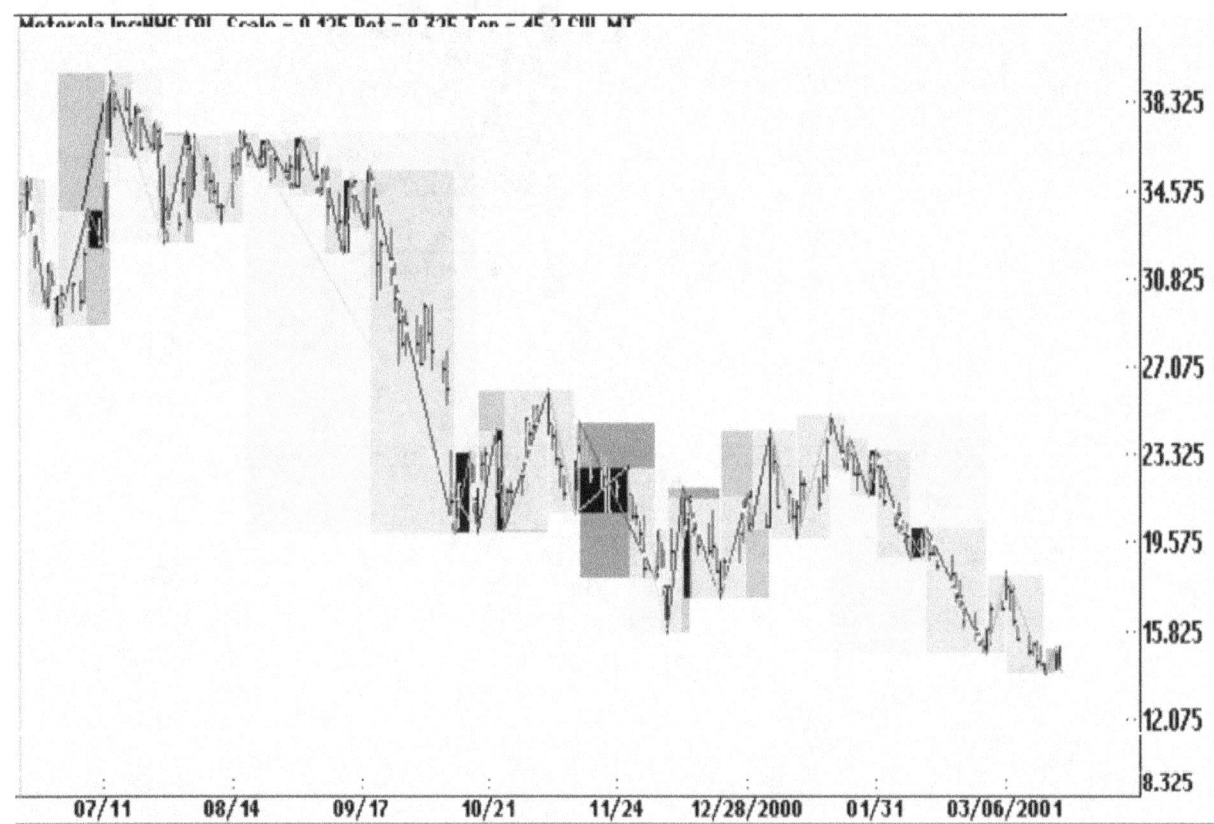
MT and SW Enhanced Swing Chart

Angles

Several types of angles are used by Gann traders. In the Ganntrader program there are several angle modes available. Under the View menu you will find All Swing Angles, Main Trend Angles, Selected Angles and Back 360 Hi / Lo Angles. The Main Trend Angles selection, shown on the next chart, draws an angle from each swing of the Main Trend Indicator. All Swing Angles is similar and draws angles from each swing of the Trend Line Indicator.

The Main Trend or Trend Line Indicator don't have to be on the screen to use these two angle modes.

The Back 360 Hi / Lo Angles will draw angles from only those highs and lows that are some multiple of 360 back from the reference point. The reference point is set to the most current date in the file but can be reset under the Setup menu. Multiples of 360 would be counts of 45, 90, 135 and 36, 72, 144 etc. These counts are the same as several natural cycle lengths and angles drawn from those points are important.

Selected Angles

Selected angles are the most used part of technical analysis according to the rules of W.D Gann. In the Ganntrader software program the Selected Angles mode to give you complete control on the location and types of angles drawn. It is a 2-step process to use this feature. First, under the View menu click on Selected Angles. The program will try to locate any selected angles and draw angles from those points. Since we have not marked any points yet you will see this reminder box. Click OK. Next, move the cursor to any desired point and hit either the <Enter> key or the <Insert> key. This will place a 1X1 angle from that point. Other angles from the same point can be applied by using the function keys. The function keys are assigned as follows:

F1= 1x1 F2= 2x1 F3= 3x1 F4= 4x1 F5= 16X1 F6= 1x3 F7= 1x4

The other lesser-used angles are activated with the addition of the <Shift> key. Use the keyboard overlay as a guide. Hold the <Shift> key and type:

F4= 8x1 F5= 16x1 F7= 1x8 F8= 1x16

Selected Angles

In the Ganntrader you can place all the selected angles on the charts using the major highs and lows and get a good idea of the relevant angles the market is following. In the above chart all the angles are displayed. Many of the angles are not important to the current market. When you find that the market is following a particular selected angle, then you can aggressively plot that angle from all major and minor highs and lows. See chart below.

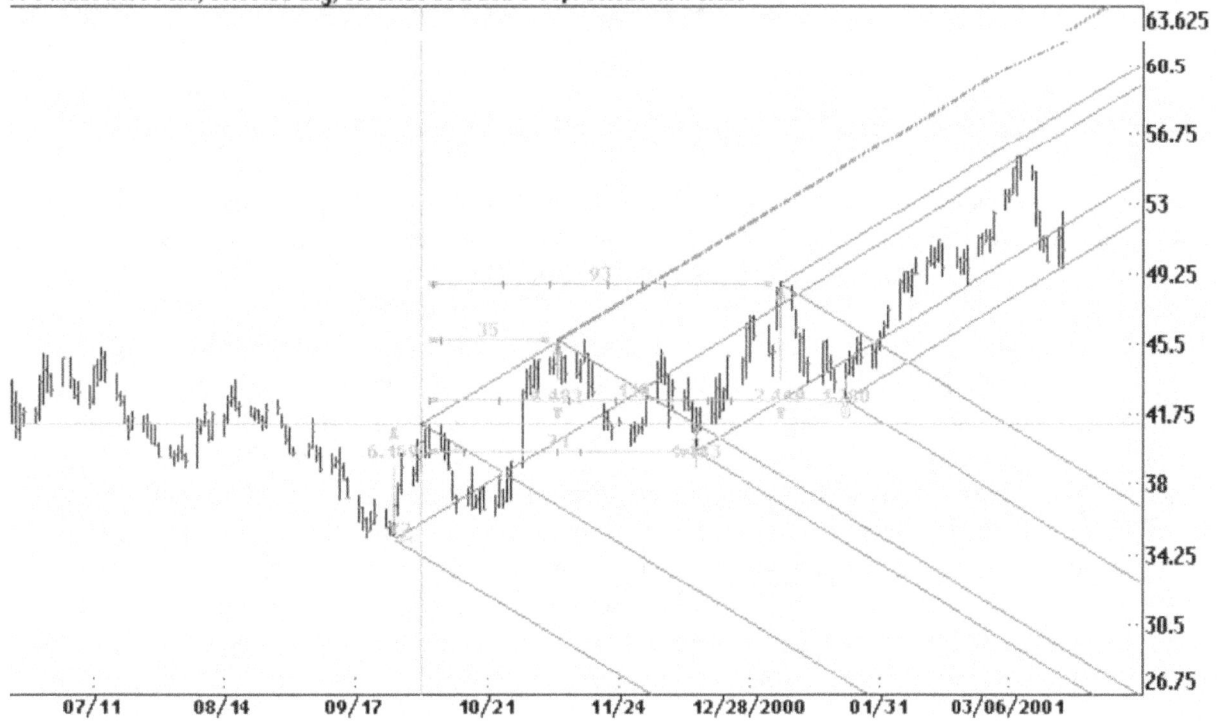

Other Selected Angles

In the Ganntrader you can move the cursor to other points and hit <Enter> or <Insert> to start angles from those points. The program will carry the current angle sets to the new marked points. Notice that hitting its function key can include any angle. If you hit the key again the angle toggles back off. If you have a cluster of angles and you want to remove all but one you can hit the appropriate function key in combination with the <Alt> key to quickly remove all but that particular angle. You will find that this exclusive mode using the <Alt><F> key is used by other modes of the program as well.

At any time you can add or remove angles from one of these marked origin points. In order to do that you must have the cursor located exactly on the point you wish to modify. To move the cursor use the <,> or <.> keys. You can also use the Tool Bar icon.

You can't simply move to a point using the regular cursor arrow keys. Use the 'Move To' keys or Tool Bar icon. Notice on the keyboard overlay that the function keys control a number of different items depending on which mode is active. You will learn later that the program can have more than one mode active at the same time. Using the Tool Bar icon or the 'Move To' keys does two things. It moves the cursor exactly onto the setup point you wish to modify and it makes that mode the last active mode so that the function keys modify the proper item. For example, you can have selected angles, planets and a square all on the screen at once. If you hit the <F1> key do you want the program to add or remove Mercury, add or remove a 1x1 angle inside a square or add or remove the 1x1 selected angle? By using the 'Move To' key or icon you remove all doubt. If you forget you will see this reminder box.

You can delete a marked point in the same way as you modify one. 'Move To' the point and hit the <Delete> key located next to the <Insert> and <End> keys. The chart above shows an angle coming up from the September low in the S&P cash. The program may also draw angles down from the low depending on the status of 'Up From Lows / Down From Highs' which is controlled by <Ctrl><F3> key. You can change this status for each origin point. 'Move To' the marked point and hit the <Ctrl><F3> keys. Selecting can save the default behavior of these Options: Configure System and hit the Save button.

Make sure you are exactly on a high or low when using this feature. The Left and right arrow keys will move you from High to High on each bar. The Down arrow will move you to the Close and then the Low of the price bar. If you are using the mouse make sure the 'Snap To' feature is active. The <Scroll Lock> key controls this or Options Snap To Hi / Lo.

The Selected angle feature can also be used to find a new up or down channel by waiting for the next high and dividing the previous range into two. See chart below:

Intersecting Angles

Intersecting Angles give you major turning points in the market. When you place these angles on highs and lows the intersection gives you a change of trend. See two charts below.

Two Different Angles

It is possible to use two angles off of one intersection to determine where a move will go to or exhaust itself. See A on the charts below:

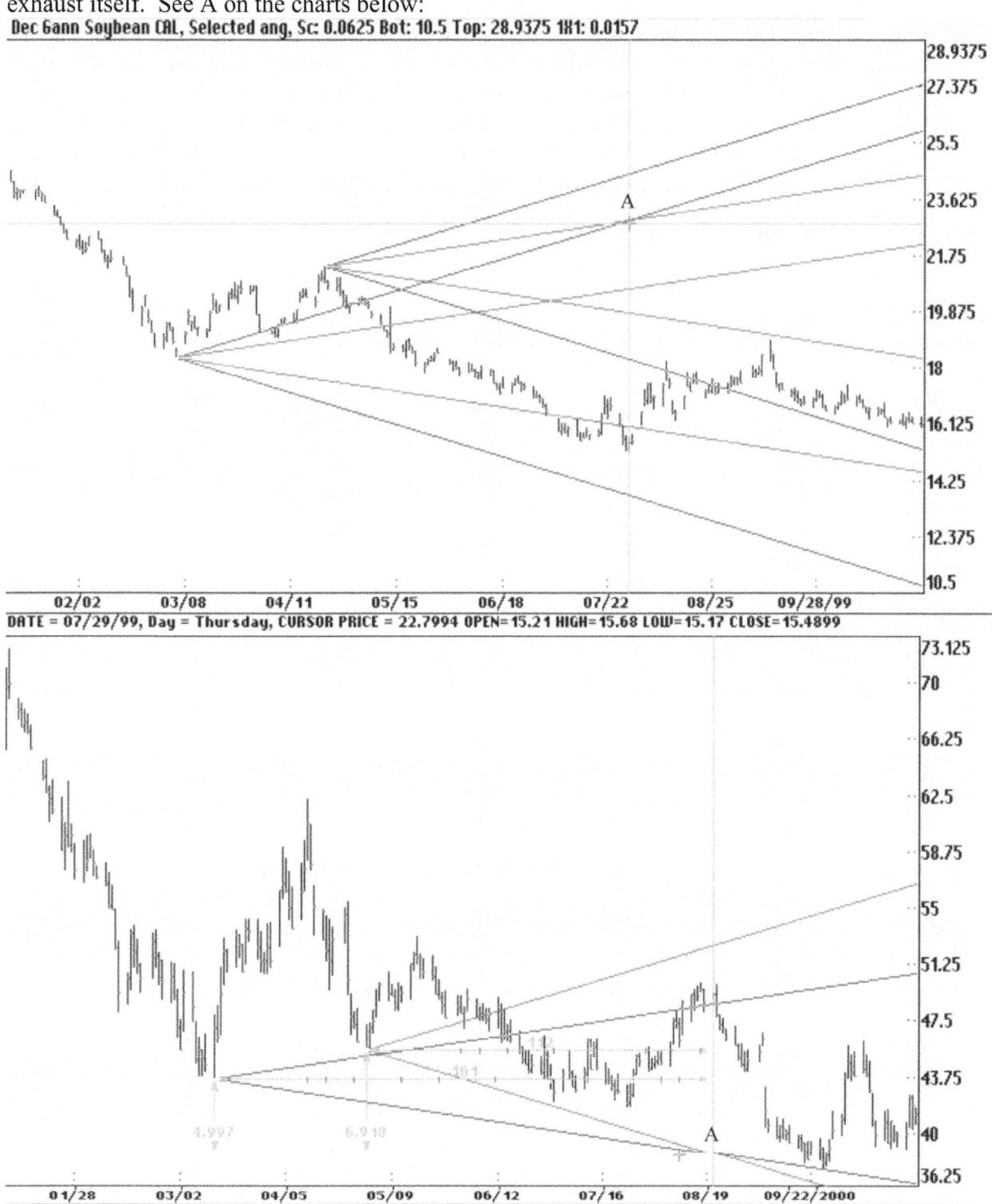

True Trend Line

Gann used the True Trend Line extensively in his trading, yet few people know about it. Most programs can do it. Gann's True Trend Line indicator is a variation on the Selected Angles mode in the Ganntrader. The following charts illustrate this example. The cursor's price line is lined up with the highs or lows pointed to by the first arrow. The cursor's time line is lined up with a high or a low point on the chart. These True Trend Lines are most impressive. Draw them on all your charts. It will be worth your time! These points are marked in the same way as a selected angle point. Move the cursor to the desired location and hit the <Enter> or <Insert> key.

As far as we know, there is no other software package on the market that can due the True Trend Line. Very few people even know of this type of trend line. The next two charts on the following two pages illustrates some more examples of the True Trend Line. Study the examples carefully. You should practice this technique on as many charts as you can. It can give you the ability to determine an aspect of technical analysis that few other people actually use.

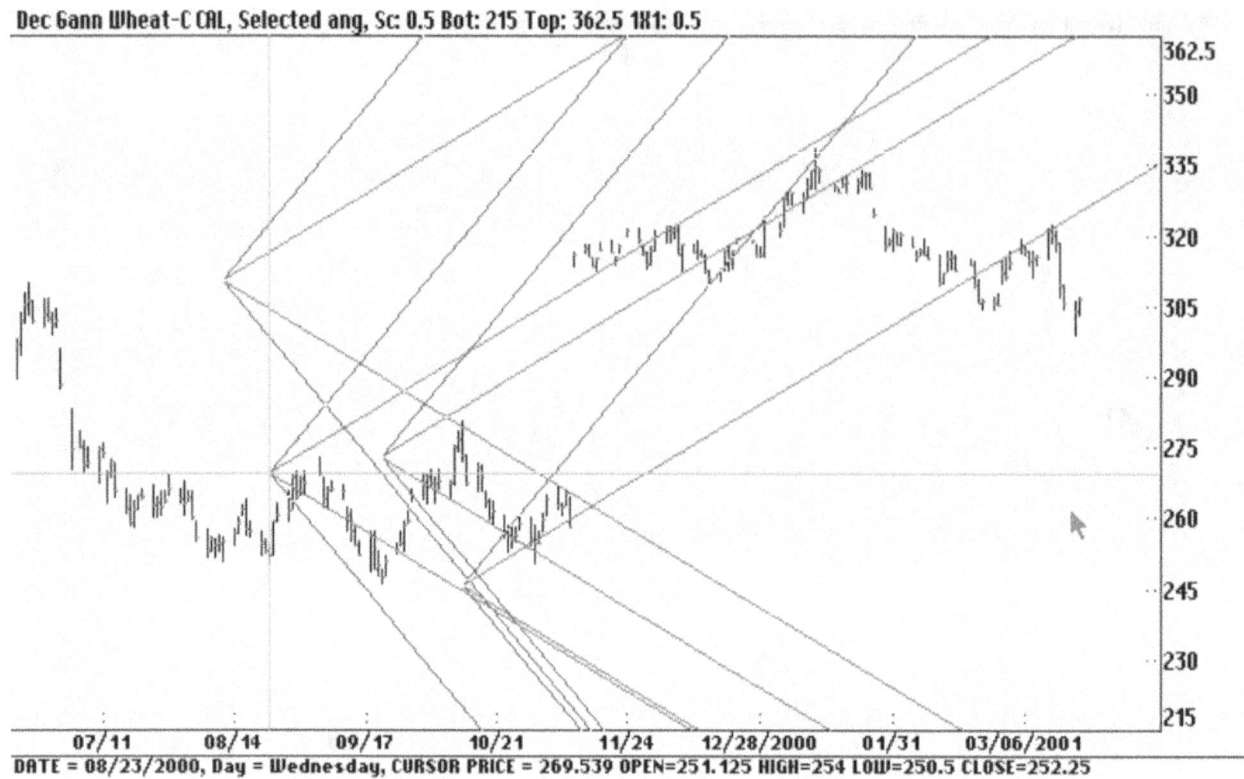

Notice in the above chart illustrating the True Trend Lines the channels that are setup using these lines. This is one way of developing channels lines that gives you unique support and resistance time and price lines. Go over many charts and try drawing True Trend Lines around major and minor bases and tops to see if you can get a handle on this particular technique. If you look over many of Gann's old charts he drew by hand, there are a lot of lines that form channels that seem to come from nowhere. Using this technique is how some of the Gann's channel lines were drawn. Other lines were planetary in nature.

Swing Angles

Some Gann traders prefer the use of using All Swing Angles. This gives you the overall trend view of the entire market. The Ganntrader program will display Swing Angles for all tops and bottoms with just a push of a button. This is generally good to view the main trends of the market. Look at the following chart. It looks like the ones Gann used to draw. It's very clear to see the channels that are forms using this technique. Notice when price gets out of a channel it's probable an ABC correction according to the Elliott Wave Theory. It will usually resume its trend once the correction is over. Also notice that in many cases the trend lines will hit more than one point usually on the outer parameters of the channels.

You will also notice in the chart example below that the more dense the lines the more tops and bottoms are in the direction on one trend and the more valid the trend is.

All Swing Angles

Dimension Lines

Gann extensively used dimension lines. He had labels and markings all over his charts. The Ganntrader program will display the price and time difference between the origin point of a selected angle and the current cursor's position. To activate or deactivate this feature select Options: Sizes, Labels & Markers. With the feature active you can also enable or disable labeling for individual marked origin points. 'Move To' the point in the usual way and hit the <L> key to turn the labels on or off for each point. <Alt><L> will quickly remove all angles and leave the dimension labels on. Notice on the time dimension line the vertical red lines mark the basic 360 time cycles. You will see a mark at 36, 72... ,30, 60... and 45, 90, 135... time periods. The time dimension label is normally the same color as the cursor lines. When the cursor is exactly equal to one of these 360 time points it will turn red in color.

When the time dimension equals the price of the origin point the label turns green in color. In other words if you were 53 days from a low of 53 the price and time would be square or equal and the label turns green to help you identify these points. This Gann technique will be covered in more detail when we get to the Squares section.

The default status of Options: Sizes, Labels & Markers can be stored by selecting Options: Configure System and click on the Save button.

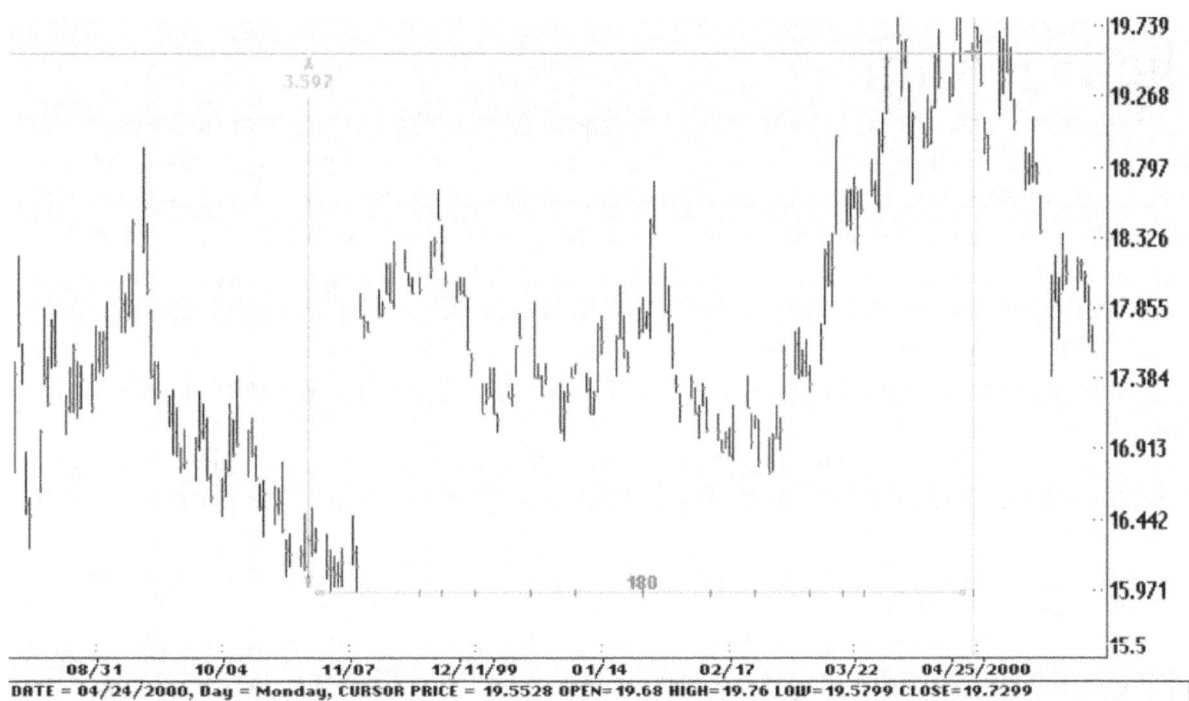

In the above example December Soybean Oil bottomed on 10/27/99 and rallied 180 days up twice that 3.60 points to square out at the top just to reverse and go down. Notice the 180 days is red because it is a circle number.

Dec Wheat on the weekly chart topped put at 632 on 9/26/99 and dropped 360 cents in 180 weeks to bottom out at 254 on 10/15/99.

The 1x1 Angle

One of the most confusing parts of Gann's work has to do with the 1x1 angle or the so called 45° angle. A 1x1 angle in its simplest form rises at the rate of 1 cents or $1 per day, week or month. In Gann's day he was charting soybeans with a chart scale of 1 cent per grid line. He wrote in his commodity course about the 1x1 angle rising at 1 cent per day. In the same course he refers to it as the 45° angle. A chart line rising at the rate of 1 cent per day will be a 45° angle if and only if the chart's scale is 1 cent per grid line. The confusion occurs when you try to duplicate Gann's work charting commodities or stocks that are trading at much higher levels. A scale of 1 cent per grid line could require a chart as tall as a three-story building. The complete Dow Industrials using 1/8 inch grid paper would require a chart 114 feet tall! In order to fit these markets on a chart we rescale the grids to something greater than 1 cent per line. The 1X1 angle on such a chart will no longer measure 45° on a protractor but as long as it rises at 1 cent per day it is still the lx1 angle.

The Ganntrader program solves this problem by allowing you to independently define the rate of rise of the lx1 angle. The program will then automatically adjust the 1x1 and all the other angles so that they will always move at the same rate you set regardless of the chart's scale. Many of the other popular trading software programs on the market do not display the correct angles according to Gann. If the program does not display the correct angles, the only way to adjust for it is to create trend line and manually calculate where it should be in the future. A 1x1 angle on a corn chart, for example, would be 1 day to every 1-cent move. Therefore in 20 days the line would be 20 cents up. You can manually plot the trend line there to give you a calculated 1x1 angle. You can then allow the program to plot its 45° angle to see how far off it is.

On the next page there is an example of the December Wheat using a 1x1 angle from the top in March of 2000. The top chart is set with a scale of 1 and the bottom chart is set with a scale of .5 The angles are flatter as the scale is increased but the angles still move at 1 cent or 2 cents per day.

If you are trading a market which is very high with a lot of volatility is will be necessary to set the scale to a higher number making the chart even flatter. Some traders prefer print out their charts because your computer screen is simply not large enough to do proper analysis and to see the entire chart at once.

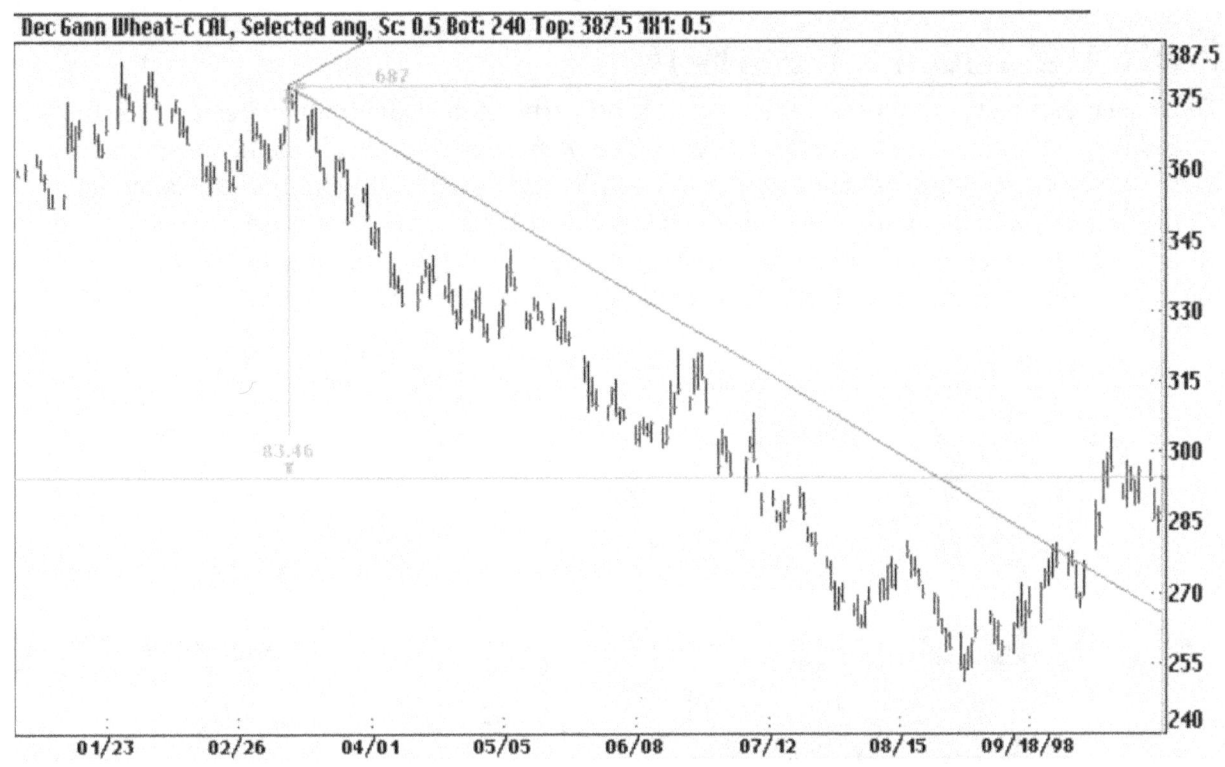

In the following chart the scale is set to 1 instead of 0.5 in the previous chart. Notice how the angles and the entire chart reformat themselves to be correct.

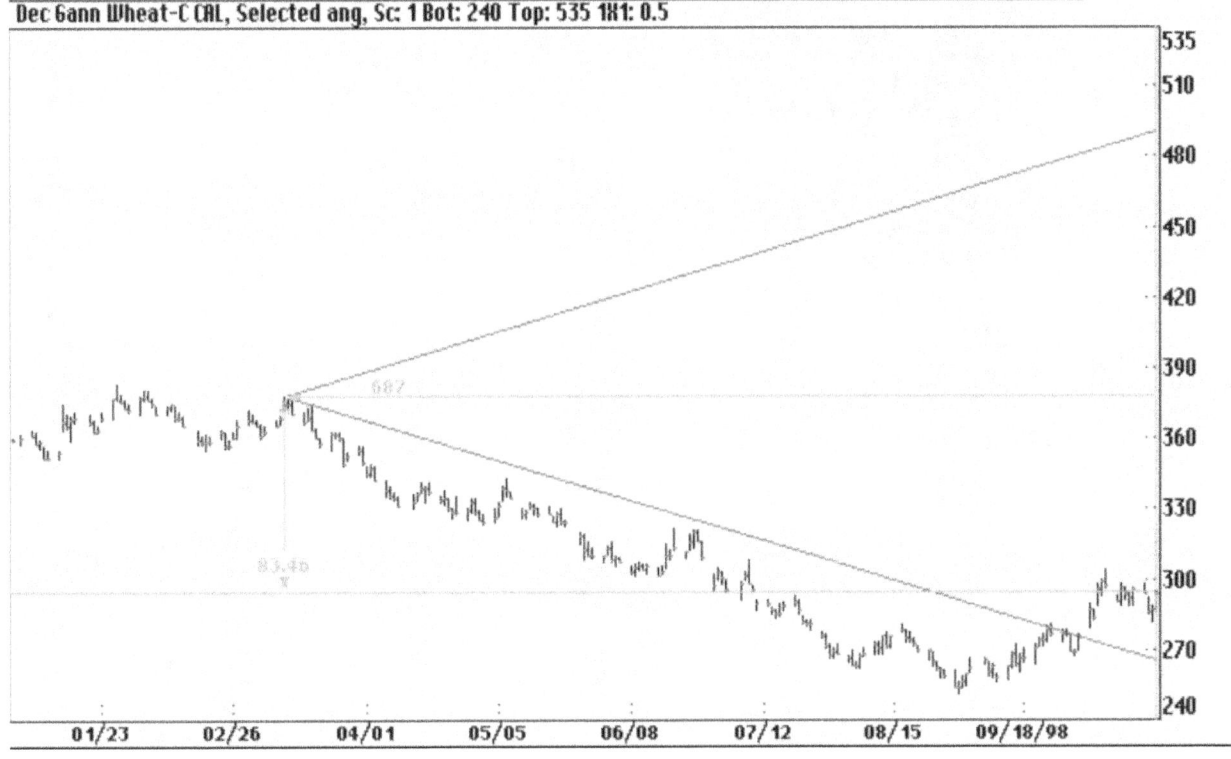

Setting the 1x1 Angle

To be successful a trader must set the 1x1 angle properly. In the Ganntrader when a file is first loaded the 1x1 angle is set to the chart's scale. The main reason for this is so the inexperienced user will see something reasonable on the screen when angles are selected. Earlier Ganntraders set the 1x1 to 1 as the default value. This value was fine for grains and most stocks but worthless on the DJIA because of its high price. As you gain experience you will most likely want to set the 1x1's value to something other than the default setting. Select Setup: 1X1 Angle to enter your own value.

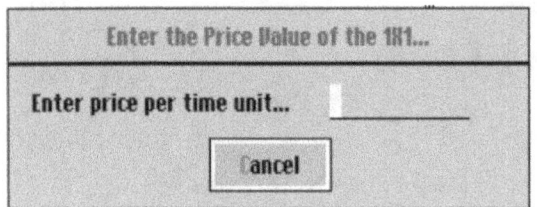

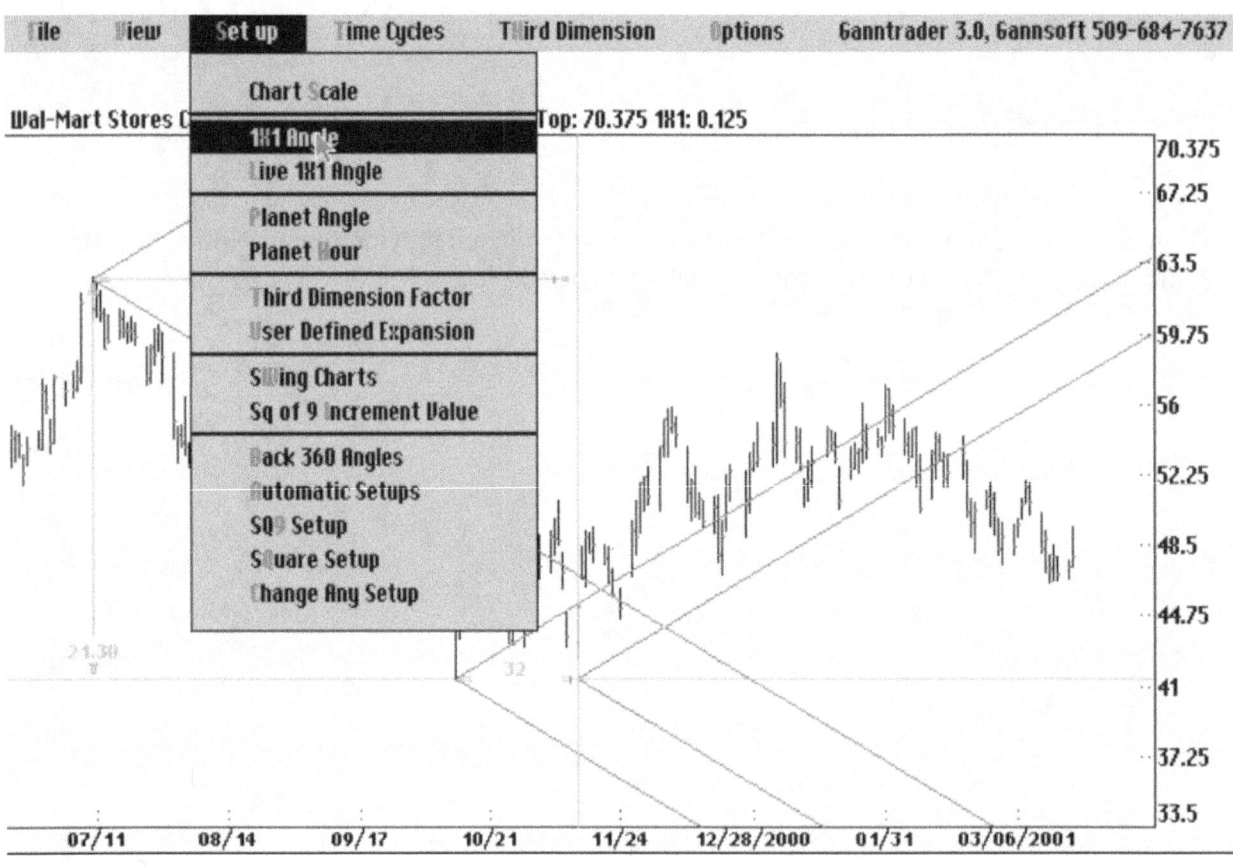

Values for the 1x1 Angle

The grains, most stocks, and the precious metals work well with the angle set to $1 or 1 cent per day. In the case of the grains Gann charted the dollars and cents as a whole number. A price of $2.50 per bushel was charted as 250 and the 1x1 would be set to 1 per day, not .01 per day. If your data appears on the screen this way you will do better if you shift the decimal point to the right using the <)> key. (<Shift>. <0>)

Gann used the circle of 360 as the basis of his numbering system. When in doubt about what the 1x1 angle should be think in multiples of 360. A grain trading at $3.00 is close to one circle of 360 so the 1x1 should be 1. A currency trading at 90 cents would work well with the 1x1 rising at 25 cents per day. The DJIA at 10000 is about 28 circles of 360 so consider a 1x1 equal to 32 or 64. Gann's angles are each double or half the next angle in the sequence. The 1x1 is followed by the 2x1, 4x1, 8x1 and 16x1 and so on. It works better if you use this same relationship when deciding on the 1x1 angle's value.

When you have the 1x1 angle correct you should see a good fit between the 2x1 above the 1x1 and the 1x2 below the 1x1. If a market breaks out above the 1x1 it should find resistance at the 2x1 above. If it breaks below the 1x1 it should find support, at least for a while, at the 1X2 below the 1x1.

The US T-Bond market is a special case. Most traders find 4/32 per day or .125 is about right. Other traders like 0.10. Most agree that a full point of 1-00 is too steep to be useful.

Here are two examples of a stock chart of Dupont. The first Chart Shows the
price per time unit set at 1 and the second chart show it set to .05. The .05 is the correct setting.

See the two chart examples on the next page. The first chart sets the price per time unit to 1 and the second chart sets the price per time unit to .05. You can clearly see that the second chart has the proper setting.

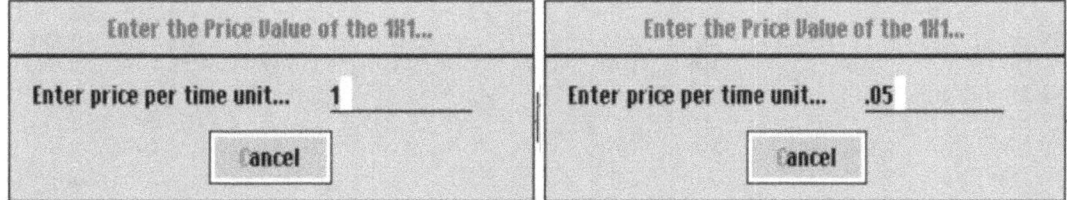

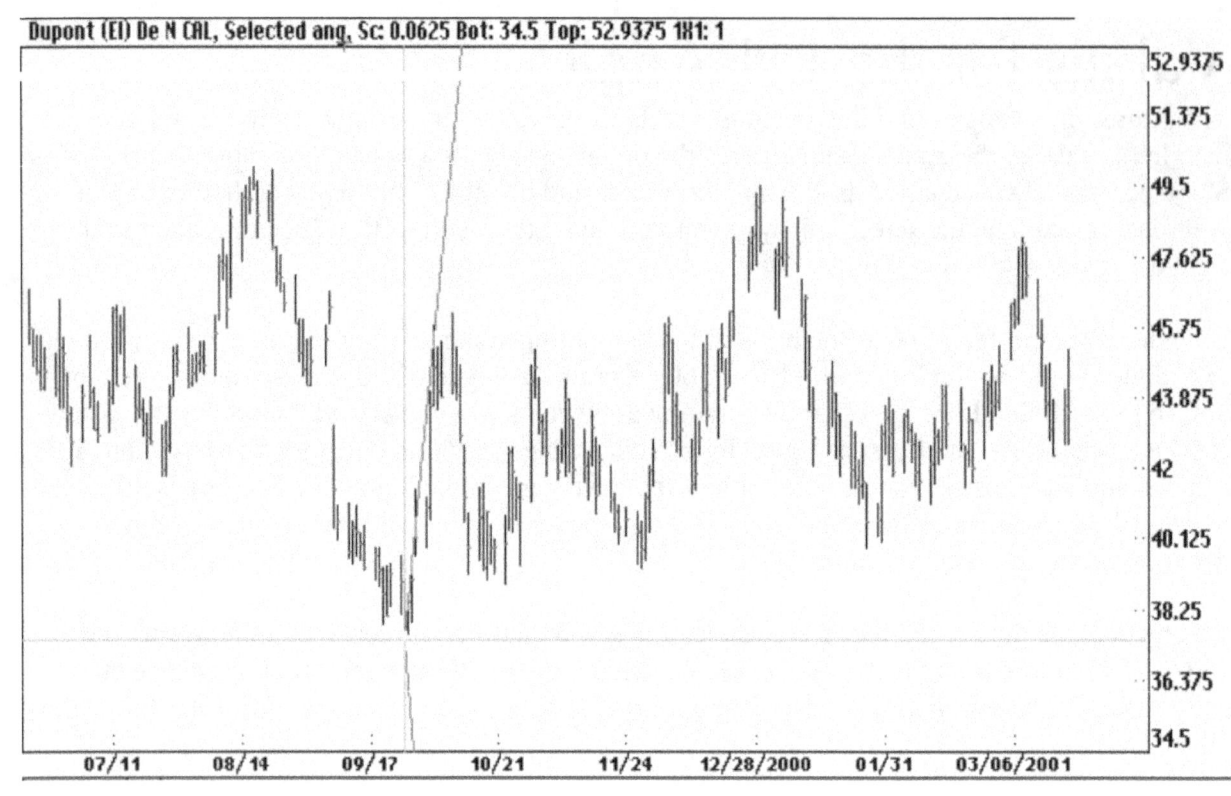

The Live 1x1 Angle

Many Ganntraders use the Live 1x1 angle. In the Ganntrader you can set the Live 1x1 Angle selection under the Setup menu. It allows you to match the 1x1 to the markets actual moves. You can connect a major low to a major high, for example, and consider that the chart's natural angle.

This feature works in conjunction with the Selected Angles mode. You must have at least one angle on the screen. 'Move To' the angle of interest and select Live 1x1 Angle under the Setup menu. Hold the Left mouse button and move the cursor to the second point. Select Live 1x1 Angle again to lock in the new setting. You will see a display of the 1x1 value as you move the cursor around the screen. In the following example of Coco Cola we set the live 1x1 from the bottom to the high. In the second example we used all complementary angles from the same bottom and the same high. See how the angles fit

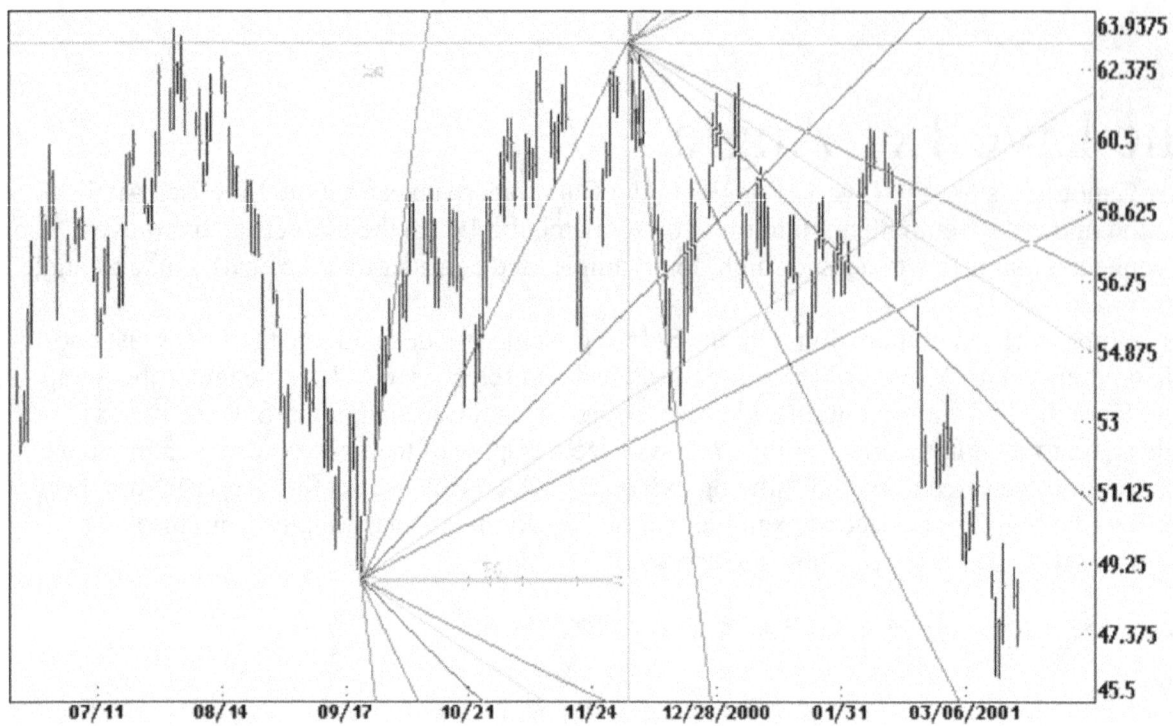

Look at the chart above on Cola Coke showing all of the Gann Angles set to the live angle. It is clear that these angles are the right ones based on how closely they fit the market.

The Live Angles can also be used to create Live Channels based on their same degree. See the chart of Dupont above.

Mirror Image Foldbacks

This feature is not a part of Gann's methods at least not as far as this author is aware. Michael Jenkins describes the method in his 2 excellent books *The Geometry of Stock Market Profits* and *Chart Reading for Professional Traders* as well as his *Complete Stock Market Trading and Forecasting Course*. He learned part of the technique from the late George Lindsay, a master technical analyst. All of Michael Jenkin's writings are available from Traders World and are highly recommended.

Briefly Mr. Jenkins and Mr. Lindsay discovered that markets often appear to reflect or mirror themselves. According to Jenkins this is most likely due to the ending of a natural cycle and the beginning of the next. For now the technique can be easily displayed using Ganntrader's Selected Angle mode. This origin point is marked in the usual way by moving the cursor to the desired point and hitting the <Enter> or <Insert> key. The default 1x1 angle was also turned off leaving only the labeling active. By hitting the <M> key on the keyboard a Mirror image of the dimension line will be displayed. This feature only works on the screen, not on the printed charts.

Here is another example of the daily chart of Dupont.

The same technique also works on weekly charts. See The Weekly Wheat Chart below.

The mirror image foldback also works on monthly charts. See the Gann Soybean Monthly below.

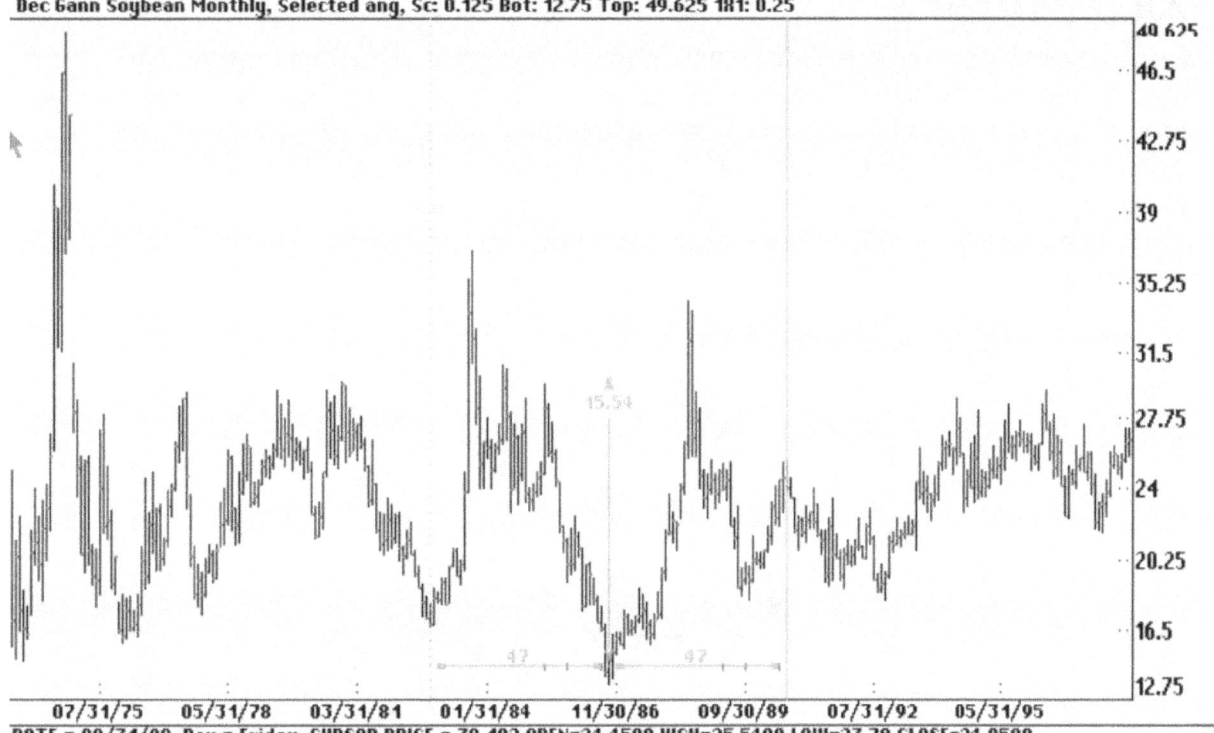

It also works on quarterly charts. See Gann Soybean Quarterly below.

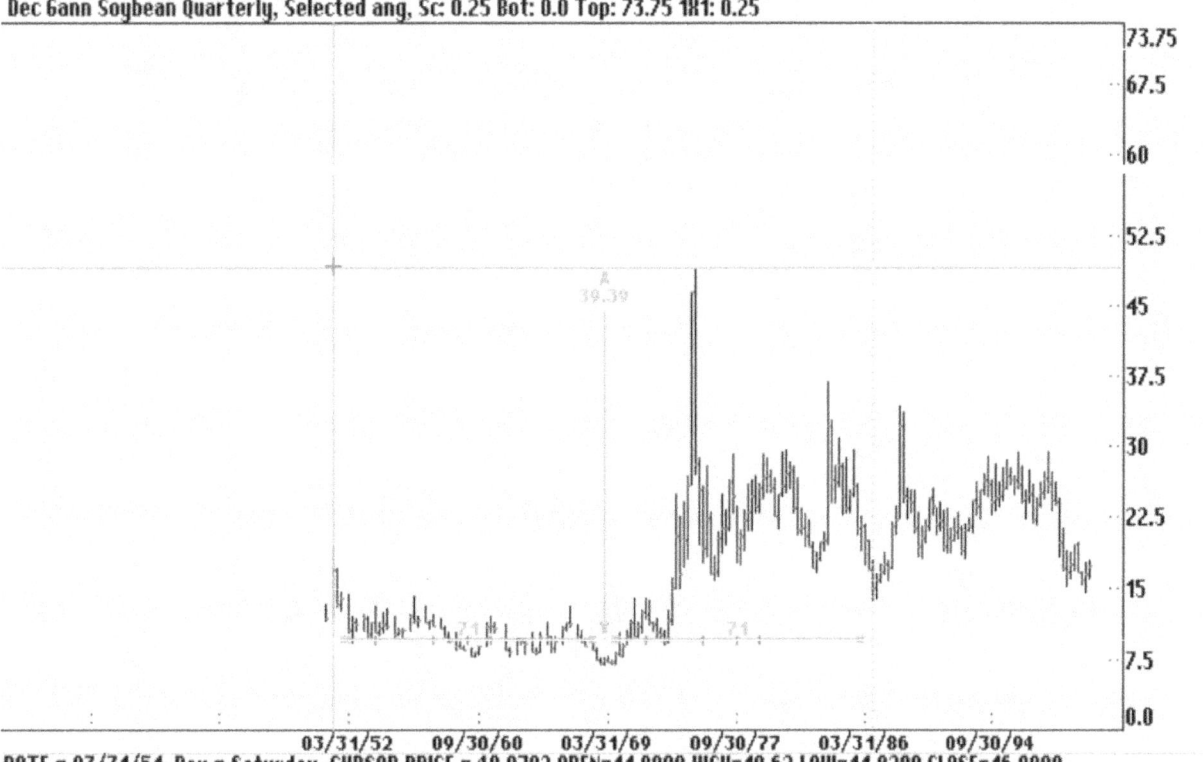

Zero Angles

Gann also charted what he called Zero angles. These are angles that rise up from zero price level and are in line with the date of important highs and lows. They are very important to watch since they often supply the last support point in a falling market. Squares of highs and lows, another Gann method, perform a similar function. To turn on Zero angles in the Ganntrader with any angle mode simply hit the <F10> key. The Zero Angle technique on high numbers works best with weekly, month, quarterly or yearly charts as you are able to see the angles coming up from zero more readily.

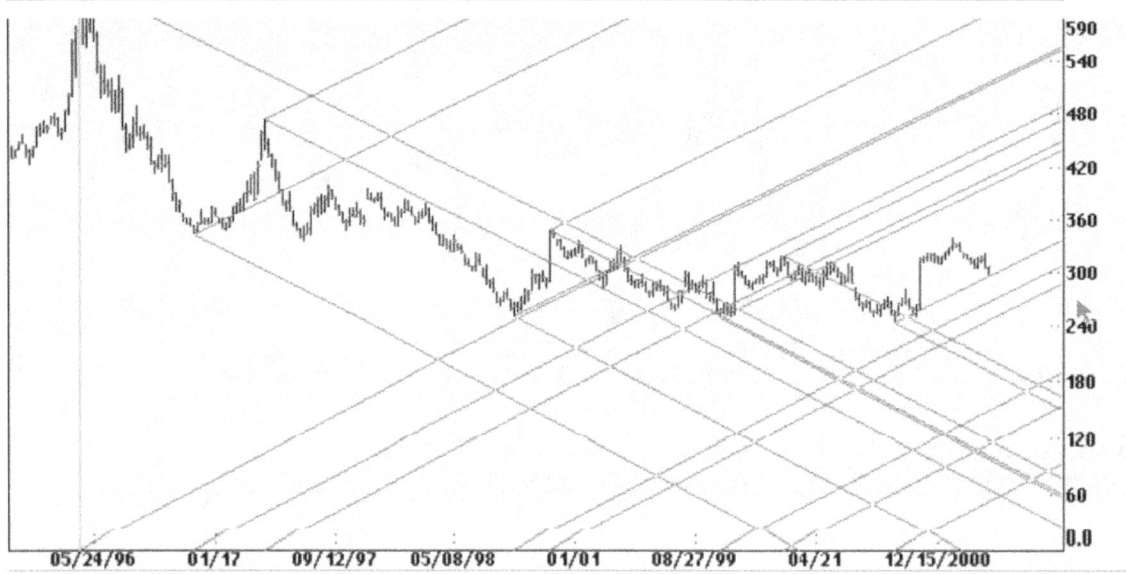

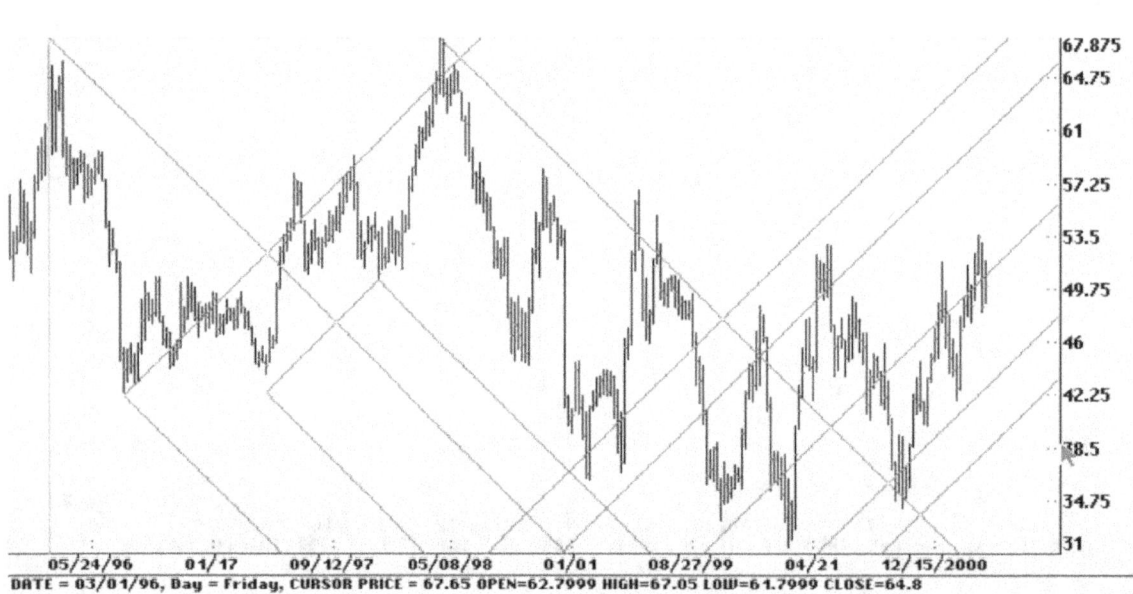

On lower prices it works good on daily charts.

The other Gann angles can also be plotted from the zero line.

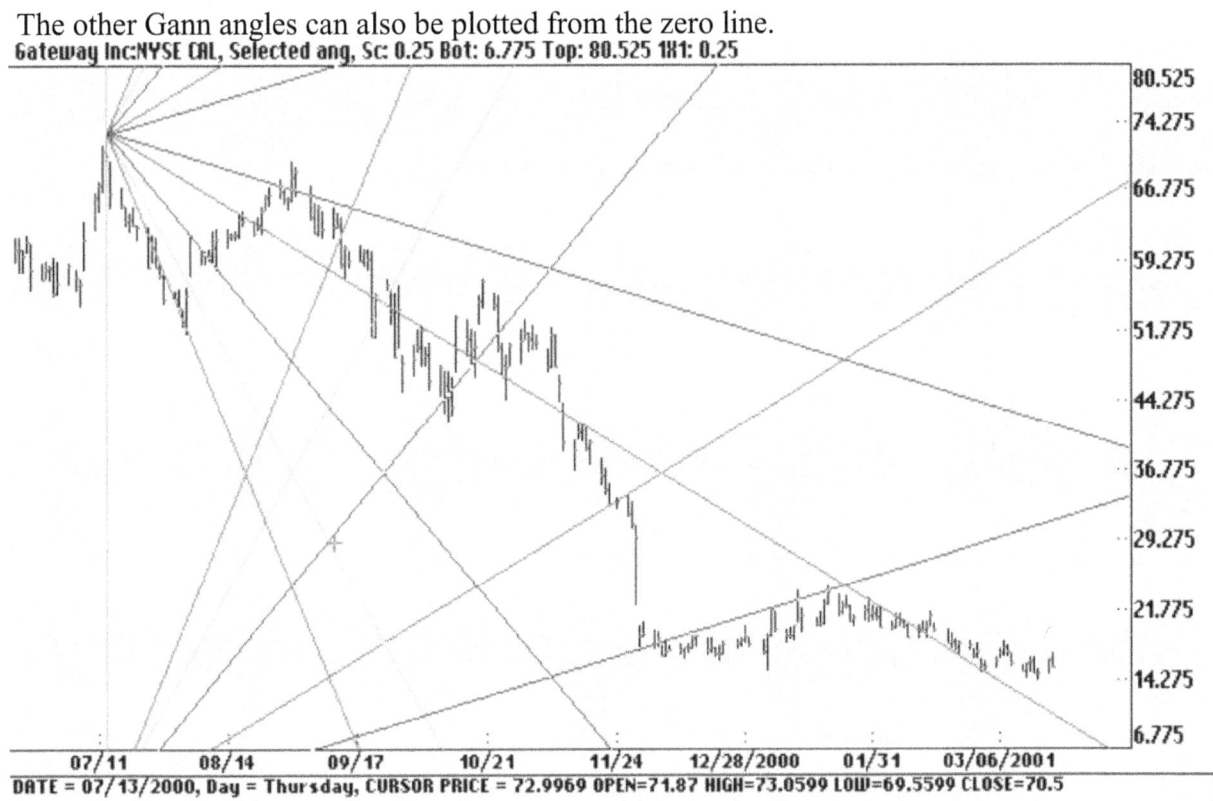

Sizes Labels and Markers

Gann used labels and markers all over his charts. In the Ganntrader you can use Sizes, Labels & Markers under the Option menu that serves several functions. In addition to activating dimension lines the option also displays a dialog box as you 'Move To' each selected angle origin point. The box indicates the price and date of the marked point as well as its active angles. Hit any key and the box will be cleared off the screen.

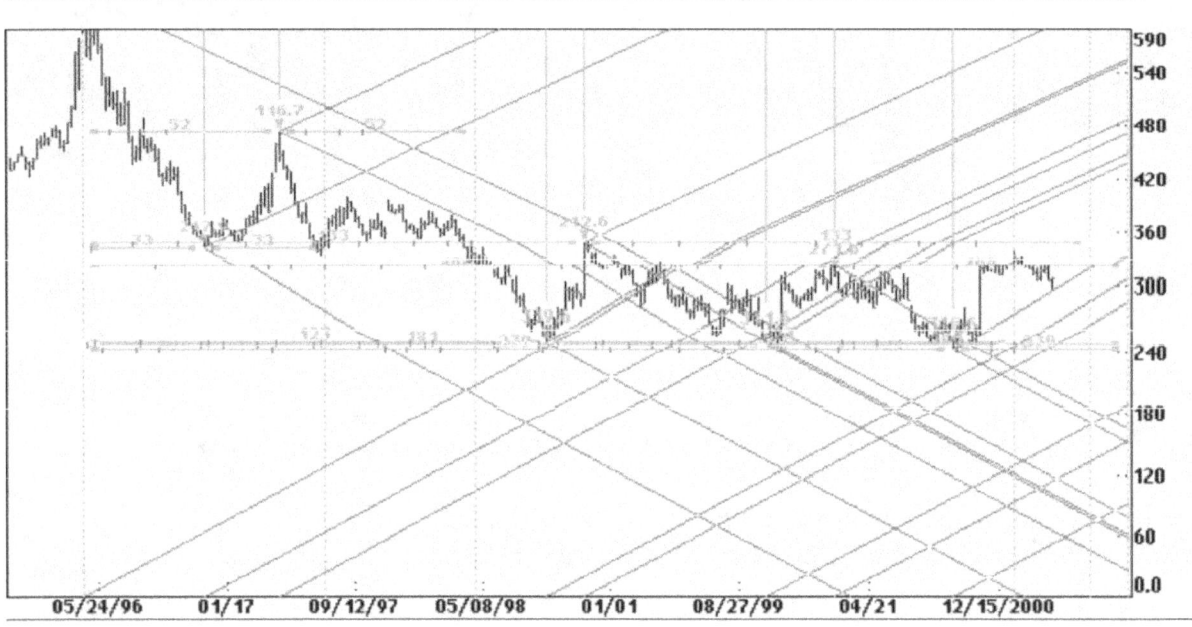

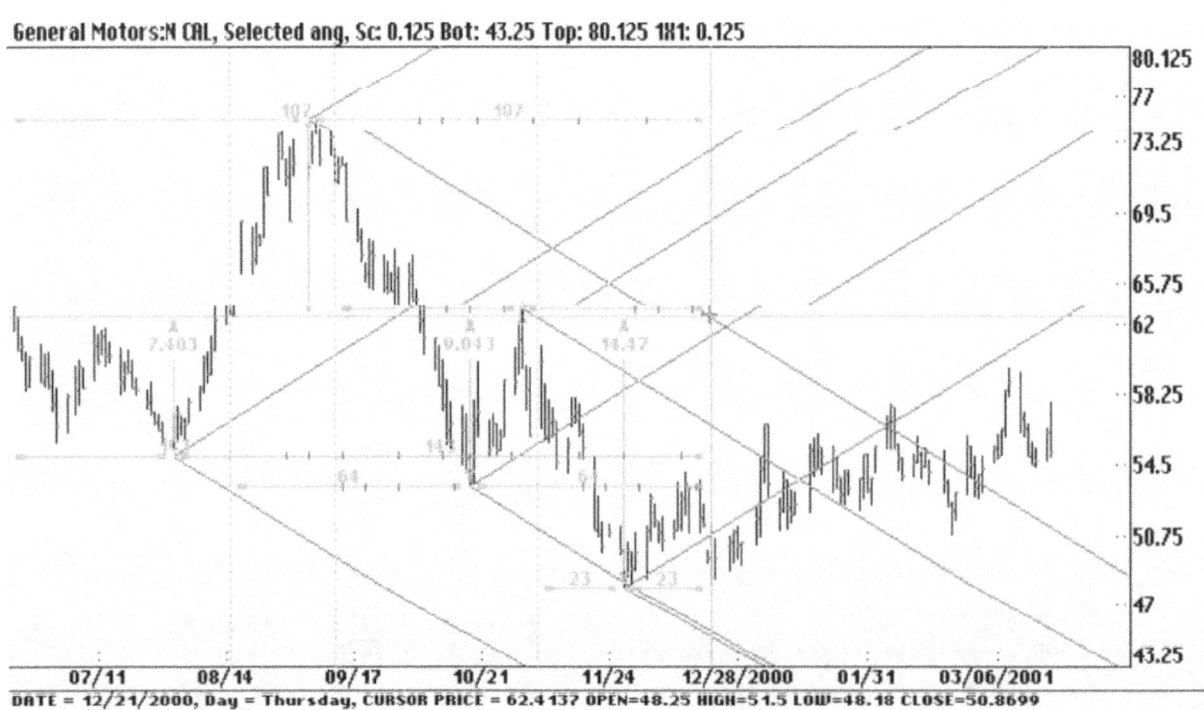

Labels and Markers are very important for timing. You can mark every important top and bottom and move over to the left and click your mouse and you can see the time and price distance from every top and bottom that you previously marked. There are very few programs on the market that have this capability. Gann believed that the more circle points that hit in one point from previous important points that there was a chance for a major change of trend. The circle points are those that can be divided evenly by the circle. For example 360, 180, 90, 45, 22 ½ 11 ¼. 360, 120, 60, 30, 15, 7 ½ and so on. Also keep in mind that if a market made a high at 47 that it would square its time and price out in 47 hours, days, weeks, months years, etc. Labels and Markets can be used to look at these points. In the example below the market made a high at 76 and if you look at the market 76 days over the market was at 25 ½ points down or 1/3 of the top at 76. Again the more point you can find that indicate a possible change of trend the more important is the pivot point.

Labels and Markers should be one of the things you most look for on a chart. You need to find several tops and bottoms with important circle number counts to one date. When you find that you have a high probability the market will turn on that point in time.

The below chart clearly illustrates the use of the labeling system using Mirror Image Foldbacks.

Squares

Gann's price and time squares are one of the most important parts of his methods. Gann's natural or permanent squares include the squares of *52,* 90, 120, 144 and 180. Gann also described methods for squaring the high, low and range of a market. Ganntrader can do all of these squares. In theory, a square is a geometric figure with equal dimensions for its price and time units. It has nothing to do with the square of a number such as the square of 5 = 25. Gann uses the archaic definition of square, which means equal. A square of 90 has 90 price units and 90 time units so that price and time are equal. A line drawn from opposite corners will rise or fall at a rate of 1 ~ or 1$ per unit of time and divides the square in half. Lines drawn vertically and horizontally through the intersection of these diagonal lines also divides the square in half and creates four squares 1/4 the area of the larger. This can be repeated to any degree of sub-division. The Egyptians used this method to measure land and money among other things and it is the basis of a number of Gann's methods.

Some squares are of a fixed size such as 144x144 or 90x90 and are often called natural squares because they measure natural time cycles. Others take the dimension of important high or low prices that have occurred in a given market. An example would be the square of 67 based on the lowest selling price for the May Soybean contract. A third type uses the range of price between an important high and low and has a price and time dimension equal to the difference between the high and low. All of these squares sub-divide an original price cycle into its natural parts. Gann considered everything to be a circle. Circles can be different sizes but they can all be divided into 1/2 or 1/4 parts either in area or by degrees.

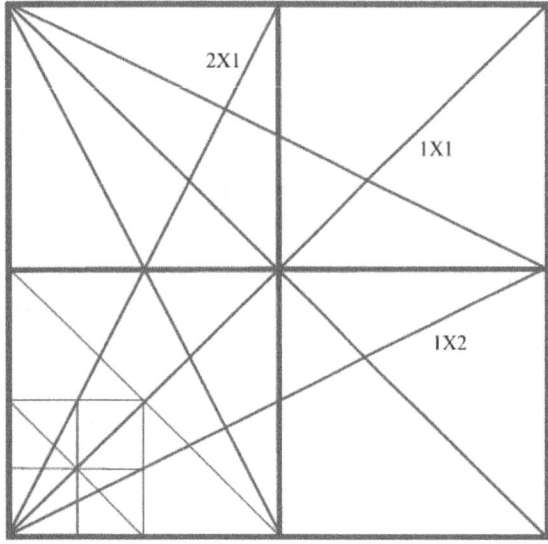

In Gann's day squares actually were square because he used a price scale of 1 cent per price division. Thus a square of 90 would be 90 grid lines up and 90 grid lines across. In today's markets it is difficult or totally impractical to use a true square. The practical solution is to use a larger scale on the chart and adjust it by making a rectangular 'Square' Computer screens offer additional problems that you don't have with a chart. The screens are seldom 'square' and there is the option of adding or removing space between the price bars. The Ganntrader draws a square that is equal in price and time units regardless of whether the resulting square is 'square' on the screen.

When the data file is loaded the program, by default, sets the 1x1 angle to equal the chart scale. Thus any square drawn on the printer will be square in physical shape but the 1x1 lines drawn from corner to corner may not move at 1 point per time period. Because of the increased price levels of today's markets, a square with a 1x1 angle equal to 1 will usually take the shape of a rectangle because of the need to use a price scale greater than 1 cent per division. They are still called squares since the relation of one unit of price to one unit of time is maintained. You can use the default value of the 1x1 or change it to any value desired. It is reset by selecting 1x1 Angle under the Set Up menu or by typing <S><X> from the keyboard.

The Gann squares on the computer are excellent and are very flexible. Some traders prefer to use printed charts. For these charts they use hand made overlays. They make the key overlays based on the circle and have them available to overlay on their charts. The material you use is .005 plastic sheets and permanent fine line magic markets that can draw on plastic. To set these up print out a blank chart of the grid per inch you are going to be working with. Tape down the chart paper and the plastic so that they are fixed on your desk. Then draw the square lines on the plastic overlay material. To draw a 144 overlay you draw it 144 grids up and 144 grids over making a 144 square. See the overlay design on the previous page for a guide.

The most popular squares traders draw are as follows:

180
 90
 45

144
 72
 36

102
 52

Natural Squares

You must know the Natural Squares listed here to trade the methods of Gann. With the Ganntrader using and applying these angles are easy to do. You should refer to the keyboard overlay while using the squares portion of the program. The numbers 1 - 9 across the top of the keyboard are a quick way to enter Gann's common square sizes. The keys are assigned as follows:

1 Special size (See Options Configure System: Preferences: Screen to change.)
2 Square of 120
3 Square of 360
4 Square of 144
5 Square of 52
6 Square of 60
7 Square of 72
8 Square of 180
9 Square of 90

To put a square on the chart simply move the cursor to any desired price and time point and type a number 1 - 9. A square similar to this square of 144 should appear. Notice at the top of the screen that the value of the 1x1 = 1 which will make the price dimension at 144 points. But, notice that the squares on the screen are rectangular. The chart's scale is 8 so the squares are automatically adjusted so that the price dimension is still 144 points.

In this case the 1x1 angle moves 1 point per day so in 144 calendar days it will be up or down 144 points.

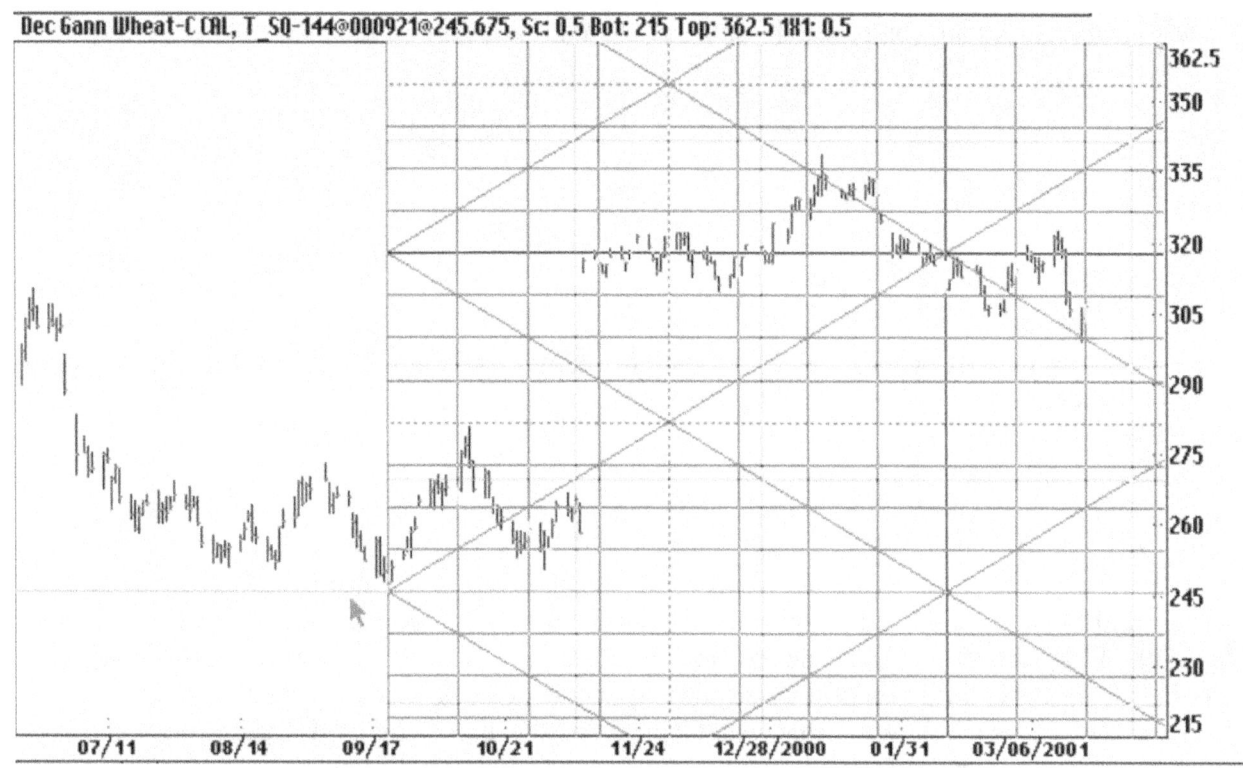

You can add or remove different angles inside the squares using the function keys. Here the 2x1 angle was added with the <F2> key and additional price and time division lines were added using the <F11> and <F12> keys. See chart below.

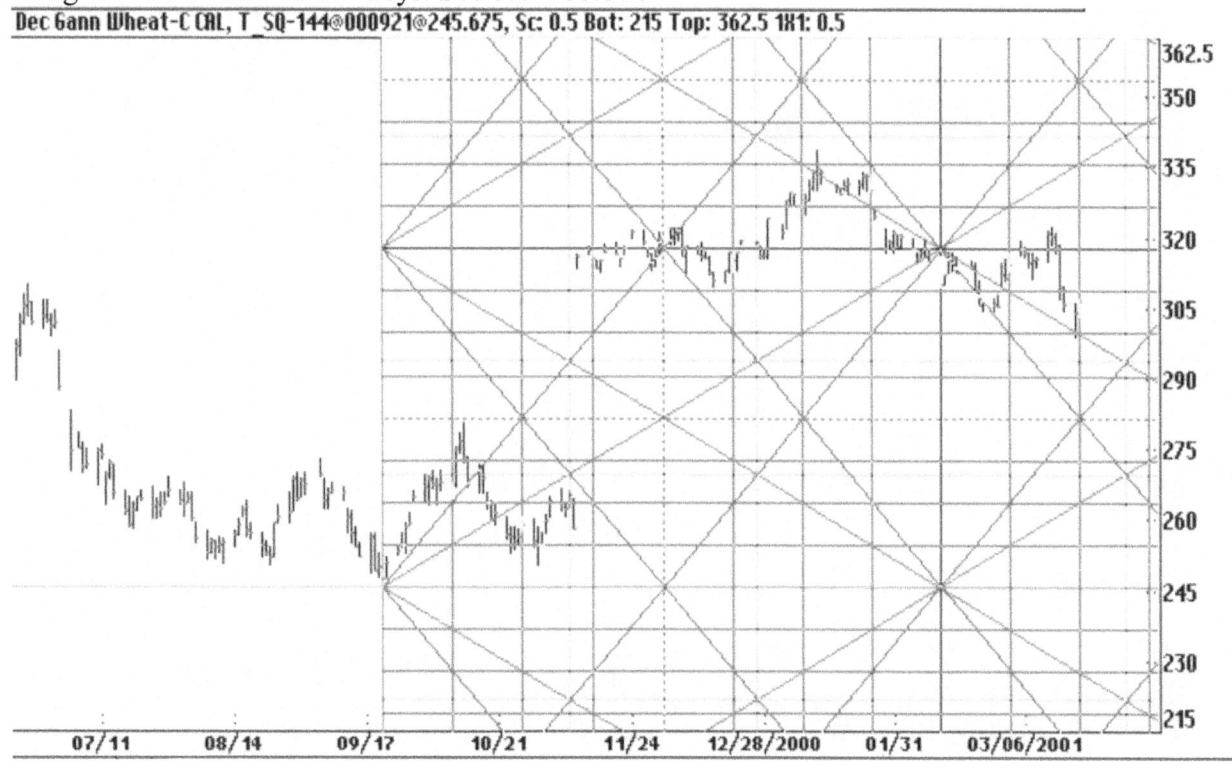

The square's angles are controlled the same as the angles portion of the program:
Fl= lxl
F2= 2x1
F3= 3x1
F4= 4x1
F5= 1x2
F6= 1x3
F7= lx4

The other lesser-used angles are activated with the addition of the <Shift> key. Use the keyboard overlay as a guide. Hold the <Shift> key and type:
F4= 8x1
F5= 16x1
F7= 1x8
F8= 1xl6

A few additional keys affect the squares only. The <F9> and <F 10> add the 1/3 or 1/6 divisions and the <Fl 1> and <F12> keys add the 1/s, 1/4 or 1/2 divisions. These keys rotate through their settings from none, third points and sixth points or none, eighth, quarter and half points respectively. The <F8> key controls what Gann called the Time Angles. They are additional 1X1 angles drawn from the corners, 1/2 point, 1/4 point or 1/8 points of a square.

Temporary Squares Made Permanent

Gann used paper charts and therefore a clear plastic overlay square. He could move it all around the chart in a temporary fashion. The Ganntrader allows you also to have a temporary square which you can make permanent. Notice these natural squares appear under the View menu as Temporary Squares. If you put up a different square the previous square is erased first. They were designed to allow quick tests of the squares. If you would like to make a Temporary Square a permanent entry under the View menu precede the natural Square's number with the letter <P>. For example, P9 would make the square of 90 an entry in the View menu. You could then move to another point and start another temporary square or another permanent square.

Squares of Highs and Lows

A Square of a high or low is a square that has a time and price dimension set to equal a significant high or low price. Here the 669 high in May Soybeans is squared. A square of 669 price and 669 time units is shown. Because of its size only about 2/3 of the total square is on the screen.

A Square of this type is easily set up. Move the cursor to the desired price and time starting point. In this case we moved to 7/25/01 on the price of 75 for a low.

Select Setup Square under the Set up menu. This box will appear...

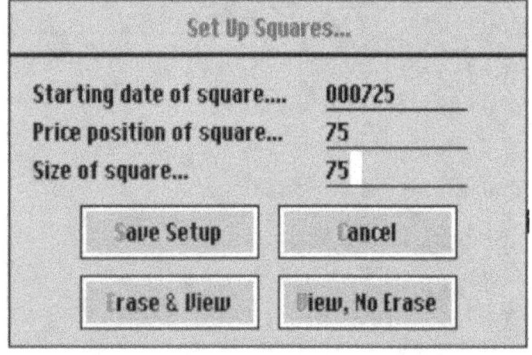

3) Click on Save Setup, Erase & View or View, No Erase. Save Setup places the square setup into the View menu for viewing at a later time. Erase & View also places the setup into the View

menu but also clears any other program features, including other squares, before displaying this setup. The third button, View, No Erase will leave anything on the screen in place and add this square. This feature permits you to place more than one square on the screen at once or to display squares, angles and planets together.

Any of these entries could have been overridden but by moving the cursor to the desired starting point before opening the box all of the desired settings will be entered for you.

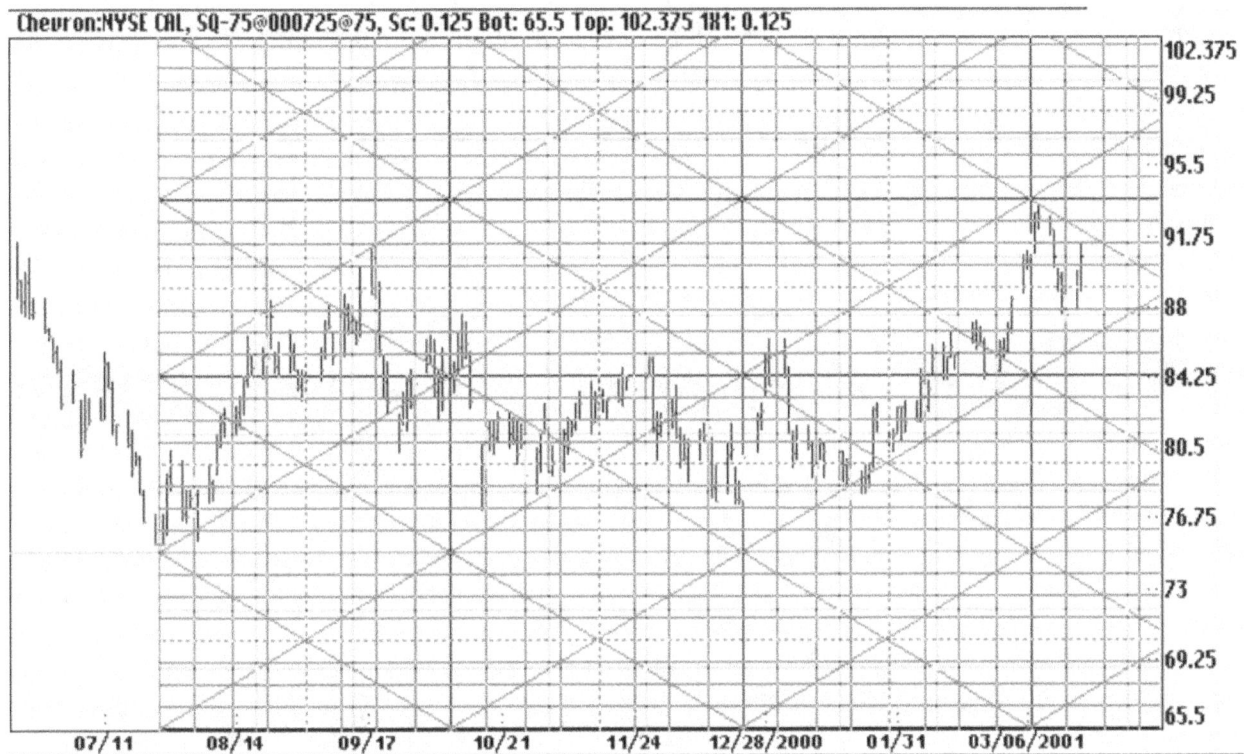

A square of a high or low is equally effective on a weekly or monthly chart.

A square will have an equal price and time dimension when the 1x1 is equal to 1 and the chart's scale is equal to 1.

A chart with a 1x1 starting at the lower left of the square will reach the upper right of the square in the number of days and points specified in the Square Setup. It would be rising 1 point per day. If the 1x1 were set to 2 per day then the top of the square would be double the number. If it were printed on a printer it would also be a rectangle.

Modifying an Existing Square

Gann many times modified his squares. Some of his charts were drawn all over with many angles and timing squares. The Ganntrader allows you to modify squares without messing up your charts. You can add or remove angles or price and time lines at any time after a square is setup. As usual you need to 'Move To' the origin of the square before changes can be made. You can use the backslash key or the Tool Bar icon. Once you are on the origin point the function keys are used in the usual manner. Since you can have more than one square set up from the same origin point use the Options: Sizes, Labels & Markers to help identify the square you want to modify.

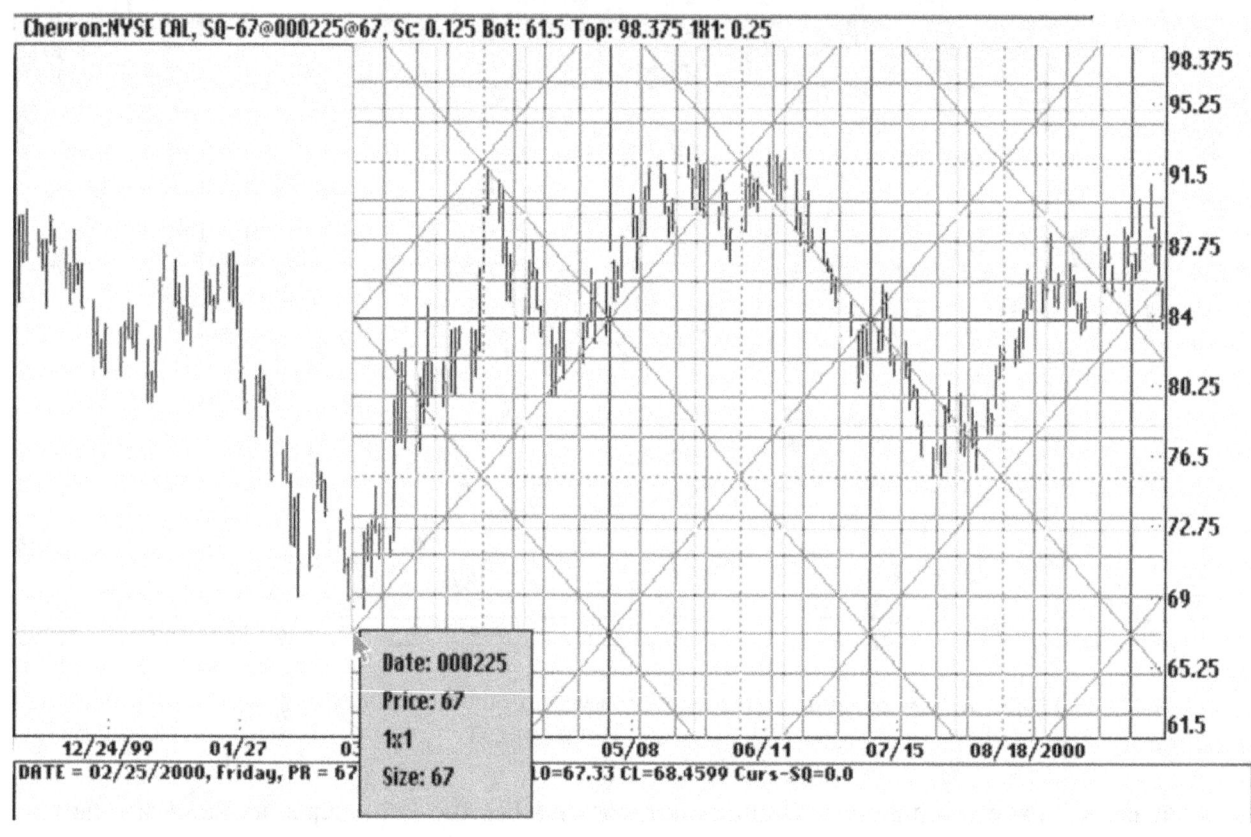

Division of the Range

Division of the Range divides a price or a range between two price levels into eighth and third parts. Gann considered 1/2 of a range or 1/2 of a high price to be very important. Of course any price range can be considered 1/2 of some larger price range so 1/4 of a range is next in importance.

A division of a range is nothing more than the price divisions inside a square. Rather than put on squares from different points it is sometimes easier to simply place the division of the ranges. To divide the range between any two points do the following:
1) Select Options: Divide Range or hit the <D> key on the keyboard. Use <Alt><D> if you want to keep any other modes on the screen without clearing.
2) Move the cursor to the first point and hit the <Enter> or <Insert> key.
3) Move the cursor to the second point and hit the <Enter> or <Insert> key again.
4) You can add or remove division lines using the <Fl0> and <F12> keys.
5) Move to another set of points and mark as many divisions as desired.
Each division will be displayed in an alternating color. There are two vertical dotted lines showing the original range that was marked. At times division lines from two different ranges will overlap one another. These are shown as dotted lines since they are often very important support and resistance points. The 1/2 points of any division are also dotted lines.
You can add or remove range division lines at any time. 'Move to' the origin of the setup and change the lines using the <F10> or <F12> keys or delete it with the <Delete> key.
'Move To' the origin using the <'>, single quote key or use the Tool Bar icon. With the Sizes, Labels & Markets active under the Options menu this box will help you identify the setup you want to modify.

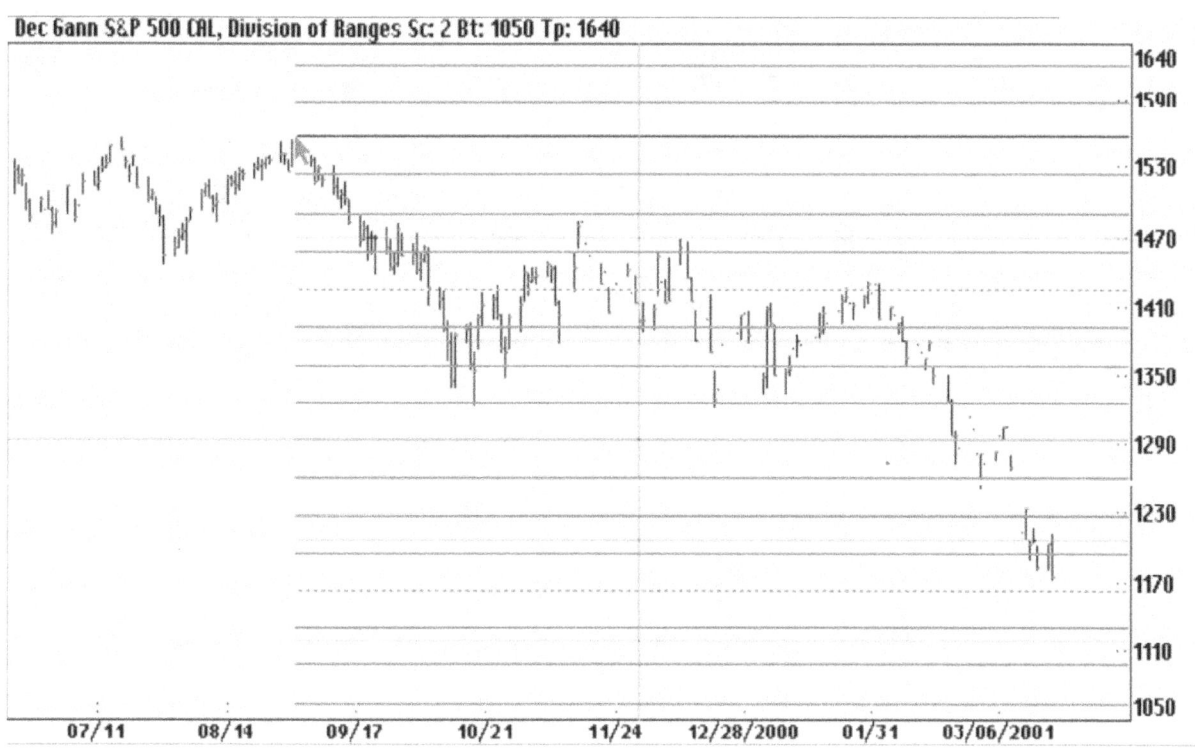

Price Targets Using Ranges

Division of the range can be used to project future price points. Gann used this all the time. You can easily do it in the Ganntrader. You have probably noticed by now that 1/2 of a range is often a point of strong price support and resistance. By locating price clustering and setting the cluster level as 1/2 of the range the top half of the range can be assumed to follow the lower half. Here is an example:

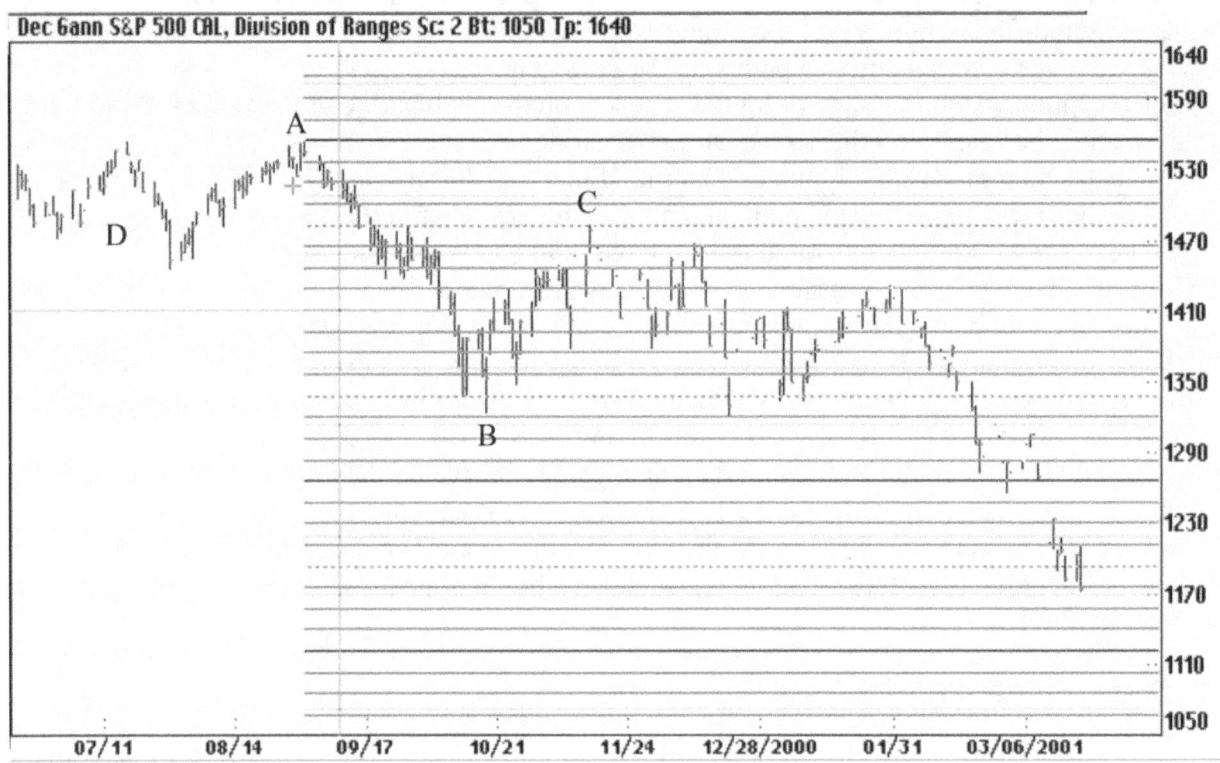

We begin by marking point 'A'. Next, by using the mouse positioned at point 'B' we stretch the lines until the dotted line 1/2 point rests on 'C'. The assumption is that point 'C' is a cluster point that often occurs at the 1/2 point of a range. Our confidence is bolstered by the cluster at 'D' as well as the support and resistance points marked by the horizontal lines. With the first half of the range fitting pretty well we can project that the rest of the chart, hidden by the box, will continue to work.

Price Targets Using 7 Times the Base

Another way to project future price points is by using the 7 Times the Base feature. It is activated under the Options menu in the Ganntrader. When active the program assumes that the range between the two marked points is 1/8 of the final range. The initial range is multiplied by 7 and that value is then added to the initial range so that it becomes the first 1/8 of the whole range. Here's an example:

The range AB, multiplied by 7 is added to AB making a range 8 times larger than AB. You can only start depending on this after you see some type of confirmation such as the support and resistance starting to form at the points marked. The rest of the chart is shown below. This method is more reliable if the same price projection is produced from different starting points.

Squaring a Range with the Mouse

You can square a range in the Ganntrader using the mouse. This is an important task to do by any serious trader of Gann. Here the range between the highest high and lowest low of Apple Computer is squared with the following procedure:

1) Make sure the Snap To function is active by pressing the <Scroll Lock> key or select Options Snap To High / Low. This will make it easier to get the mouse cursor exactly on a high or low.

2) While holding down the Left mouse button move the cursor to the first point, in this case the high at A. The cursor will snap to the high when you are on the price bar and towards the top of the bar.

3) Hold down the <Alt> key.

4) Without releasing the Left button move the mouse to the second point. You will see a box being drawn with the price difference between point A and B displayed.

5) At any time you may release the <Alt> key.

6) When you release the Left mouse button the square will be drawn. See the second chart of Eastman Kodak. The square extends to the right.

This will produce a temporary square of this range. You can erase the square by holding down the <Alt> key and clicking the Right mouse button. The square will also erase when you start drawing another one.

Gann found that squaring of ranges as one of him most important techniques. You should always square previous ranges to find the important support and resistance points of today's market. After you square the range Ganntrader will draw a square to the right of the square with the square and the angles inside of it. If you look at the example below, you will be amazed at how accurately the square fits the market.

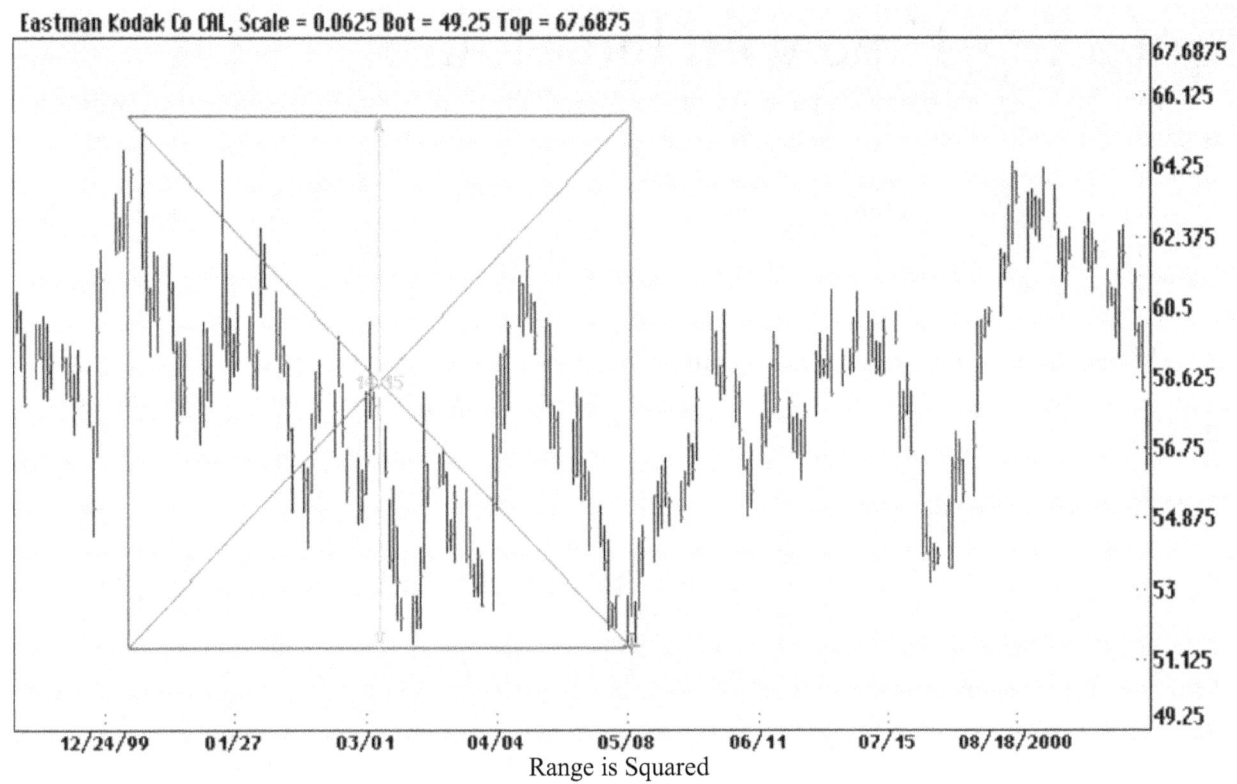
Range is Squared

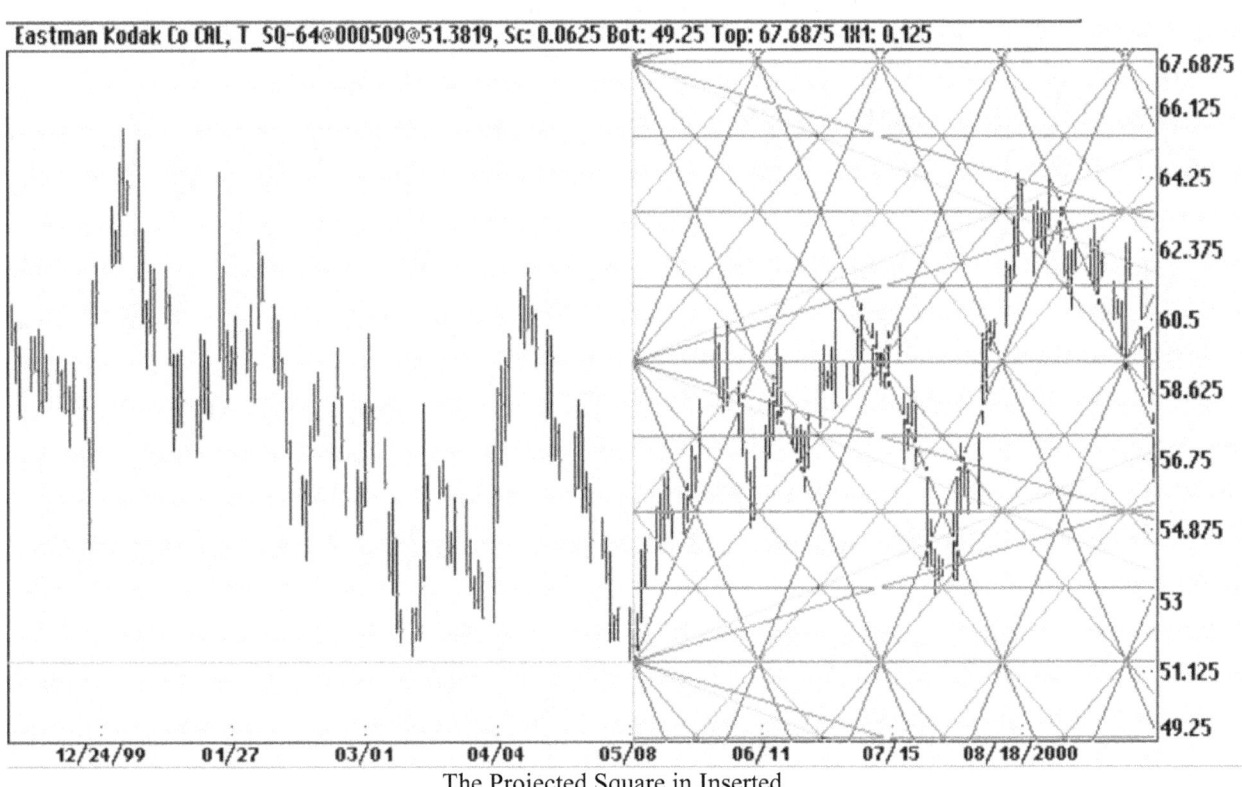
The Projected Square in Inserted

Squaring Time with the Mouse

The time between two points can also be squared. Here the time between a high and a lower high is squared by the following procedure in the Ganntrader:

1) Make sure the Snap To function is active by pressing the <Scroll Lock> key or select Options Snap To High / Low. This will make it easier to get the mouse cursor exactly on a high or low.

2) While holding down the Left mouse button move the cursor to the first point, in this case the high at A. The cursor will snap to the high when you are on the price bar and towards the top of the bar.

3) Hold down the <Ctrl> key.

4) Move the mouse to the second point. You will see the following box being drawn with the time difference between point A and B displayed.

5) At any time you may release the <Ctrl> key.

6) When you release the Left mouse button the square will be drawn. This will produce a temporary square of this time range. You can erase the square by holding down the <Ctrl> key and clicking the Right mouse button. The square will also erase when you start drawing another one.

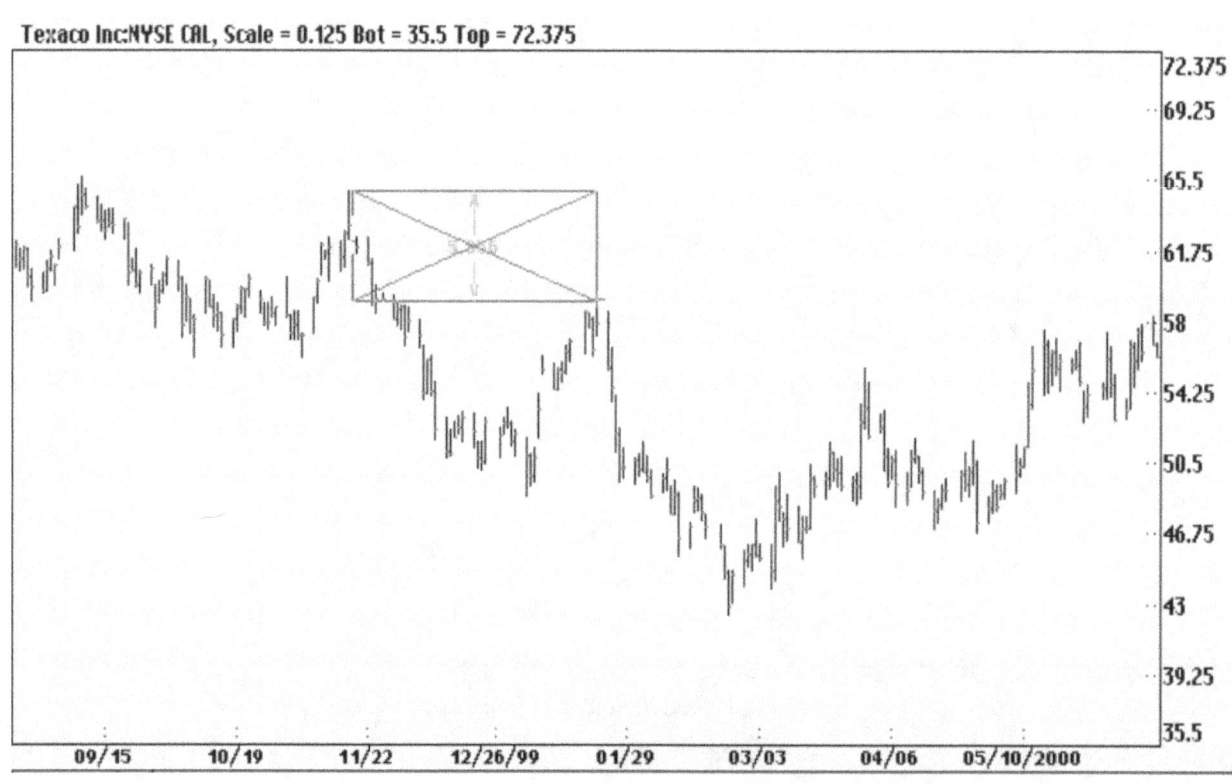

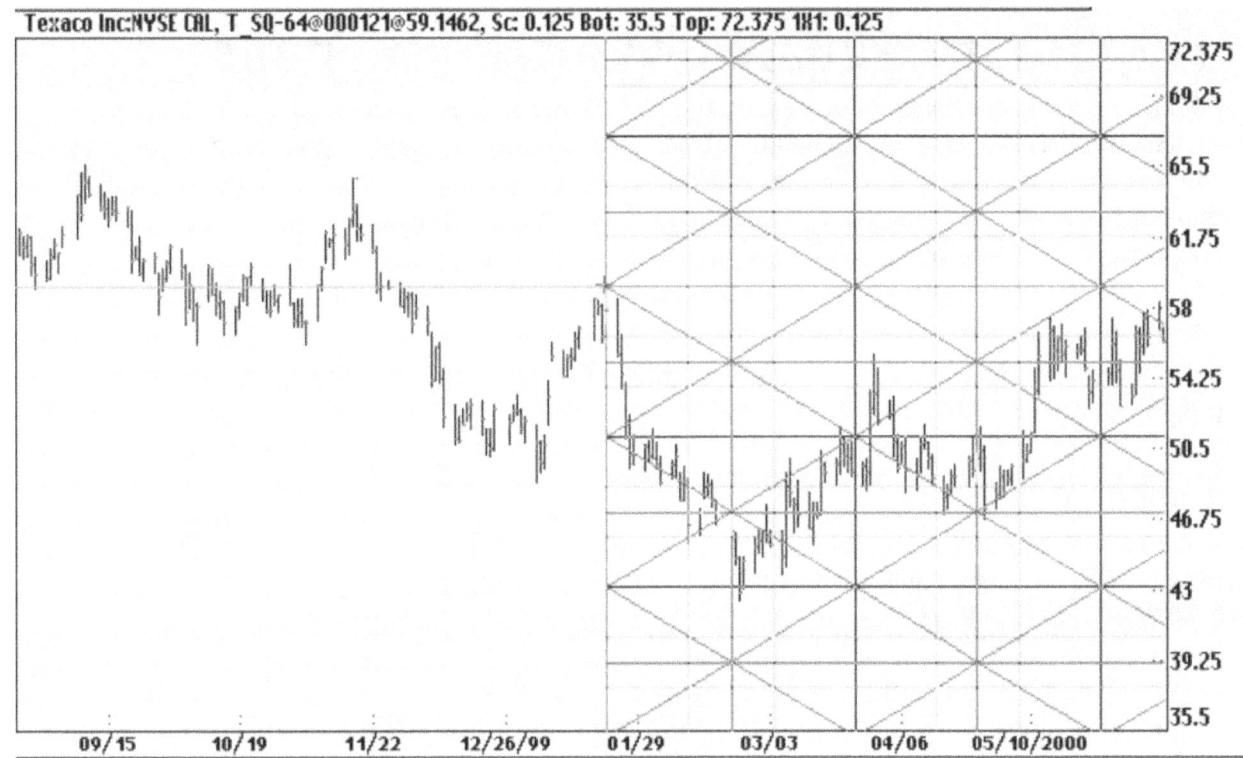

It's quite amazing how the trend on the second chart takes hold. Both time and price points are nearly perfect in the above example of Texaco. Look how accurately the upward trend channel holds the bottom of the market formed in early May of 2000. Also see how the top of the price trend is restrained by the highs hit late in the month. This method used by Gann is clearly one of the most valuable ones around.

As you know, most of the current crop of software trading programs will not make squares on your chart or keep your chart square all the time. That's what really sets the Ganntrader apart from these other run-of-the-mill programs. Ganntrader is truly a professional trading and research program for serious Gann students.

Temporary Squares Made Permanent

Squaring price or time using the mouse produces Temporary Squares under the View menu in the Ganntrader. They were designed to allow you to quickly move through a chart trying various square setups. If you find a setup that you'd like to make permanent draw it again in the usual manner but hit the <P> key prior to releasing the Left mouse button. This will make a permanent entry under the View menu.

Deleting a Square

You can delete a square in a number of ways depending on whether it is a permanent or temporary square.

Temporary Squares:

If the square is a Natural Square that you create using the number keys simply hit the same number again and the square will be erased. For example, the number <9> key puts on a square of 90. If you hit the key again and the square clears off the screen.

If you squared the range using the <Alt> + Left mouse button or squared the time using <Ctrl> + Left mouse button you can clear the square from the screen by holding either the <Alt> or <Ctrl> key and click on the Right mouse button.

Permanent Squares:

Permanent Squares will be listed under the View menu. There are several ways to delete them from the list:

1) 'Move To' the origin of the square using the </> backslash key or the Tool Bar icon and then hit the <Delete> key.

2) Select List Square... under the View menu, select the square and hit the Delete button.

3) Select Change Any Setup under the Set up menu, select the square and hit the Delete button.

Square of 9

The Square of 9 is one of Ganntrader's most powerful tools. Before you can understand what the program is doing with the feature you have to be familiar with how the basic Square of 9 works.

On the next page we have a copy of the Square of 9, which is also available in a Microsoft Excel template version included with the CD in the back of this book. Please look at the square in front of you as we try to explain its use.

The chart consists of a spiral of numbers beginning with '1' in the center and expanding outward in a clockwise direction. It is often called the 'Square of 9' because of the fact that the first square in the center ends on the number '9'. The real Square of 9 is something altogether different but the name has been used enough that we will refer to it as the 'Square of 9' rather than the 'Master Price and Time Calculator' as Gann named it. Notice the numbers 9, 25, 49, 81... running along the Southwest corner of the square and the numbers 4, 16, 36, 64, 100... running along the Northeast corner. These are what Gann refers to as the odd and even squares of numbers. The odd squares are 3x3 = 9, 5x5 = 25... and the even squares are 2x2 = 4, 4x4 = 16... In theory the numbers could be expanded to infinity; Gann had squares that extended to 1089 (33x33) or 2025 (45x45). Over the years there have been Gann Wheels produced that extended to over 10,000. In all versions the odd squares are along one corner and the even squares along the opposite corner.

Note that each 3600 ring from odd square to odd square increases by 8 points over the previous ring. From 1 to 9 is 8 points, from 9 to 25 is 16 points, from 25 to 49 is 24 points and so on. A 3600 move on the wheel follows the mathematical formula $(\sqrt{n} + 2)2$. Take the square root of any number 'n' on the wheel add 2 and square the results. For example, the square root of 25 is 5, add 2 give 7. Squaring 7x7 gives 49 which is 3600 out from 25. Any other degree position is derived by using fractional parts of 2. A 900 move is 0.5 added to the square root of the original number, for example. This formula, used by the program, produces results, which are more accurate than the mechanical square's number distribution.

Notice that the even squares should be exactly 1800 from the odd squares using this formula but that would require adding a little more space in the first 1800 of a turn and a little less space between numbers in the second 1800 swing. In the 1930's Gann was laying these charts out on regular graph paper and being that precise was not possible. Imagine what he could have done with a computer! Keep this fact in mind when you compare the program's output with the actual chart's numbers.

Because of this square root expansion there are more numbers between the corners of the chart the further out from the center you go. This explains why higher priced markets move a greater number of points up or down than lower priced markets do. There are simply more numbers between the corners and sides which are the stable points in the chart.

The Square of 9 also contains a calendar distributed around the outside of the square of numbers. There are two squares that Gann used. One has the March 21, 0° point, on the right side of the chart and the other has the March 21 point on the left side of the chart. In one case the degrees increase from 0° to 360° in a clockwise direction and the other in a counter-clockwise direction. I have heard several theories on why Gann had the 2 different charts but to my knowledge he never explained the reason. In my opinion one works better in a down market and the other works better in an up market. The Ganntrader is programmed to handle both charts equally well. Notice this calendar divides the 365.25 days of the year evenly around a circle of 360°. On both charts June 21 is always on top and December 21 is always on the bottom. Every 15° move of the Sun is also shown marked off You will often see markets make highs and lows on these natural divisions of the yearly cycle.

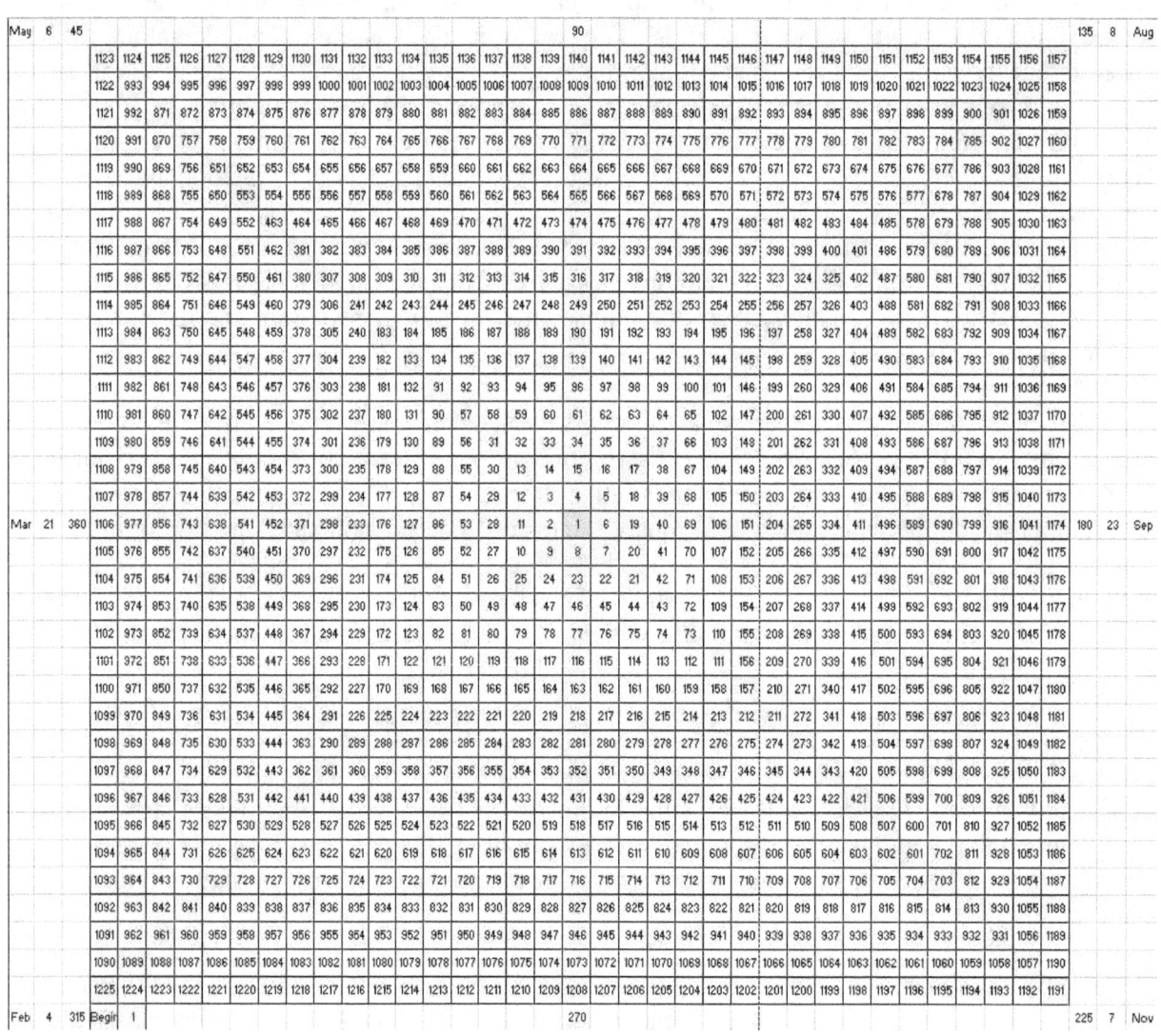

Square of 9 on the Natural Cycle of 365.25

One of the most common ways to use the square is on the natural divisions of the year. We will start with a chart of Apple Computer and show why the prices changed direction when they did using both the program and the mechanical Square of 9. Of the 2 squares provided in the back of the manual we will duplicate the clockwise item with March 21 on the left side. Notice the date of Feb. 4 is on the SW corner. We will use that date as the starting point for the square. Select Setup SQ9 Setup and the following entry box will appear:

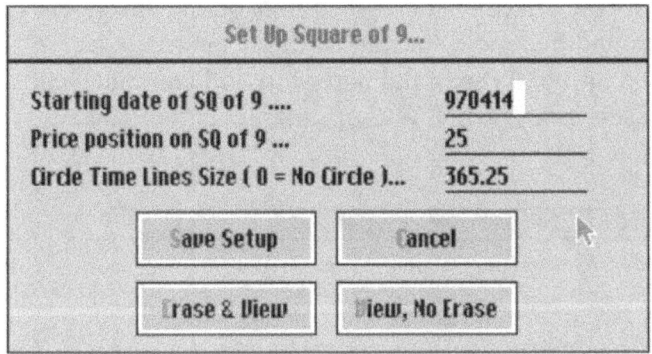

We are entering February 4, 1997 as the starting point of the square. The price position can be any odd square such as 25, 49, 81... All of the other odd and even squares will be generated from this starting point so any odd square will do. The circle size represents the number of time periods represented by the outer circle of 3600. In this case a calendar year of 365.25 days will be spread around the wheel. If we were using a trading day chart this circle size would be 261 (5/7 x 365.25) or perhaps 250 to exclude the holiday market closings during the weekday. It is far simpler to use a calendar day chart with this value set to 365.25. If you enter 365.25 and the chart happens to be a trading day chart the program will suggest that you switch to a 7-day chart. You can set a default circle size by selecting Options: Configure System: Preferences:

Erase & View will clear whatever might be on the screen and put this setup in its place. View, No Erase will leave whatever setup is on the screen in place. Save Setup will save this Square of 9 setup for later display.

Clicking on Erase & View will produce a chart like the one on the next page.

Notice how the chart prices hit the vertical and horizontal lines so perfectly. If you set the chart up correctly using the Square of 9 you will find that it is a valuable chart to have on hand.

Square of 9 Time Divisions

The vertical lines divide the time circle of 365.25 days into 1/4, 1/2, 3/4, 1/3 and 2/3 parts. The magenta lines are the 90° and 270° 1/4 and 3/4 points. The dotted red line is the 180° 1/2 point, and the green lines are the 1/3 and 2/3 120° points. Locate these dates on the Square of 9 chart: May 6 at 45° in the NW corner, August 8, the 1/2 point at 135° or 180 away from the February 4 starting point at 315° and November 7 at the 3/4, 270° point. Use the clear overlay dial by placing the '0' arrow point on February 4 and locate the 120° and 240° points on the dates of June 6 and October 8. These are 1/3 and 2/3 around the circle starting from the February 4 corner. These lines evenly divide the calendar year into its seasonal parts and will continue year after year hitting these same dates. As you can see from the below chart, markets often make a turn on these yearly cycles and fractional parts.

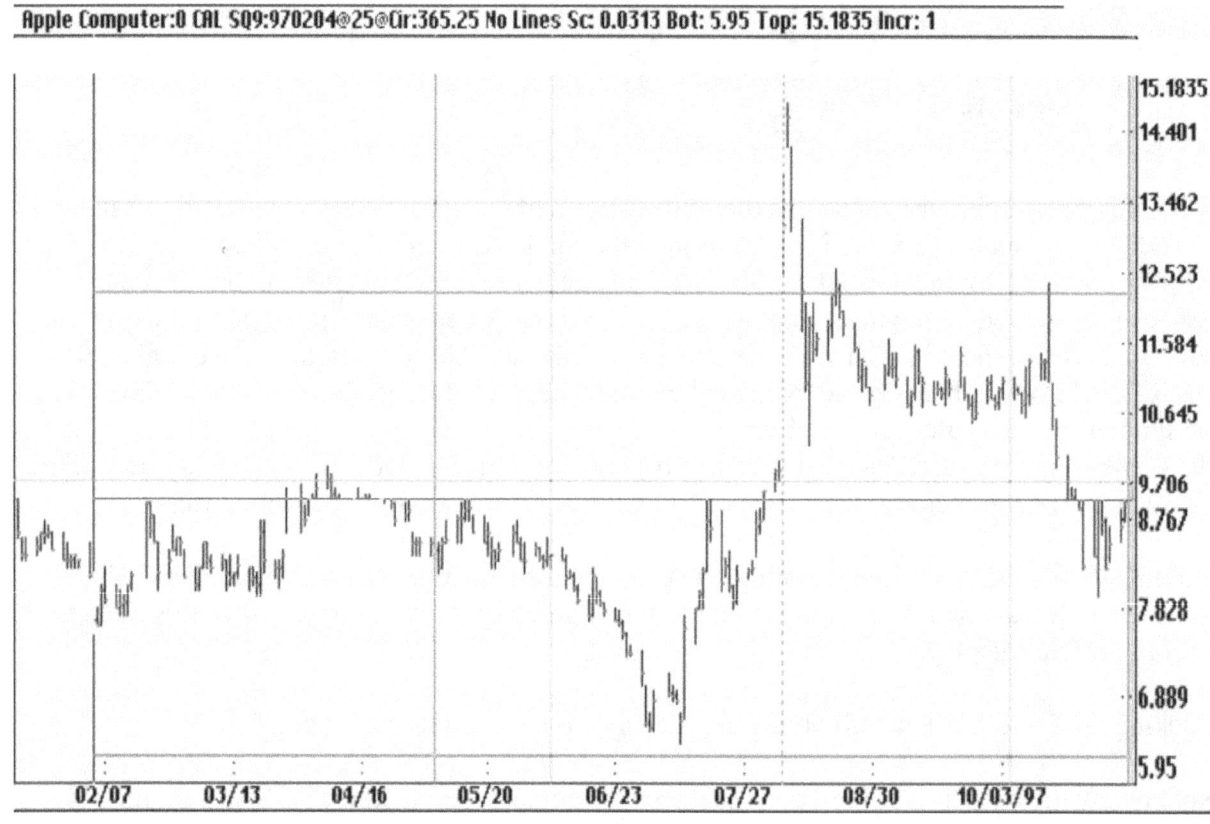

Square of 9 Price Divisions

Price divisions of the Square of 9 divide up the square into 900 and 120° increments but the division lines are not linear from the bottom to the top of the chart. The prices expand by a factor of 8 points as the prices move into each higher odd square. In the previous chart the difference in price from the 90° line at 12.25 and the odd square line below it at 9 is 3.25 points. (12.25 - 9) The difference between the odd square line at 25 and the 90° line above it is 5.25 points. (30.25 - 25) One of Gann's discoveries was that markets become more volatile at higher price levels. The distance from corner to corner on the Square of 9 expands as you move out from the center. Gann developed the Square of 9 as a tool to measure and predict this expansion.

The previous chart of Apple Computer shows that the prices find support and resistance at 16, 20.25 but when there is a breakout above 25 the market moves all the way to 30.25. When it broke 25 it went into a new energy level between 25 and 49 and the full circle is 24 points (49-25) rather than 16 points in the previous ring. (25-9). If the price resistance levels of the previous ring had prevailed the price should have stopped at 28.25 (25 + 3.25) or 29.25 (25 + 4.25) but instead it went all the way to 30.25 which is the new resistance level in the new energy ring of 25 to 49. Compare the price levels calculated by the program and the prices on the mechanical wheel. Starting from '9' the numbers 90 degrees clockwise are 13 followed by 17, 21, 25, and 31. This is as accurate as you can get using a mechanically drawn figure. The more precise values are 12.25, 16, 20.25, 25 and 30.25. (3.5, 4, 4.5 and 5.5 squared) This Apple Computer chart is proof that the calculated values are more correct than the mechanical wheel's numbers.

Other Price and Time Divisions

The default price and time divisions of the Square of 9 are 900, 1800, 2700, 1200 and 2400. The function keys, as shown on the keyboard overlay, control which angles are displayed on the Square of 9 as follows:

Key Degrees
F1 = 11 ¼°
F2 = 15°
F3 = 22 1/2°
F4 = 30°
F5 = 45°
F6 = 60°
F7 = 72°
F8 = 90°
F9 = 120°
F10 = 180°

You may find the 450 increments useful at times. The sample charts shown in this section have the 45° lines turned off for clarity but they often produce more hits in both price and time. The finer divisions of 11 1/4° and 15° work best on intra-day charts. If you want to quickly change the angles hold down the <Alt> key and the desired function key. All other angles will be removed.

Increment Value

Sq of 9 Increment Value under the Setup menu permits you to change the increment value from the default value of 1.0. All calculated values are multiplied by this value before being displayed. Some markets such as T-Bonds might work better with an increment of .125 (4-32) rather than 1.0. The increment value effects the horizontal price division lines as well as the trend lines covered in the next section. This feature is mainly included for experimentation purposes. It is difficult to find a market example that shows the need for this feature. Most charts work well with a value of 1, the default.

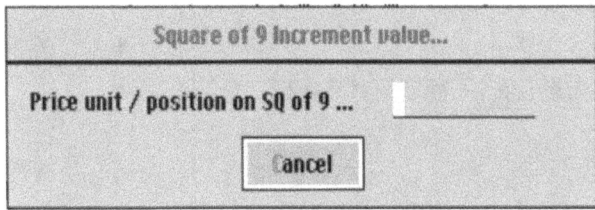

Square of 9 Circle Price Lines

This is a Square of 9 chart of Apple Computer with its origin point on February 4, 1997, prior to its all time low. It matches the clockwise rotating square with March 21 on the left, The starting price was 25, an odd square. The time and price divisions as described previously are shown. In addition, a series of upward moving Price Circle trend lines are included. These price lines are turned off by default but can be activated by hitting the <P> key on the keyboard. Each time the <P> key is hit it rotates from 'No Lines', 'Origin Lines', up down and both and these 'Natural Lines', up, down and both for a total of 7 possible settings. We will discuss 'Origin Lines' later. The lines on this chart are the natural divisions of the odd and even squares and are thus labeled the 'Natural Lines'.

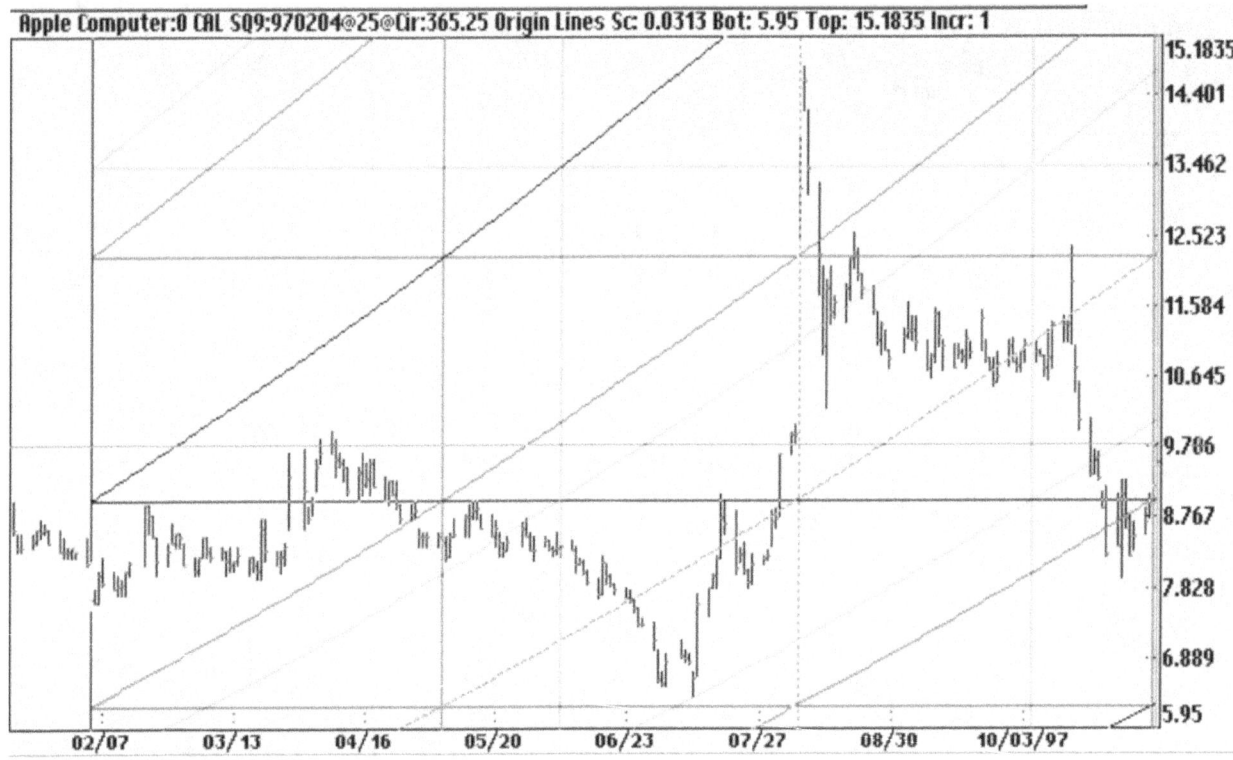

There lines connect the odd square price level to the next odd square price level, the even square to the next even square and all the lines in between to their corresponding points. At the end of each circle the lines have moved up one ring of the Square of 9. They become steeper and steeper in a gradual curve as they reach the beginning of each new circle of 365 days or in this case every February 4. The trend lines are slightly faster with each energy level as shown by the 2 lines drawn near the point E.

Gann tried to keep track of these points using a mechanical wheel. He most likely missed many setups. The Ganntrader makes them all very easy to see.

In this chart we have added the down Natural Angles by hitting the <P> key until both the up and down angles are displayed. These down angles hit most of the reactions in this bullish chart. Had

we started these charts from November 7, the counter-clockwise chart, instead of February 4 we would have seen a similar cluster of lines in the same locations. On one chart a 90 degree line might be a Square line or a 180° line but they would be plotted at the same points on the chart. Notice on the two squares that February and November 7 are 90° apart. In the up and down 90° angles are displayed in a single chart started from either November 7 or February 4 will suffice. Try it yourself.
]

You can add or remove any of the angles in an existing Square of 9 simply my moving to the origin of the square and then hitting the appropriate function key. 'Move To' the origin using the <?/>, forward slash key, or use the Tool Bar icon.

The Circle Price Lines are modified for all squares on the screen by alternating through the <P> key. The settings are No Angles, Up Origin Angles, Down Origin Angles, Both Origin Angles, Up Natural Angles, Down Natural Angles, Both Natural Angles and back to No Angles again.

Square of 9 from a High or Low

We have moved the cursor to the low of 12.75 on December 30, 1997. Next we selected Setup SQ9 Setup and this box will appear. All the information is already entered for us so a simple click on Erase & View will put the chart below on the screen. With this technique the program will draw price and time divisions starting from 12.75 and the date of 12/30/97. With the dial locate the '0' arrow point on December 30. The 900 dates work out to be March 31, July 1 and September 30. The 1200, 1/3 points are May 1 and August 30.

Now move the dial arrow to the price of 12.75. The 900 moves will be at 16.57, 20.89, *25.71* and 31.03. The 1200 points are at 15.24 and 17.95. With this chart and the previous ones every turn in AAPL can be determined.

Here the lines were switched to Origin Lines meaning they build from the origin price of 12.75 rather from an odd square price level. You can also use Natural Lines from the same starting date. These often provide some interesting results.

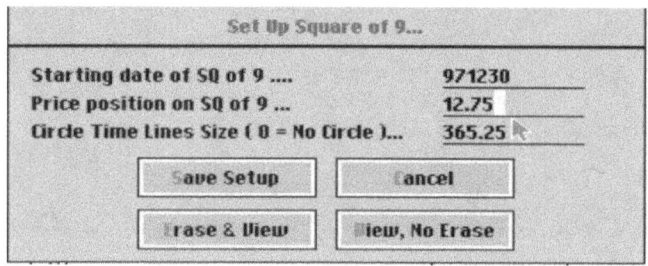

Other Square of 9 Circle Sizes

We mentioned using 261 or 250 for a trading day chart. Another size you will want to use is 52 on a weekly chart. What you are specifying is the number of time period that are represented by a circle or cycle of 360°. If you think about it any Time Cycle can be represented on the square of 9. Mercury has an 88-day cycle and Venus is 225 days. The ambitious student will want to try them all! Since a picture is worth a thousand words is an example of December Corn.

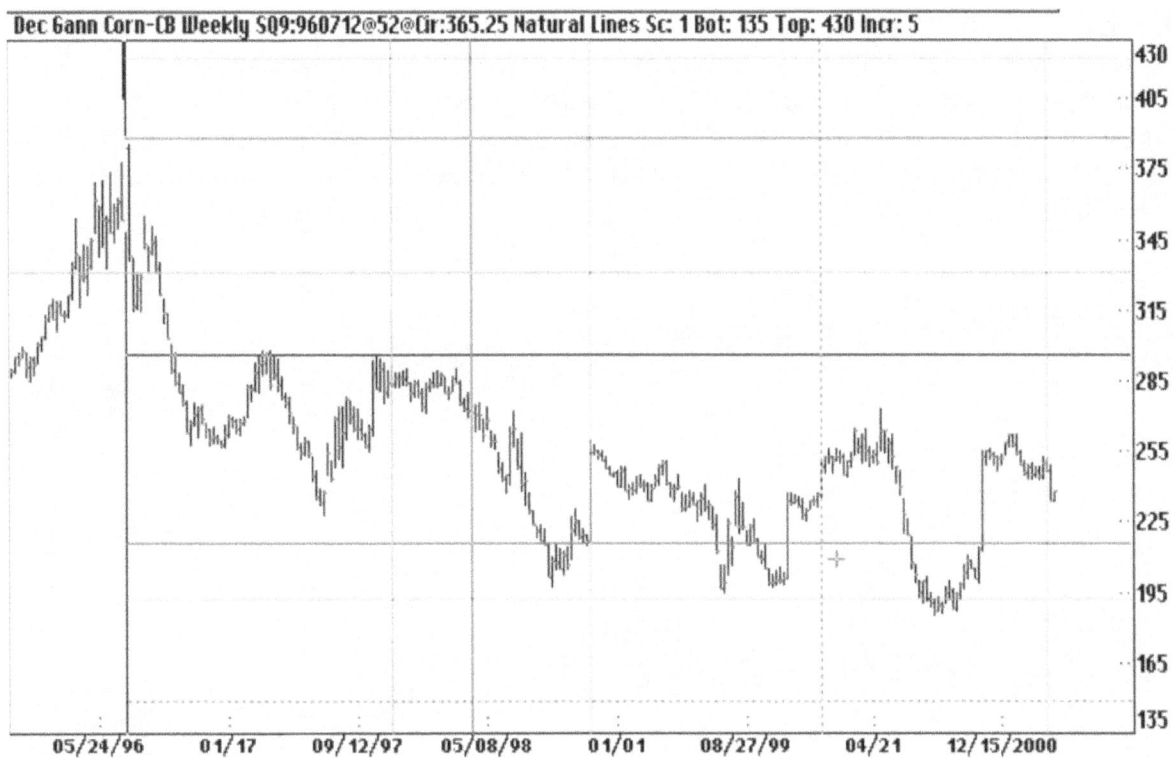

Time Cycles

Gann's use of Astrology in the markets has always been controversial. Some people have chosen to exclude the subject from any serious consideration. That, of course, is their privilege. Gann used it throughout his career and managed to accumulate a great deal of money in the markets. As a student of Gann, it would seem logical that you would want to try to duplicate everything Gann was doing. We aren't going to try to make a true believer out of you but please keep an open mind while we try to demonstrate what is known and not known on the subject.

Gann wrote little on the subject of Astrology, so our major sources of information are his old charts and copies of Astrology books contained in his personal library. Fortunately, most of the books he owned have been reprinted by a few publishers and are still available. Gann wrote two letters on the subject, one on coffee and the other on soybeans. They are reproduced in Appendix B. We have analyzed most of his planetary charting techniques and have duplicated them in the planet portion of the program.

What is Astrology?

For our purposes, Astrology is defined as the study of the correlation between the planetary positions and the market's activity. No cause and effect relation is claimed or needs to be claimed. The idea that the planets 'rule our destiny' was actually fostered by contemporary writers, not by the ancient Astrologers who studied the subject. The earliest studies in Astrology had to do with determining the time of the seasons for planting and harvesting. As time went on certain correlations between the planet's positions and the happenings of the country or region were discovered. The occurrences of such things as wars, famines, and floods were predicted based on the recorded planetary positions of the last similar occurrences. Later, the planetary positions at the time of birth of the country's ruler were added to the pot.

After the invention of the printing press in 1450, planetary ephemeredes became readily available. For the first time, the commoner was able to have his own horoscope calculated. It was during this period that some of the most ridiculous writings on the subject began to appear. Determining which books are valuable and which is garbage is, unfortunately, a good part of the study of Astrology today. Even in modern times the true workings of Astrology is a well-guarded secret. Walter Gorn-Old writing under the pen name 'Spherical' was banned from a professional astrological society for revealing too much in his books. We can only assume that the books Gann owned contained at least some truth or he wouldn't have had them.

Keep in mind that you're looking for correlations but not necessarily causation. Almost all technical trading is based on the correlation of a certain set of rules and the markets past performance. If you buy when a market forms a double bottom you do so because double bottoms in the past have proven to be a good place to buy. In the final analysis, the act of buying is still a declaration of faith that this double bottom will react like past double bottoms. If you discover a 75-day cycle in the gold market that has repeated itself 100 times in a row, you still have to assume the 101st cycle will perform the same way. The actual cause of the 75 day cycle is not the major concern as long as it has repeated itself often enough to rule out a chance happening. Conversely, if you only looked back far enough to see the last two 75 day cycles, it would be foolhardy to invest your money on such a 'discovery'.

A similar situation exists for anyone searching for planetary to market correlations. An Astrology book might say something like: 'The evil aspects of Saturn cause depressed markets'. Whether or not Saturn 'causes' depressed markets is of little concern to you. The statement from the book should be mentally converted to: 'Certain aspects of Saturn have shown a strong correlation with depressed markets'. How strong the correlation actually is can only be determined by asking: 'Out of the last 100 or more occurrences of these 'evil' aspects, what percentage have been associated with a depressed market'. The planet portion of the Ganntrader program offers a systematic method for testing such claims. Whenever you see the word 'Time' in Gann's writing you would be well served to substitute the word 'Planet Cycle' since Gann is never talking about civil time when he uses the word 'Time' especially when the word is capitalized.

After loading any file try selecting Geocentric Planets from the View menu. Geocentric

Geocentric Planets

Planets are the longitude of the planets as viewed from the perspective of the Earth.
On a trading day file notice there is a small jump in the plot between Friday and Monday. This is normal since the planets continue to move on Saturday and Sunday and this jump reflects the amount they moved over the weekend. For the smoothest daily file plots select 7-Day Chart under File: Daily File Type.

Along the bottom of the screen the longitudes of each planet are displayed for the date of the cursor. To the right of the longitude the planets latitude or declination is also displayed. The planets that are activated will be plotted on the chart and the same color is used in the box at the bottom. For a daily file the program, by default, plots the faster planets. With a weekly or monthly file the program plots the slower planets and turns off the faster ones. The longer market trends are normally seen on a monthly chart and are best predicted with the slower planets. Shorter trends are predicted by using the faster planets.

Any of the planets can be added or removed by using the following function keys:

F1 = Mercury
F2 = Venus
F3 = Sun or Earth
F4 = Mars
F5 = Jupiter
F6 = Saturn
F7 = Uranus
F8 = Neptune
F9 = Pluto
F10 = Signs of the Zodiac
F11 = Moon
F12 = Moon's Node

Hit the key and the planet comes on. Hit it again and it goes back off. If you want only one planet on and erase all the others then hold the <Alt> key while pressing the function key. This will turn on the selected planet and turn off all the others. The <Alt> key acts as an exclusive key and the plain function keys act as on / off toggles. This feature works the same as the angle and square portions of the program. The geocentric planets are available under the View menu. This is a view of the planets from the perspective of the Earth rather than the Sun. Both methods are valid Gann techniques and are available in the program. Notice that the geocentric view has a more curved plot. This is due to the retrograde position of the planets. In short, the planets appear to reverse course and move backward in relation to the stars in the background. This is due to the geocentric point of reference and is not present with the heliocentric plots. Markets often change trend during this retrograde period. In the following pages we have plotted these planets on the December Daily S&P 500 in the Geocentric mode to give you an idea of how these planetary lines work with the price plots.

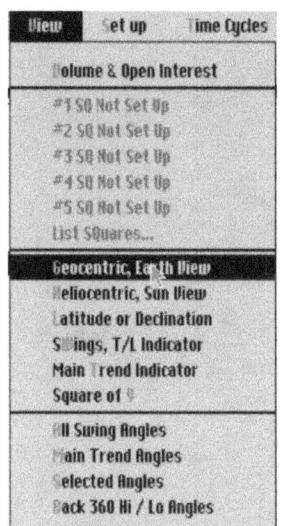

F1 = Mercury

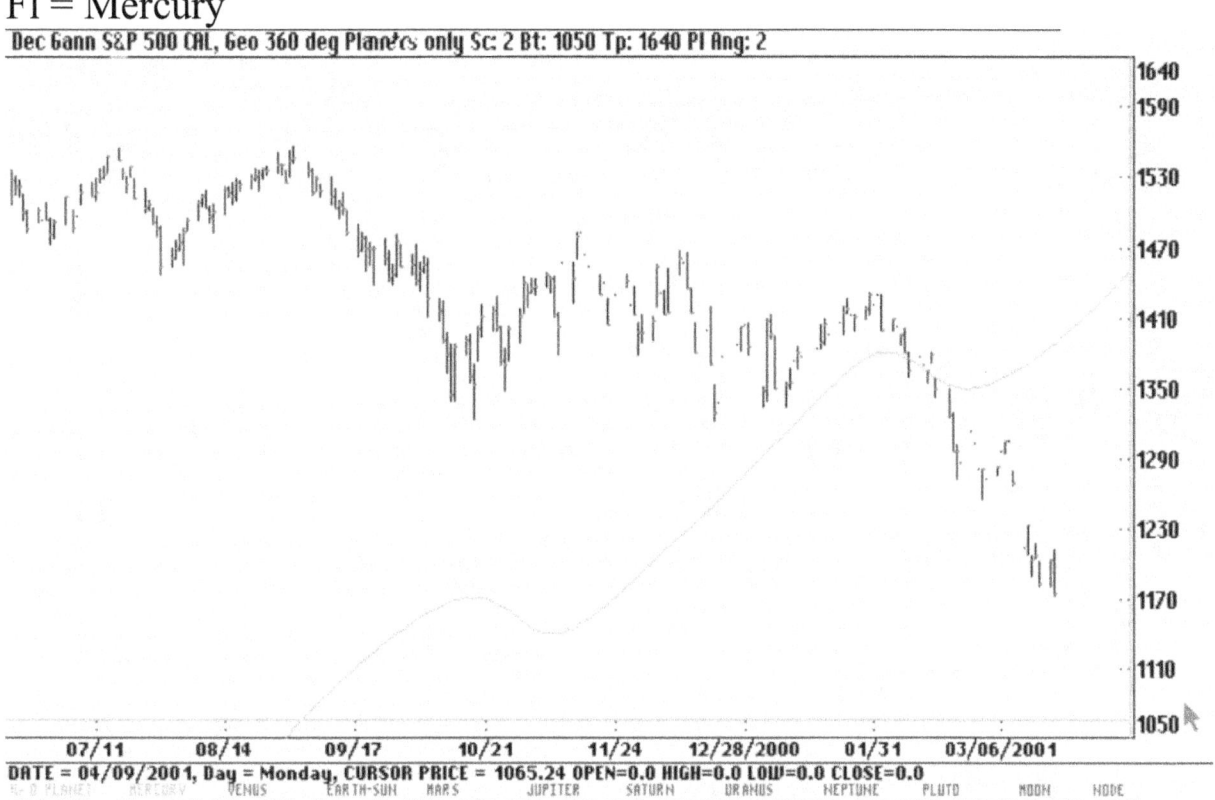

F2 = Venus

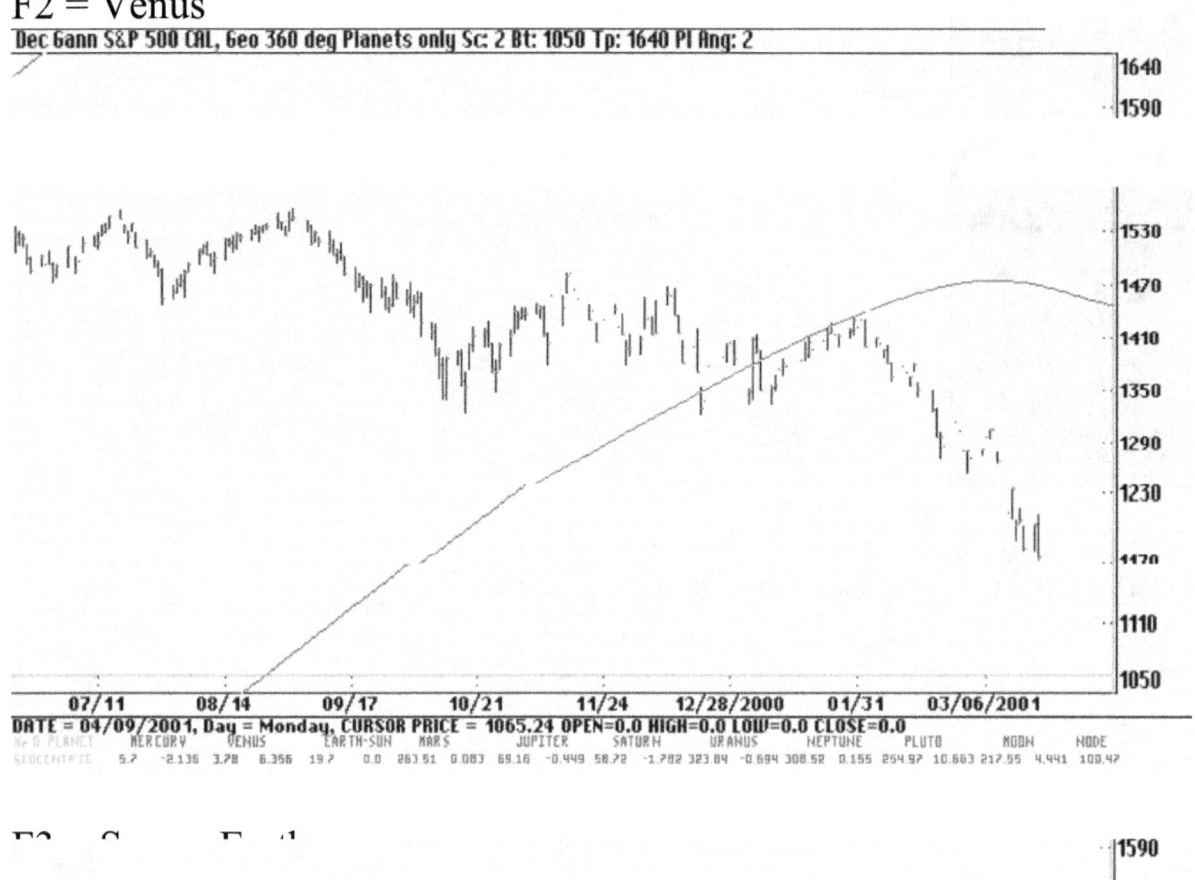

F3 = Sun = Earth

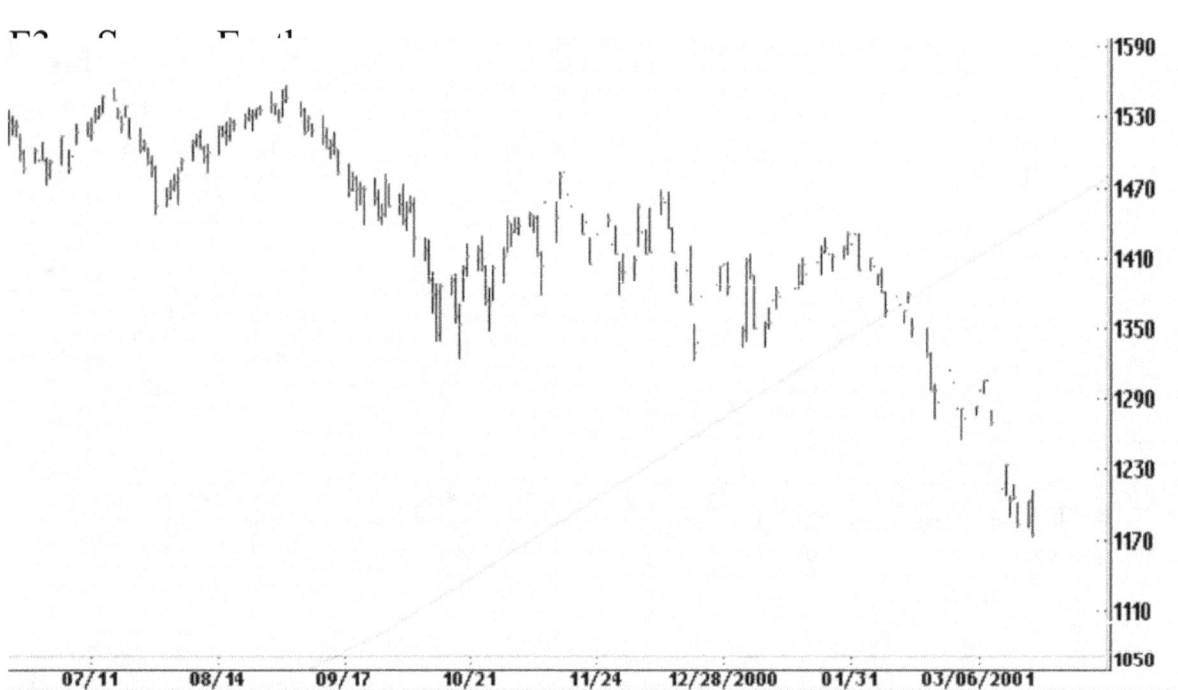

F4 = Mars

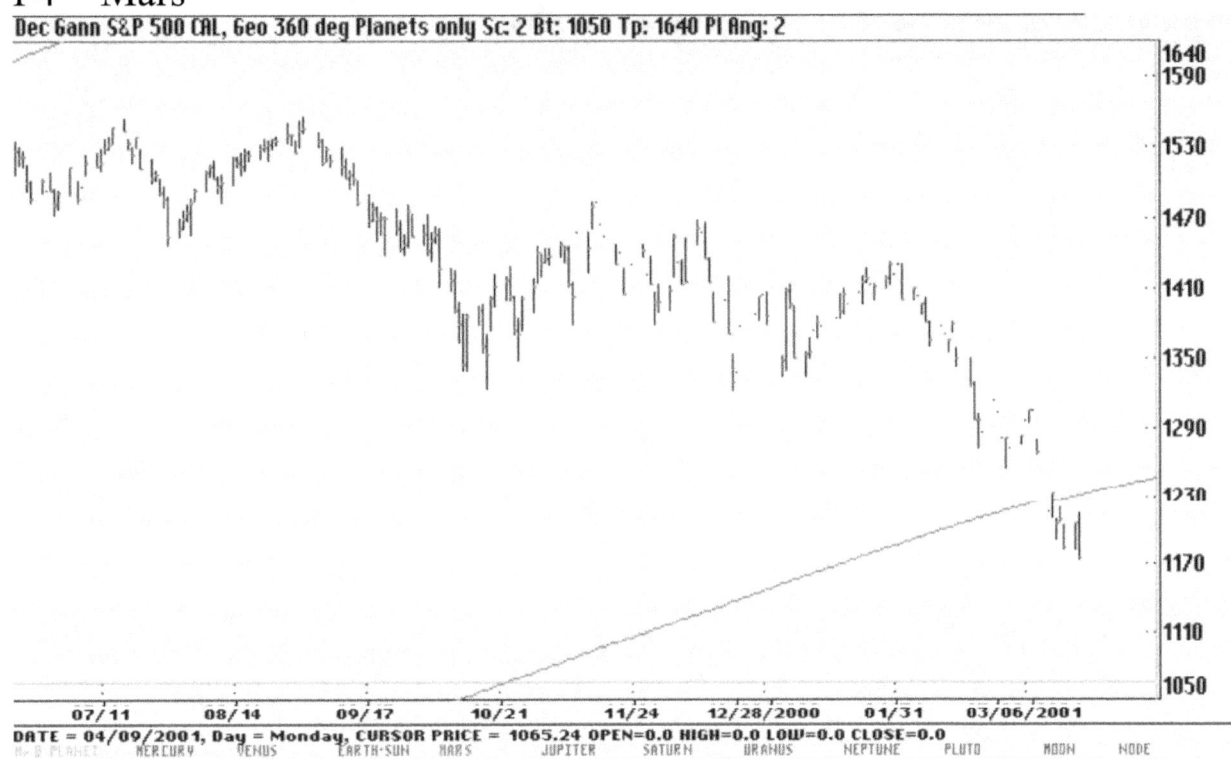

F5 = Jupiter

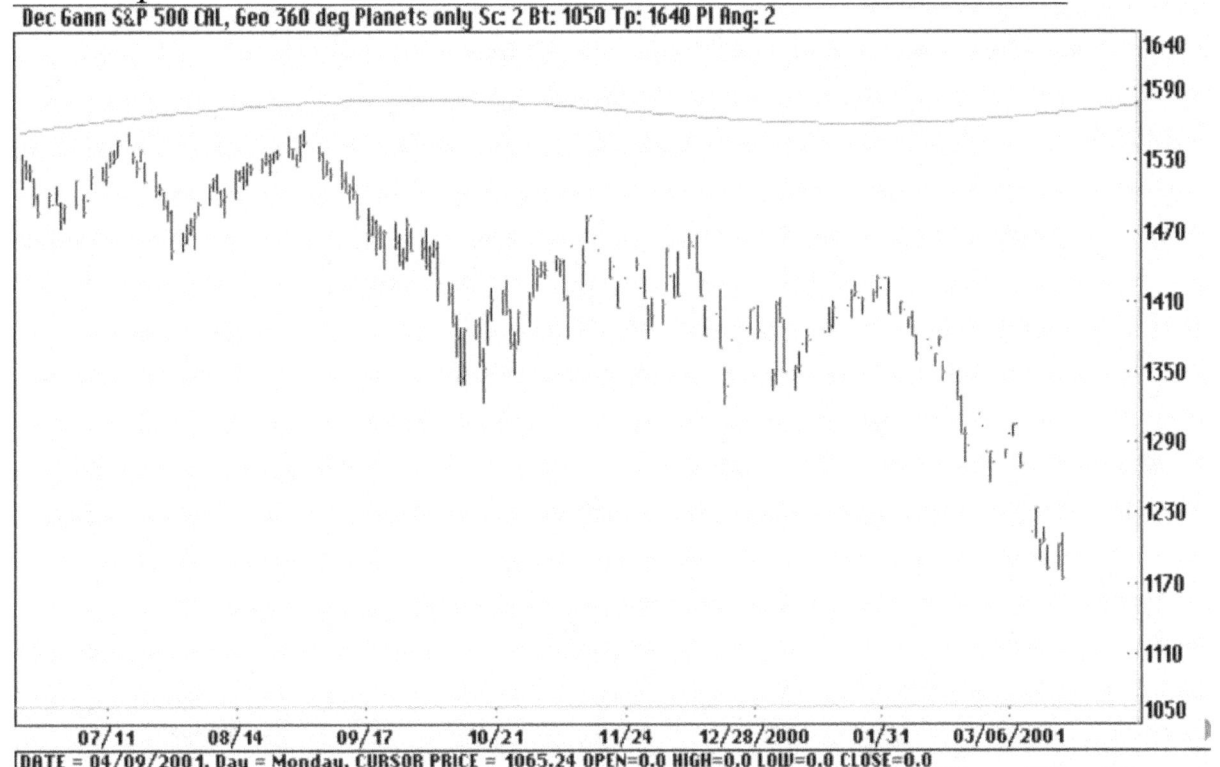

F6 = Saturn

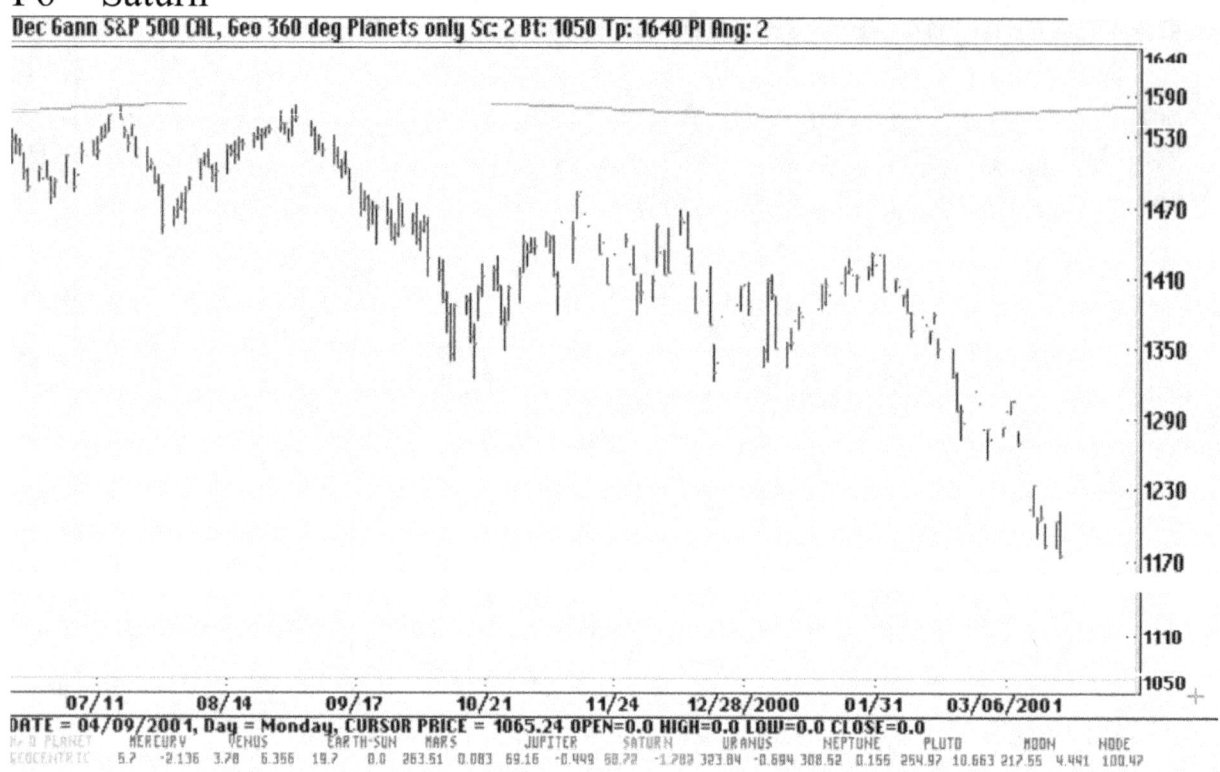

F7 = Uranus

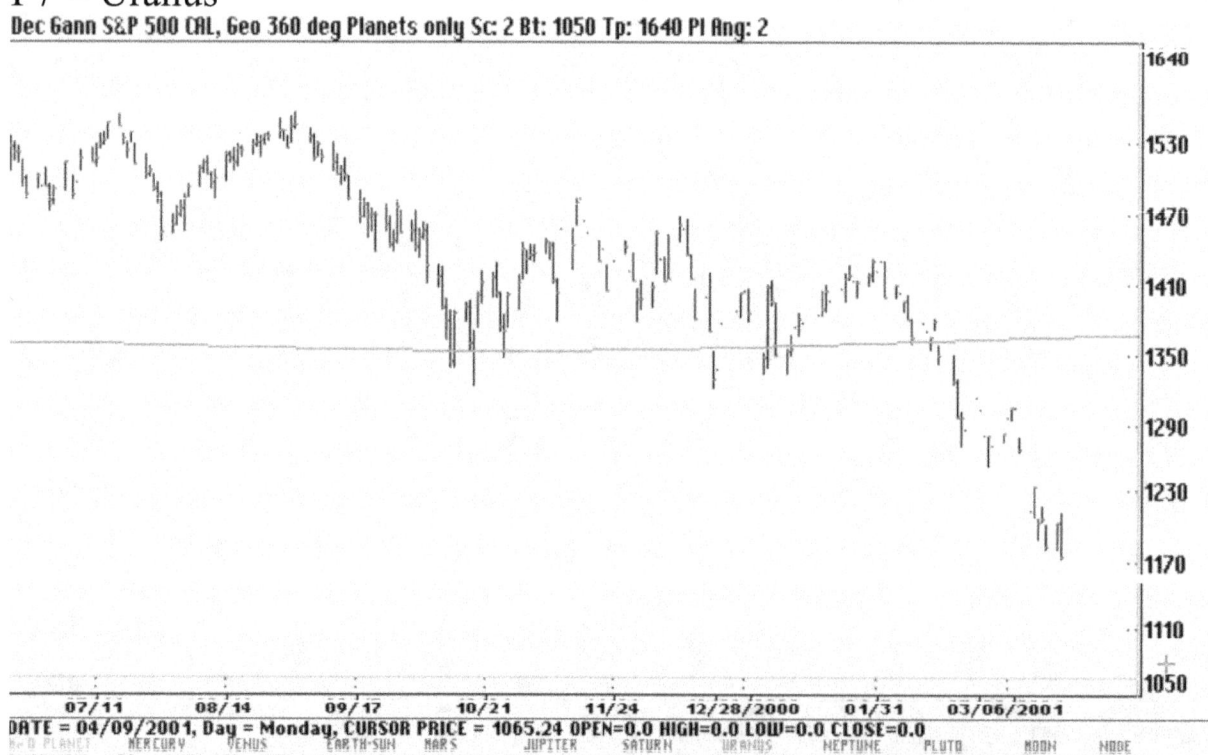

F8 = Neptune

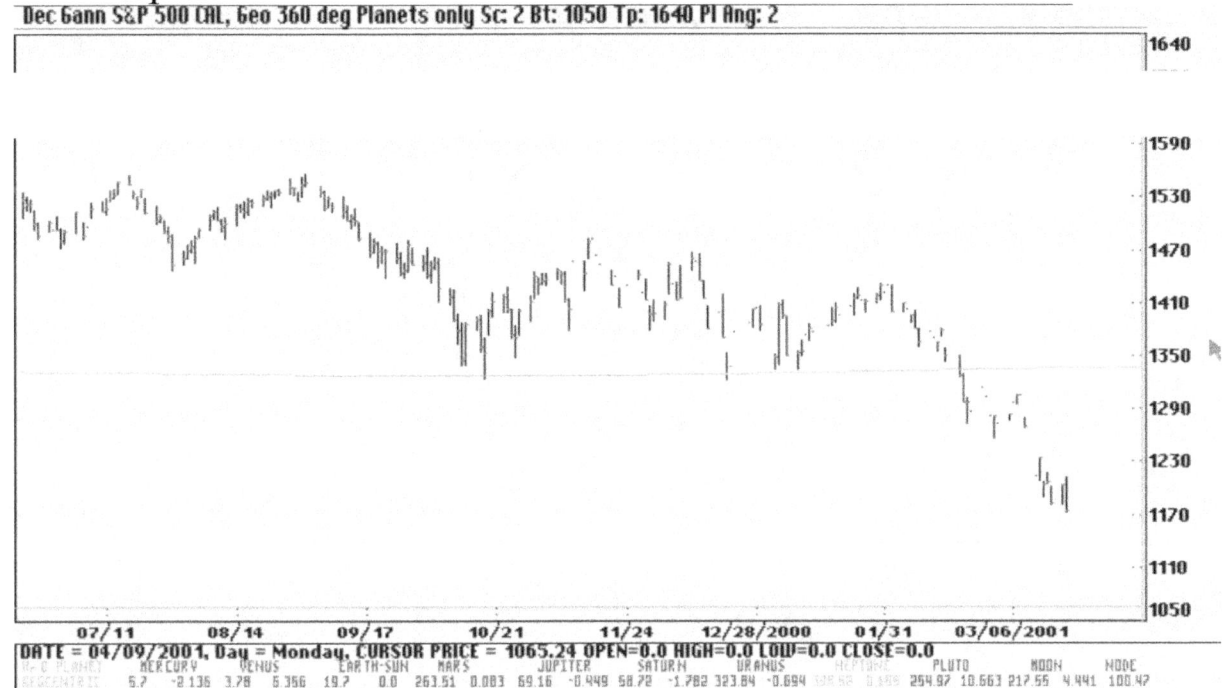

F9 = Pluto

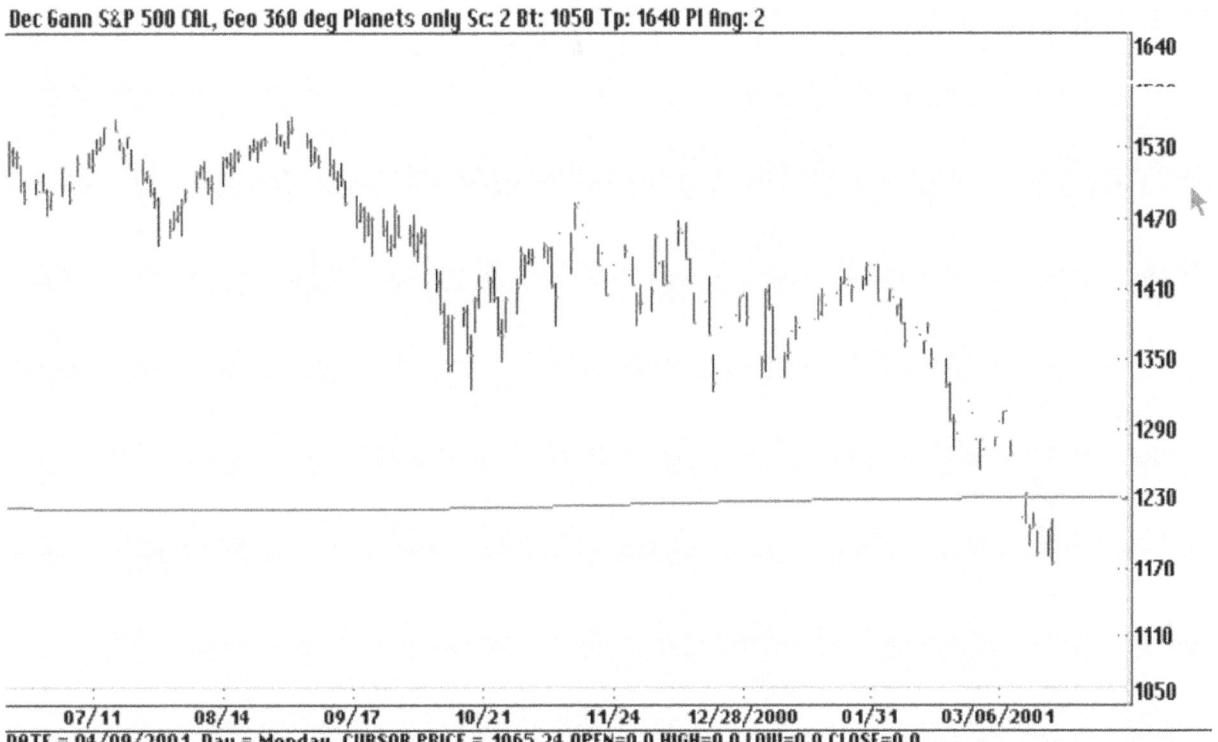

F10 = Signs of the Zodiac

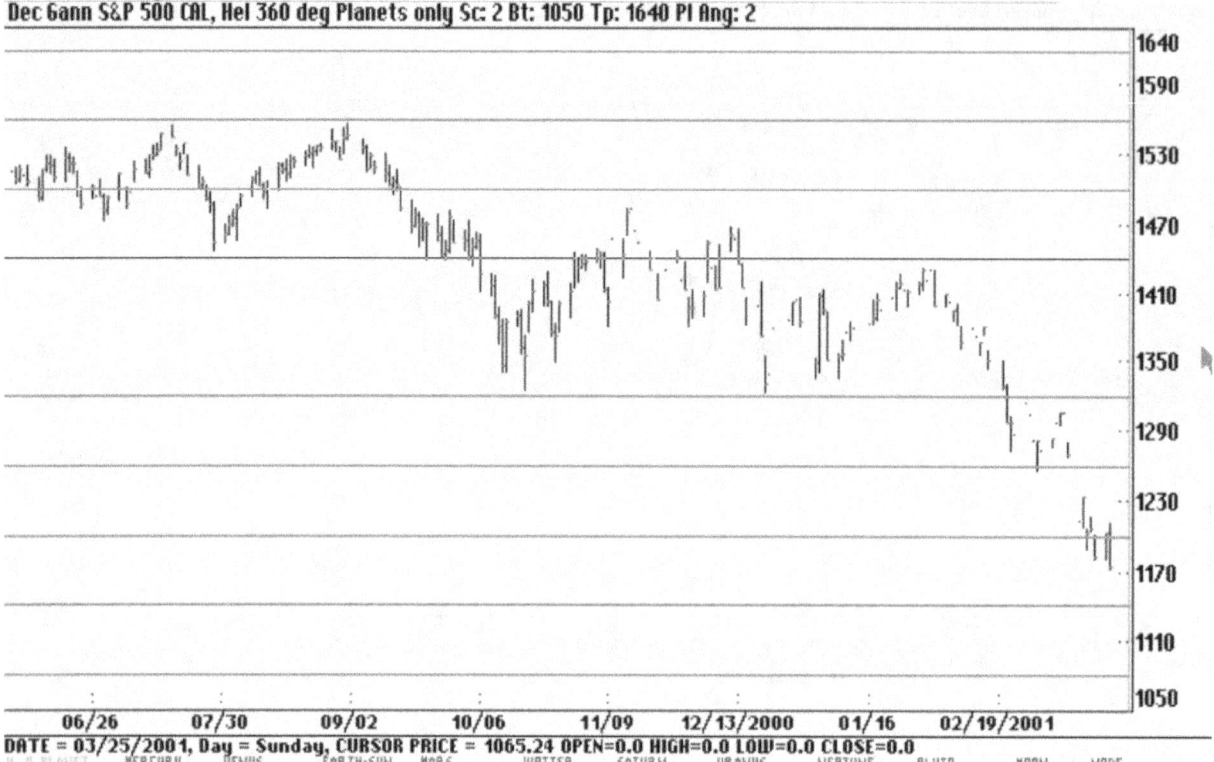

F11 = Moon

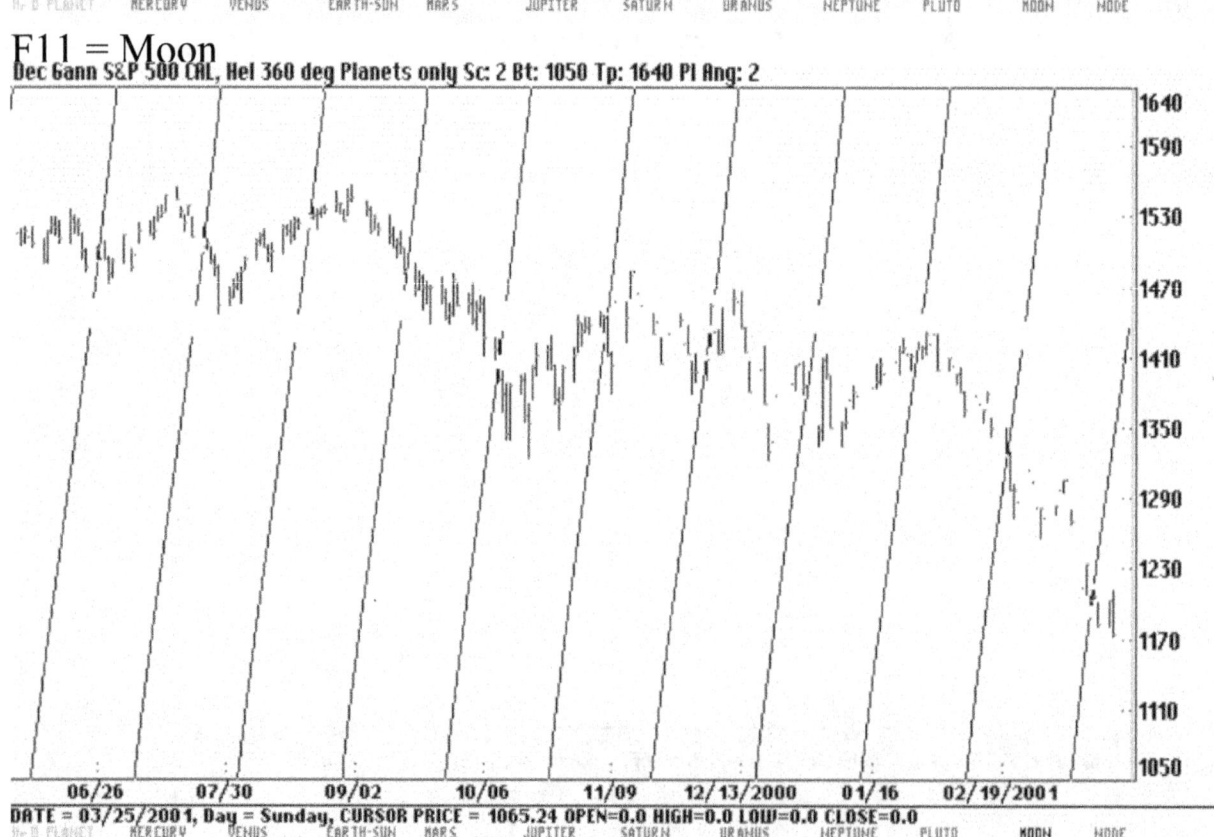

F12 = Moon's Node

Heliocentric Planets

Any of the planets can be added or removed by using the following function keys:

F1 = Mercury
F2 = Venus
F3 = Sun or Earth
F4 = Mars
F5 = Jupiter
F6 = Saturn
F7 = Uranus
F8 = Neptune
F9 = Pluto
F10 = Signs of the Zodiac
F11 = Moon
F12 = Moon's Node

Hit the key and the planet comes on. Hit it again and it goes back off. If you want only one planet on and erase all the others then hold the <Alt> key while pressing the function key. This will turn on the selected planet and turn off all the others. The <Alt> key acts as an exclusive key and the plain function keys act as on / off toggles. This feature works the same as the angle and square portions of the program. The heliocentric planets are available under the View menu. This is a view of the planets from the perspective of the Sun rather than the Earth. Both methods are valid Gann techniques and are available in the program. Notice that the geocentric view has a more curved plot. This is due to the retrograde position of the planets. In short, the planets appear to reverse course and move backward in relation to the stars in the background. This is due to the geocentric point of reference and is not present with the heliocentric plots. Markets often change trend during this retrograde period. In the following pages we have plotted these planets on the December Daily S&P 500 to give you an idea of how these planetary lines work with the price plots.

F1 = Mercury

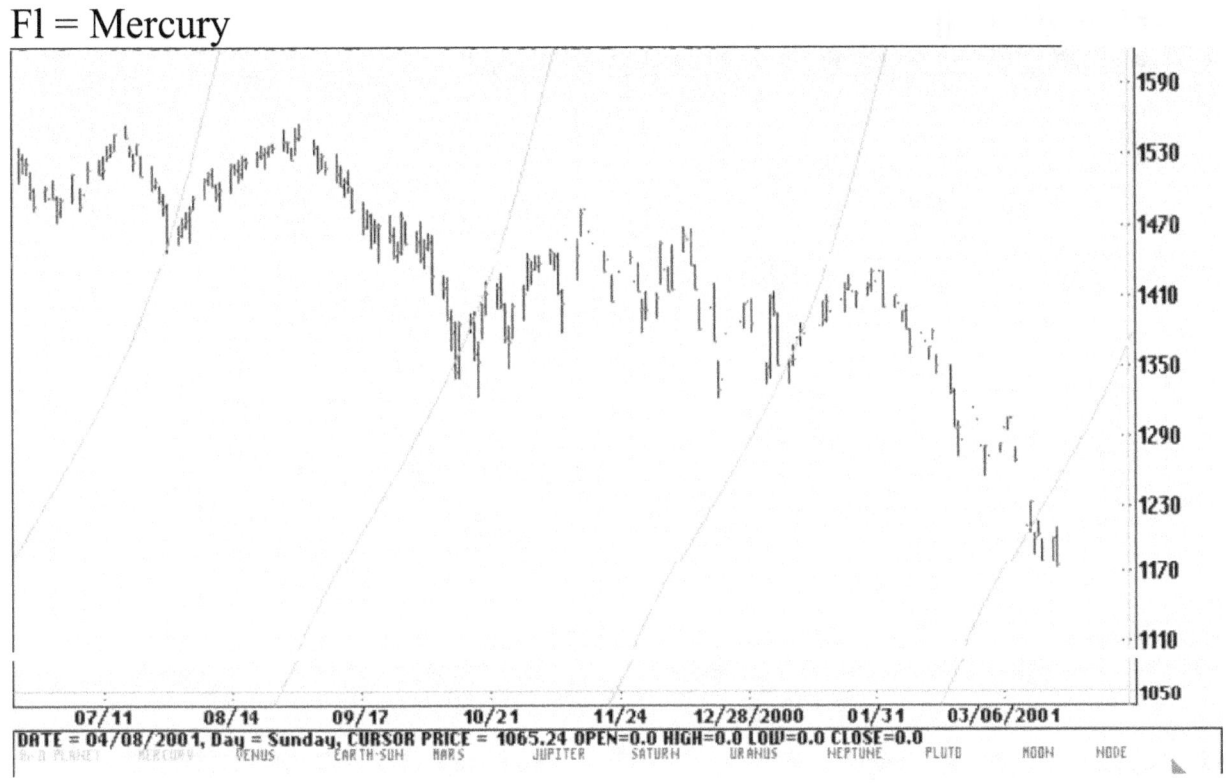

F2 = Venus

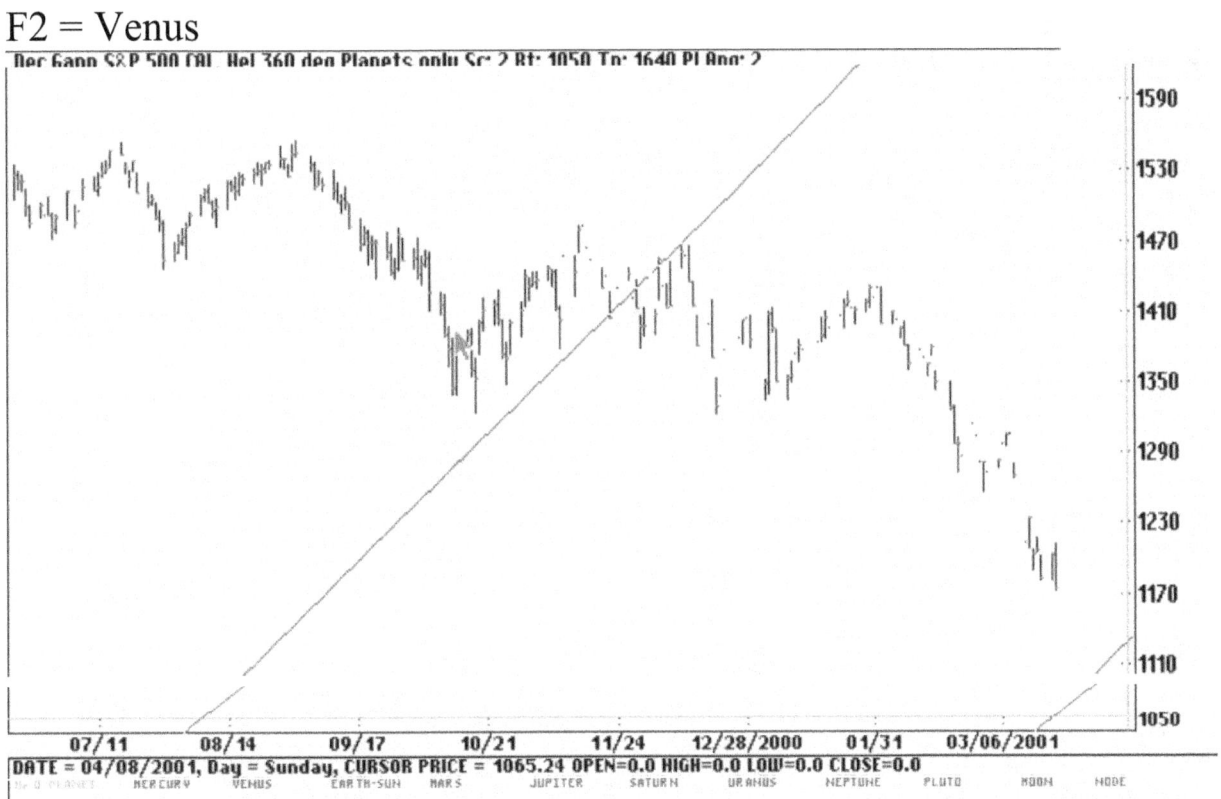

F3 = Sun or Earth

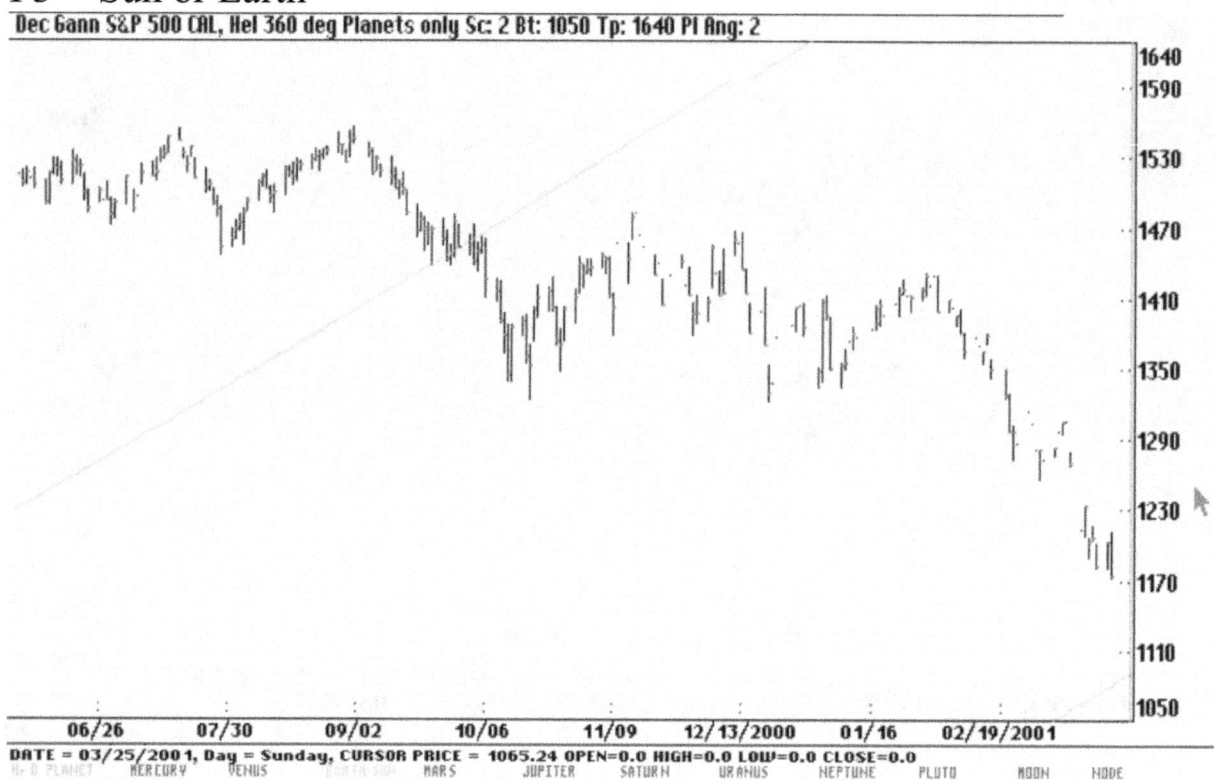

F4 = Mars

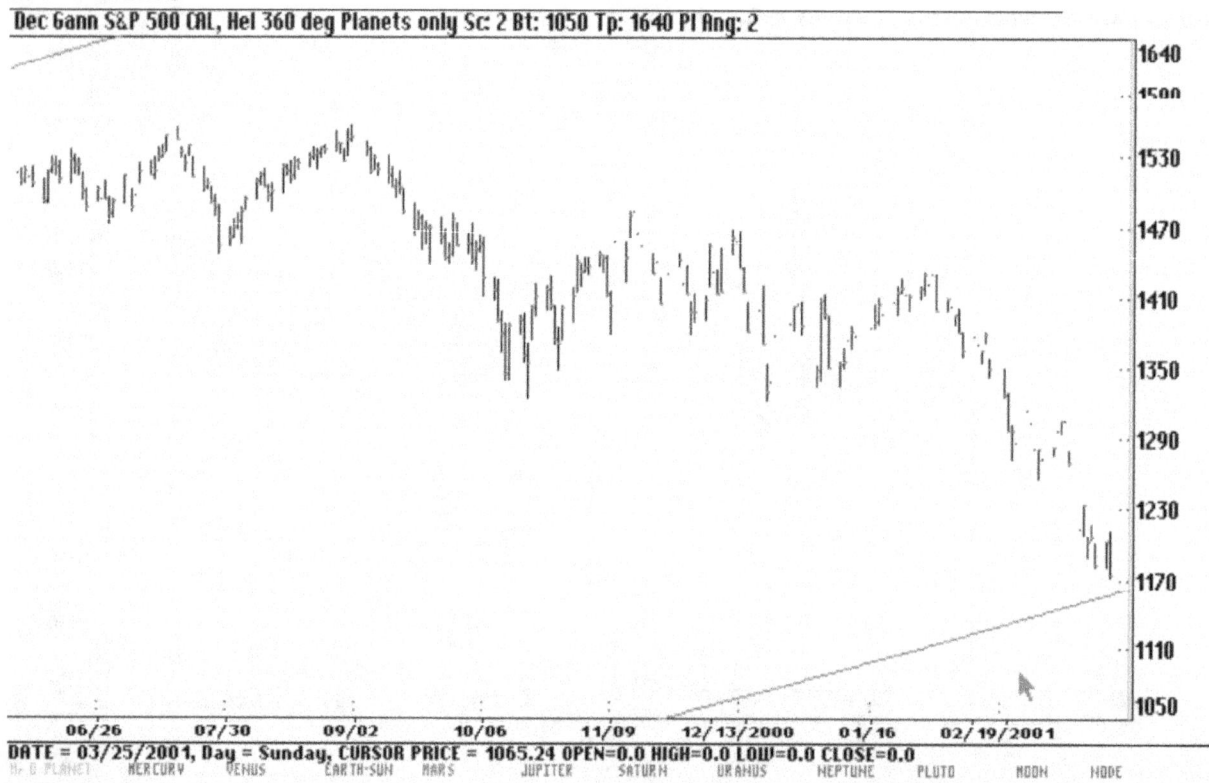

F5 = Jupiter

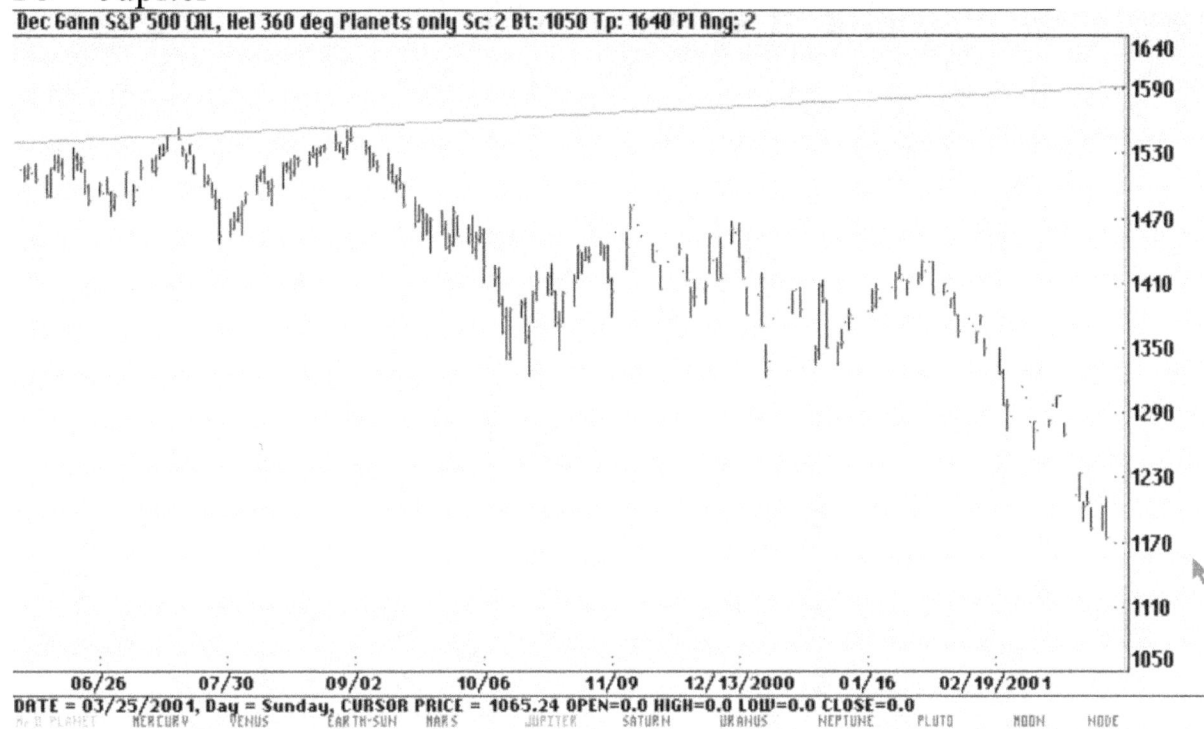

F6 = Saturn

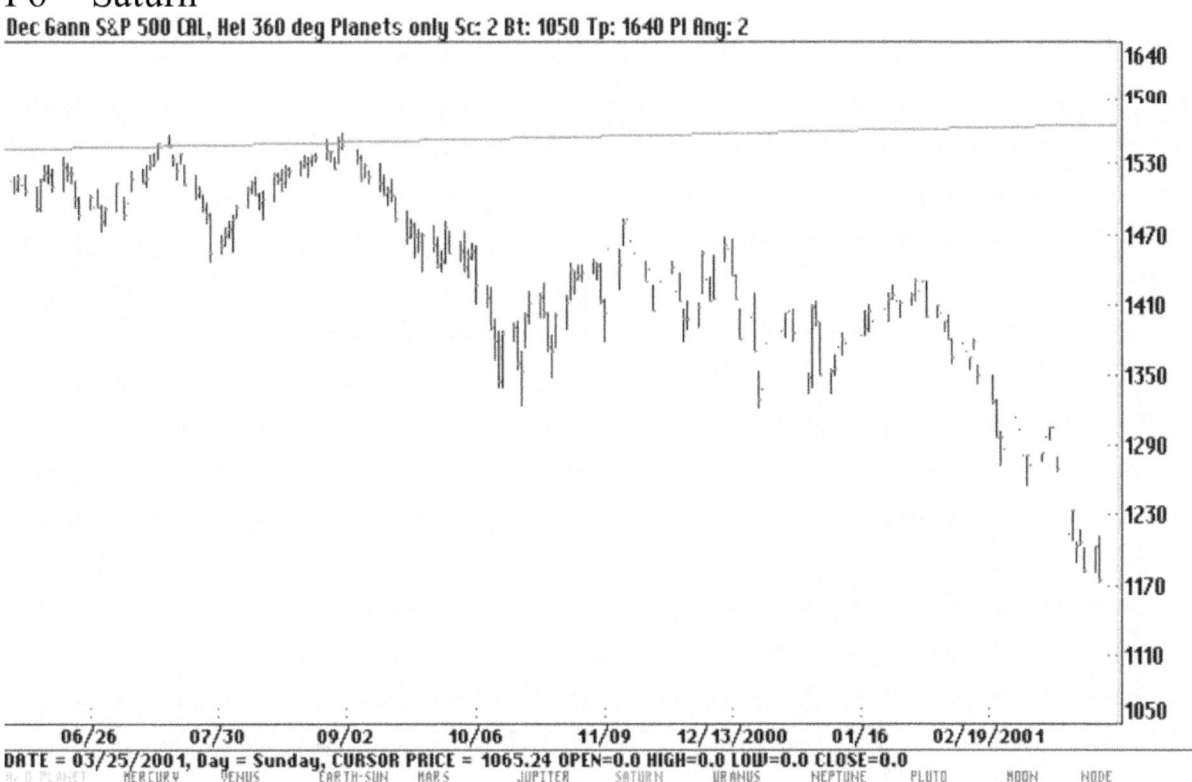

F7 = Uranus

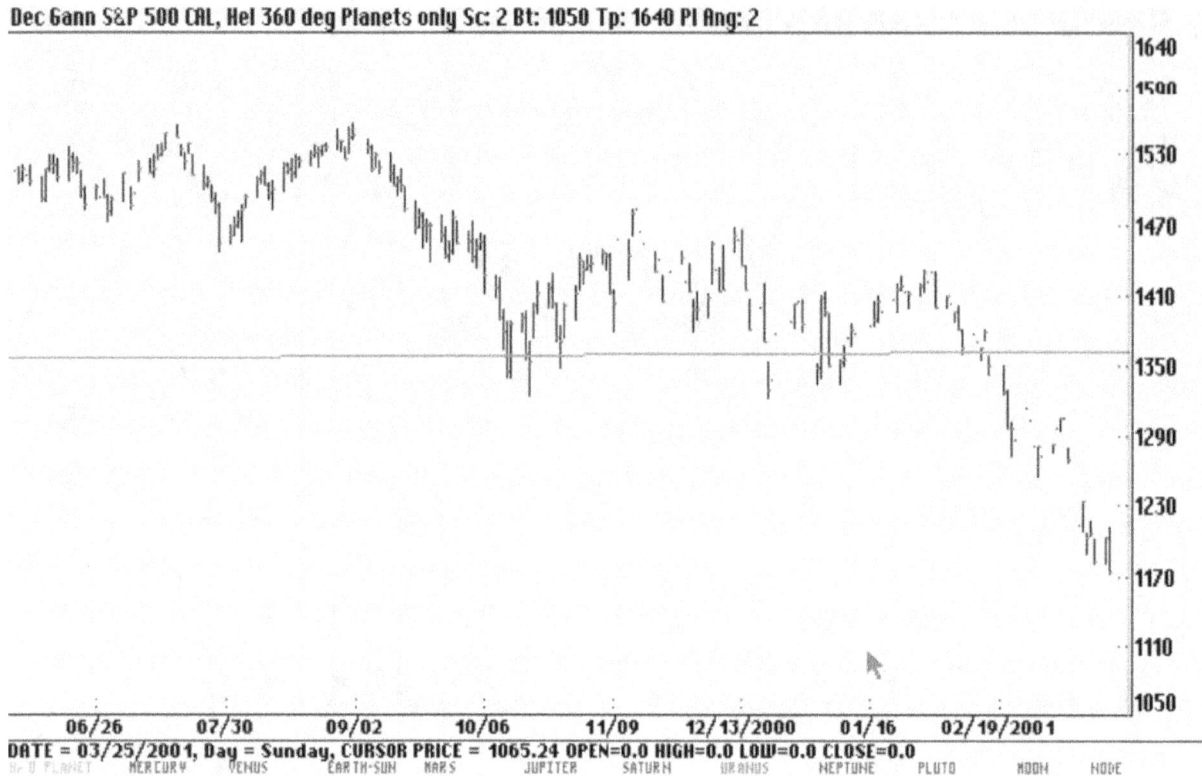

F8 = Neptune

F9 = Pluto

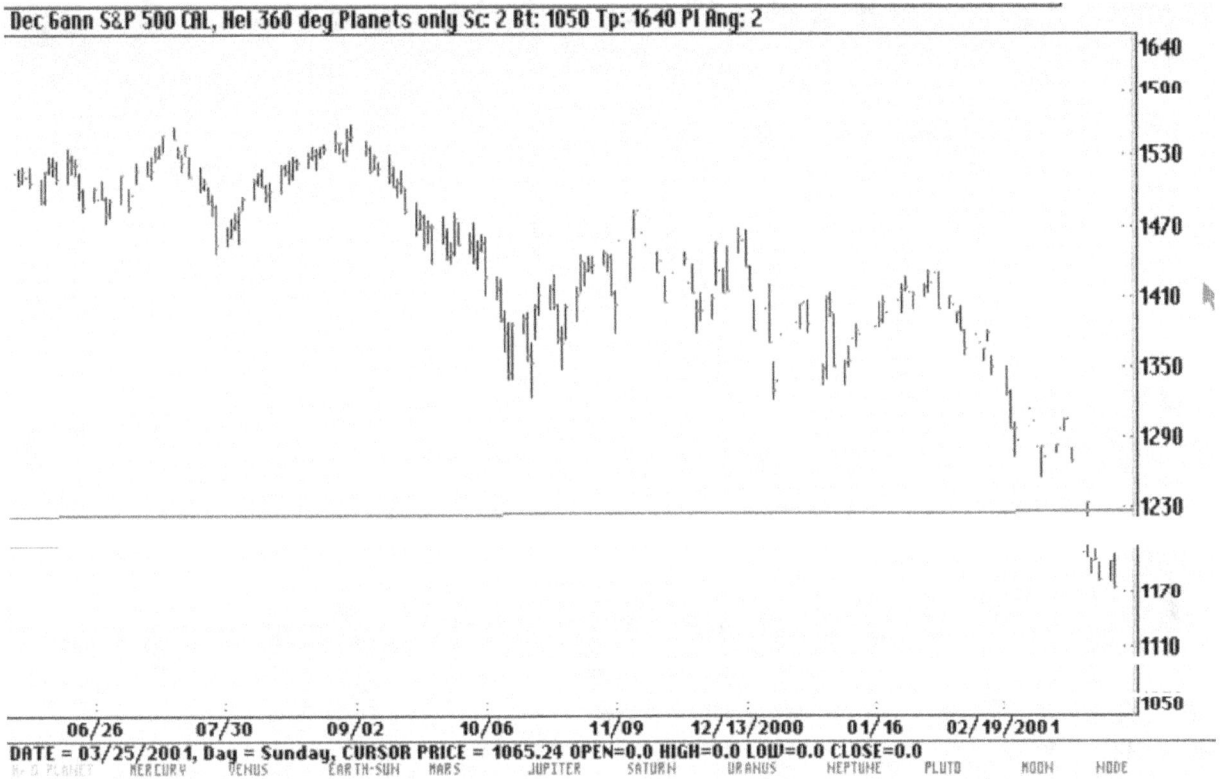

F10 = Signs of the Zodiac

F11 = Moon

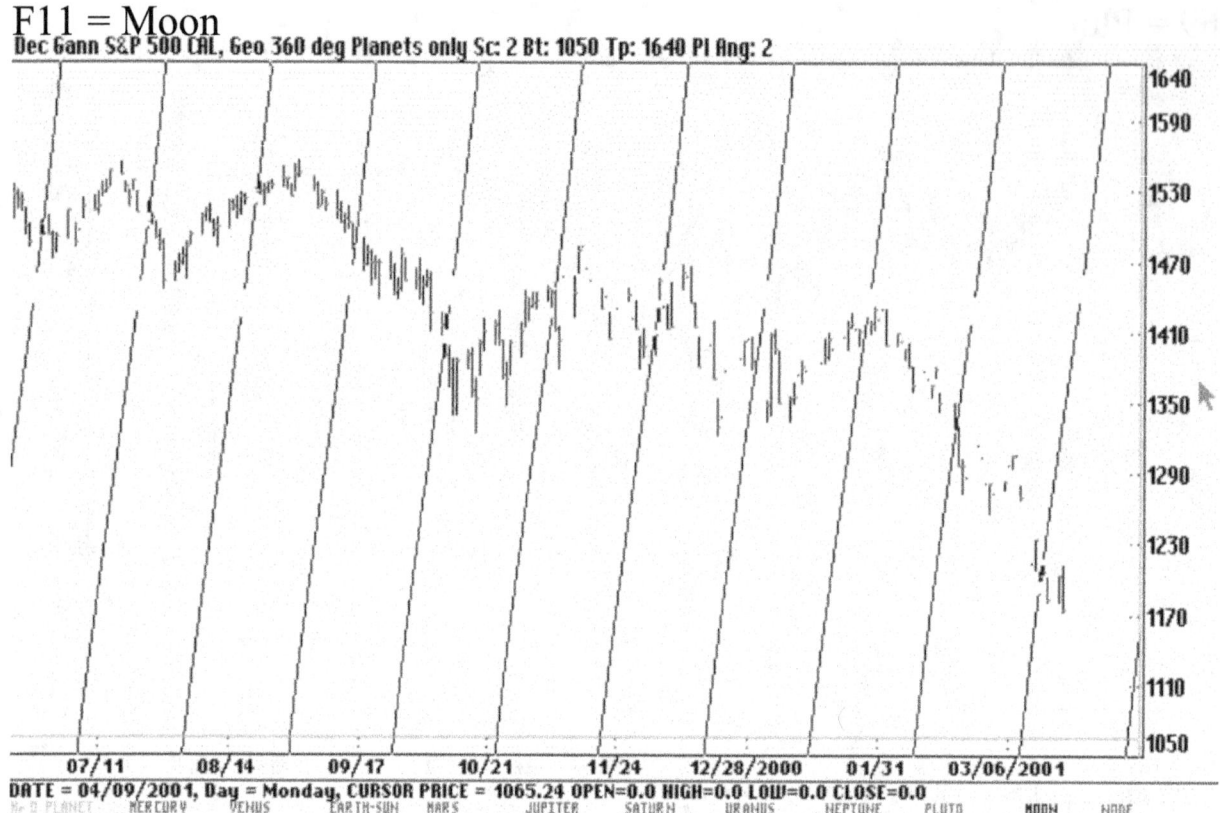

F12 = Moon's Node

Planet Angle

The planet angle offers a method for adjusting the planet plots to fit the type of data loaded. When Gann plotted the planets on a chart he took the degree position of the planet and assigned it to the same price level on the chart as its degree value. If the planet were at 123 degrees in the sky he would mark it on the chart at $1.23 or 123 cents. If a market were trading at a price greater than $3.60 he would simply add 360 degrees to the planet's longitude. Thus, a planet degree value of 123 degrees would be equal to $1.23 or $4.83. (123 + 360) The soybean and coffee letters in the appendix show this technique. By default, the program makes the planet angle equal to the chart's price range divided by 360 degrees. This produces a plot on the screen that is at least usable. The problem with using Gann's methods with today's market is similar to the problem with the value of the 1x1 angle in the angles and squares. Today's markets are trading at such high levels that the 1 degree = 1 cents is no longer practical for some markets.

The planet angle is simply a multiplier for the planet's longitude. If it is equal to 1 then 360° = 360 cents and the planet would be plotted every 360° on the chart. If it is equal to 2 then 360° is plotted at 720 cents, 1440... on the chart. Notice on this Corn chart at the top of the screen that the planet angle is equal to 1. On the two points circled the degree position of Jupiter convened to price was at the same level as the prices.

The ability to set the planet angle makes it possible to do planetary work on any market. Some markets such as the currencies will need a very small planet angle in order to produce a usable planet plot. For example, a currency that had a low of 35 cents and a high of 75 cents would have a price range of only 40 cents. If you use Gann's method of converting 1 cents = 1° you would only have 40° of the 360° in the sky represented on the chart. There might be no planets appearing on the screen unless one of them happened to be in this narrow wedge of the sky. The chance would be 1 in 9 since 40 is 1/9 of 360. If you used a planet angle of 0.1 in this example then 360° would become 36 degrees and all the planets would be seen on the screen.

Time Cycles as Support and Resistance

The chart below shows support and resistance on the 45 degree Saturn lines. Note at the low Saturn's geocentric longitude is 19.82, which is below the bottom of the chart. The dotted line near the low is actually at 244.82, which is 225 + 19.25. Five times 45 is 225 so this is the fifth line above the actual location of Saturn's longitude.

On the next heliocentric chart the planet angle is equal to .0001 and the Saturn Time Cycles are included. The Time Cycles are selected under the Time Cycles menu and display additional aspect lines. The aspect lines run parallel to the actual planet's longitude line and are displaced a fixed number of price units equal to the degree value of the aspect.

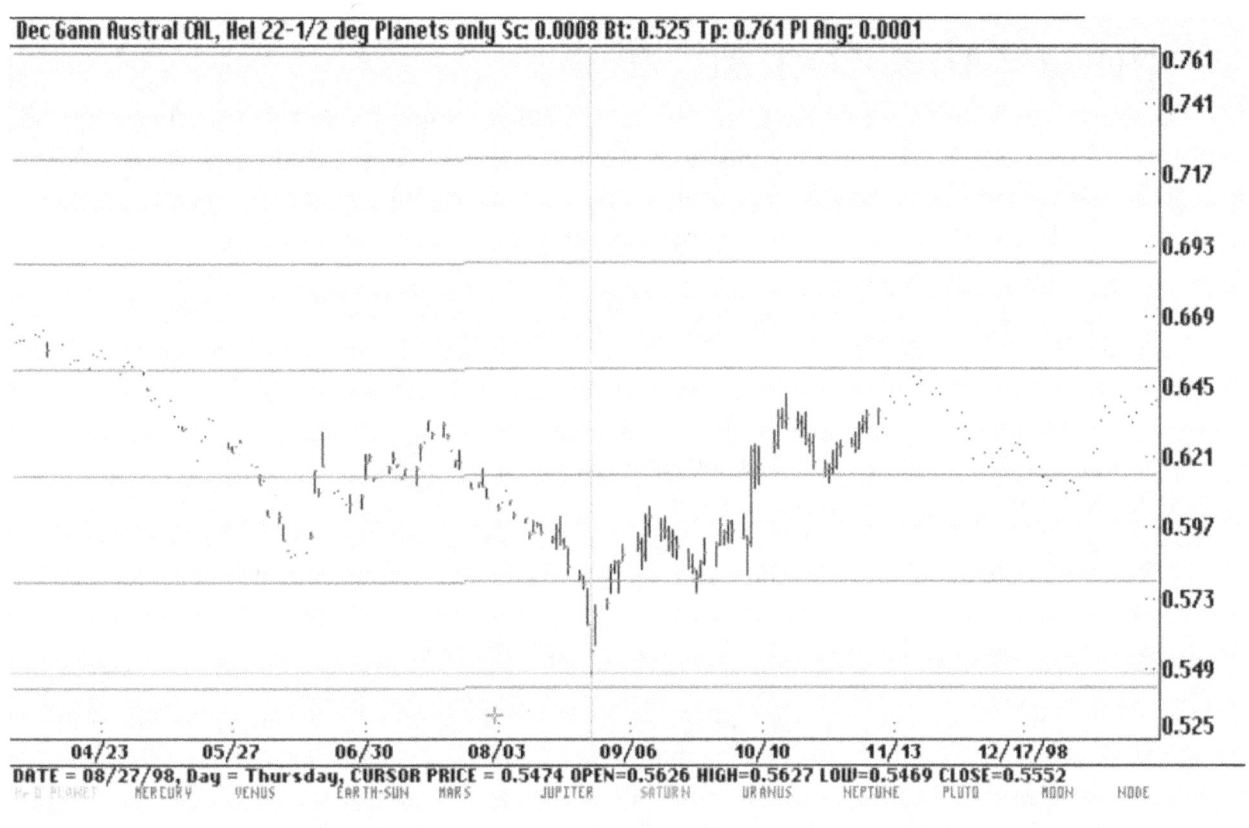

Notice how the Saturn planetary lines give you clear support and resistance lines. If you use these Saturn planetary lines or other ones along with many of the other Gann methods it gives you high reliability in trading. All of Gann's techniques should be used together and never just alone. The secret is to know which of Gann's techniques work on each market. You determine which techniques to use by trial and error. Gann wanted you to experiment with these techniques on past market to prove it to yourself that they work. This gives you the proper psychology to trade with confidence.

Signs of the Zodiac

In Astrology the heavens are divided into 30° sectors called 'Signs', with Aries starting at 0° and Pisces ending at 360°. The planetary positions are described as being in a certain number of degrees of a specific Sign. That is, Jupiter in 8° of Leo or Saturn in 29° of Libra, etc. If a planet happened to be in 15° of Cancer, it was plotted on the price chart at 105. Cancer is located between 90° and 120° therefore 15° Cancer would be 90 + 15 = 105. The program's longitude display makes this calculation for you so you will see a longitude at say, 105° rather than Cancer 15. Since we are convening degrees to price this is a more useful format. The signs can be turned off and on with the <F10> function key. The lines are shown in red and are all 30° apart.

Planets in certain Signs are said to be stronger or weaker in their effect depending on the nature of the planet and the Sign it occupies. In Astrology jargon, the planets can be in their ruling sign, fall sign, exaltation sign or their detriment sign. As an example, the Sun 'rules' Leo and therefore its effects on the market, whatever they may be, would be enhanced whenever it occupied Leo. A full discussion of which planets are effected by which Signs is beyond the scope of this User's Guide. This information is well covered by most Astrology books.

The movement of a planet into a new sign is generally associated with a change in mood of the market. A change of trend often occurs each time a planet changes sign. This effect will usually be within one day for Mercury, Venus, Sun and Mars. Note the crossing of the Venus lines with the horizontal Sign lines on the next chart.

Time Cycles and Time Measurement

The original of this next chart has been reproduced in several books about Gann's methods. On Gann's original chart the astroglyphs for both planets are clearly visible. The deciphering of it was critical in the development of the planetary portion of the Ganntrader program. Here the actual positions of Jupiter and Mars are shown. At the point the two lines cross is what is called a conjunction.

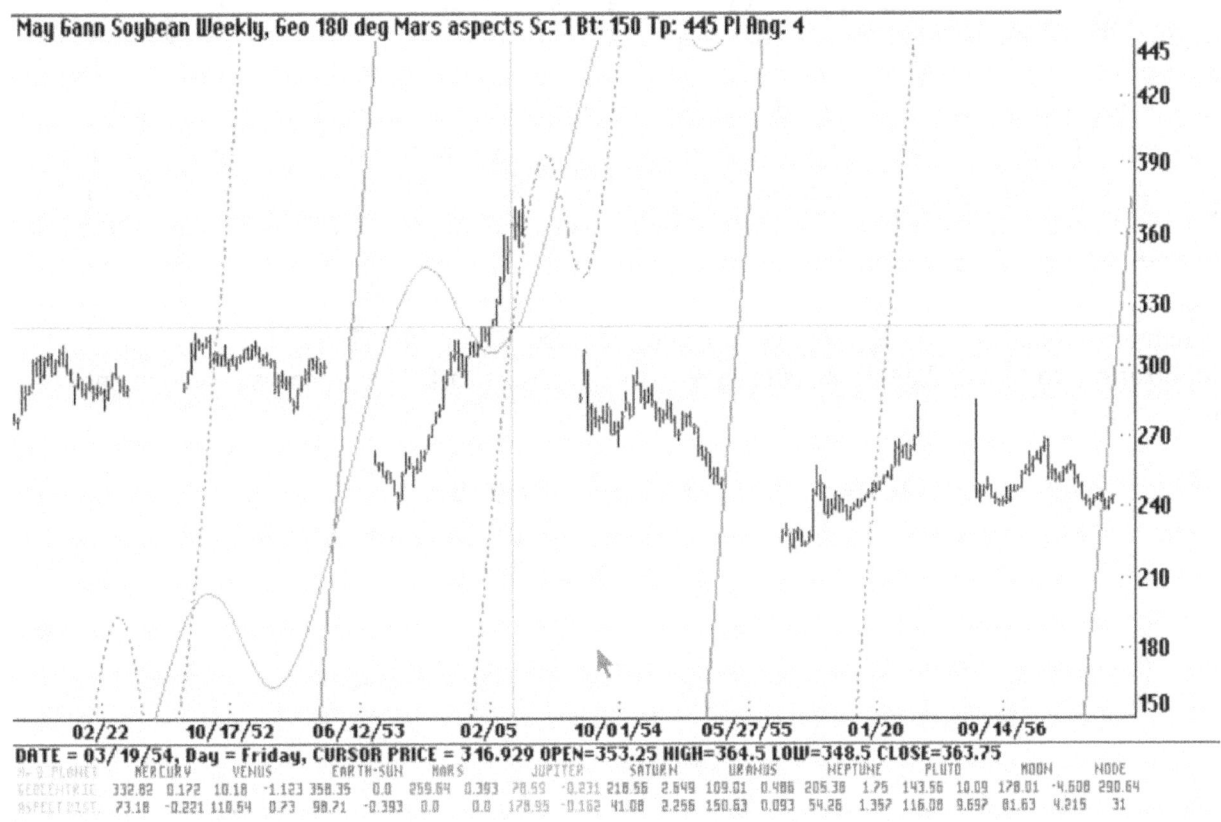

Taking the previous chart a step further, the 90° aspects to Mars were added. This is done by selecting the Time Cycles menu, Mars aspects, the fault aspects are 90 degree but any separation can be selected using the function keys:

<Ctrl> F1	5 5/8°
<Ctrl> F2	7 ½°
<Shift> F1	11 ¼°
<Shift> F2	15°
<Shift> F3	22 ½°
<Shift> F4	30°
<Ctrl> F7	36°
<Ctrl> F5	40°
<Shift> F5	45°
<Ctrl> F6	51.43°

<Shift> F6	60°
<Shift> F7	72°
<Shift> F8	90°
<Shift> F9	120°
<Shift> F10	180°
<Ctrl> F10	360°

These are every common aspect used by Astrologers plus others such as 40, 51.43 and 36 degrees that might be good for research purposes.

In the chart below there are 3 dotted lines between the solid Mars lines. These represent the 90, 180 and 270° aspects. The 270° aspect is really a 90 degree aspect since no two planets can ever be more than 180 degrees apart. Since the planet angle value is 1 these lines are 90° apart. There is more than one Mars line because there is more than a 360 degrees/cents chart range. Each solid Mars line is 360 cents from the next one.

When the Jupiter line crosses a dotted line is considered 'square' to Mars. At 180° it is in 'opposition' to Mars. The 90° crossings are marked on the chart. The cursor is placed at one of the crossings.

Transits or Time by Degrees

Gann treated a major high or low as a new birth date for a market. He then noted the positions of the planets at the date of the high or low and watched as the planets moved 45, 90 or 180 degrees from its original place. The astrological term for this is a 'Transit to Natal Position'. See the coffee letter in the appendix under 'Geocentric Maps Movement' for more information on this method. The simplest way to measure a transit is to move the cursor to the high or low, note the position of the planet and then add 15 or 45° increments to the starting position. Move the cursor to the right and, using the display at the bottom of the screen, find the new longitude positions. A pocket calculator with a constant key can be useful with this technique.

The following approach combines the planets and a square of 120 to measure 15° planet movements. A square can have up to 8 price division lines and since 120 price units are the same as 120° a square of 120 divided by 8 would be 15° per cent. As long as the 1x1 angle is 1 and the planet angle is also 1 the technique will work. Here is an example using the July 12/96 high in July corn. We will measure the Jupiter transits.

1) First turn on Geocentric planets followed by <Alt><F5> to remove all planets except Jupiter.

2) Next use the GoTo function under the Option menu to move to the July high and at a price level equal to Jupiter's longitude on that date. In this case the longitude is 281.73° which is the same as 281.73 cents on the chart.

3) Set up a square of 120. In this case make sure you click on the View, No Erase button or Jupiter will be removed from the screen.

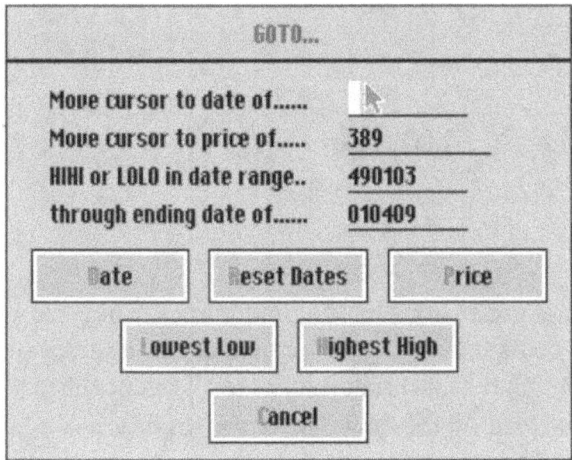

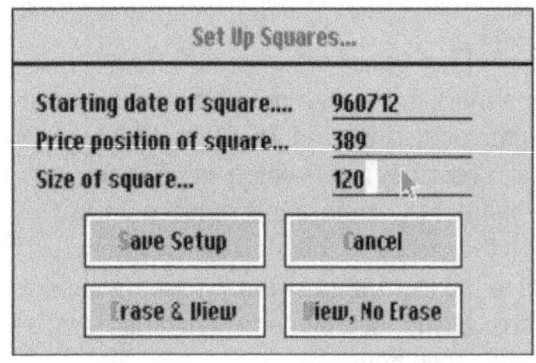

The points of interest are the crossing of the horizontal green lines by the planet lines. They are marked below. Since each square division line is 15 cents these lines also represent 15 degrees of movement. This technique should be used with all the planets, both heliocentric and geocentric. Look at only 45 or 90° moves for the faster planets instead of 15° as we have shown here.

If the 1x1 angle were set to 3 instead of 1 the price dimension of the square of 120 would become 360 and each of these horizontal lines would be 360/8 or 45°.

Averages of the Planets

Gann also used the average of various planet longitudes as support and resistance points and transit time measurements. Under the Time Cycles menu you can select any of the following:

Average of 5
MOf, Mean of 5
Average of 6
CE, Circle of 8
Average of 9
Mars through Neptune
Jupiter through Pluto
Mars through Pluto
All except Sun in Geocentric, All except Earth in heliocentric
All planets and the Sun/Earth

In addition you can select Avg Planets on Screen or Keep Planets & Avg. These will calculate the average of the planets on the screen and can be used to get an average for all other possible planet combinations. The Tool Bar icon can also be clicked. The program will make an average out of any planets that are on the screen.

Average of 5

Here is the average of the 5 planets (Mars, Jupiter, Saturn, Uranus, and Neptune) plotted on the General Motors daily chart. See how nicely the planetary lines hits highs and lows.

MOf, Mean of 5

In this example we have plotted the MOf 5 planets - Jupiter, Saturn, Uranus, Neptune and Pluto. Apple Computer follows these lines very nicely.

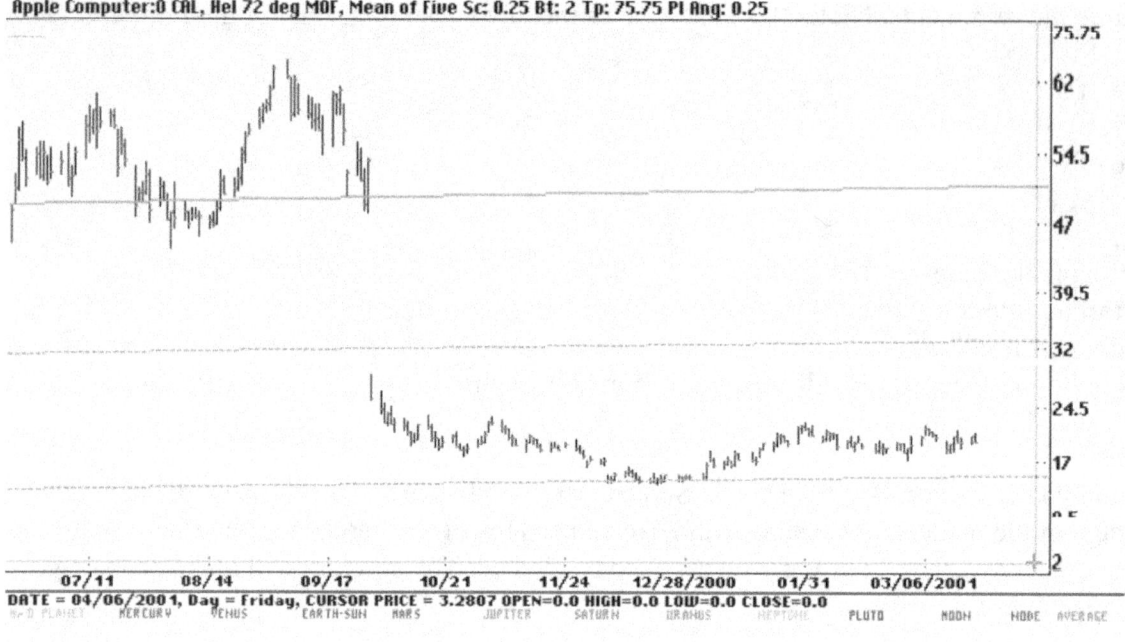

Average of 6

In this example we have plotted the Average of e six planets Mars, Jupiter, Saturn, Uranus, Neptune, and Pluto on the Gateway chart.

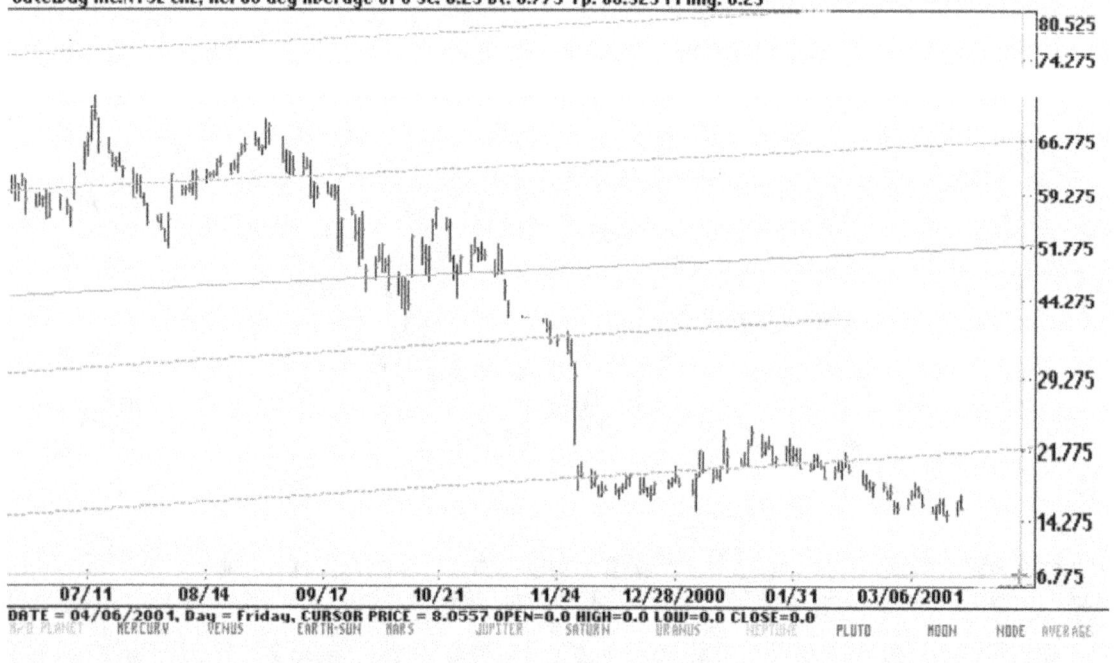

CE, Circle of 8

In this chart we have plotted the Circle of 8 planets on PPG Industries chart.

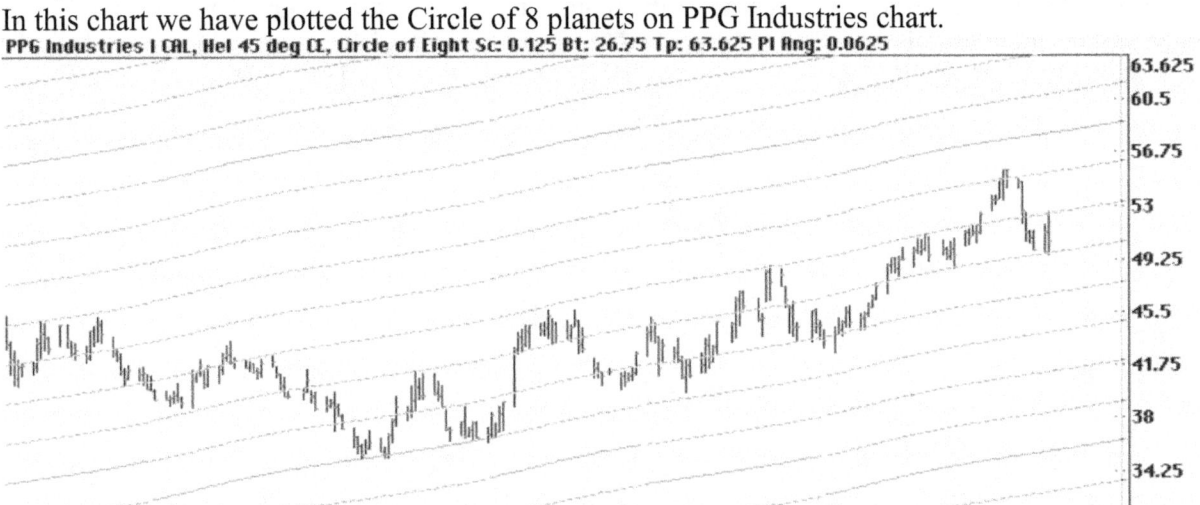

Average of 9

In this chart example we have plotted the average of 9 planets (Mercury, Venus, Earth-Sun, Mars, Saturn, Neptune and Pluto on the Dec Oats Chart.

Mars through Neptune

In this chart we have plotted the average of the planets (Mars, Jupiter, Saturn, Uranus, and Neptune) on the December Soybean Chart. The lines seem to hit fairly good in this example.

Jupiter through Pluto

In this chart we have plotted the average of Jupiter, Saturn, Uranus, Neptune and Pluto on the December Soybean chart. In this example the lines fit almost perfectly.

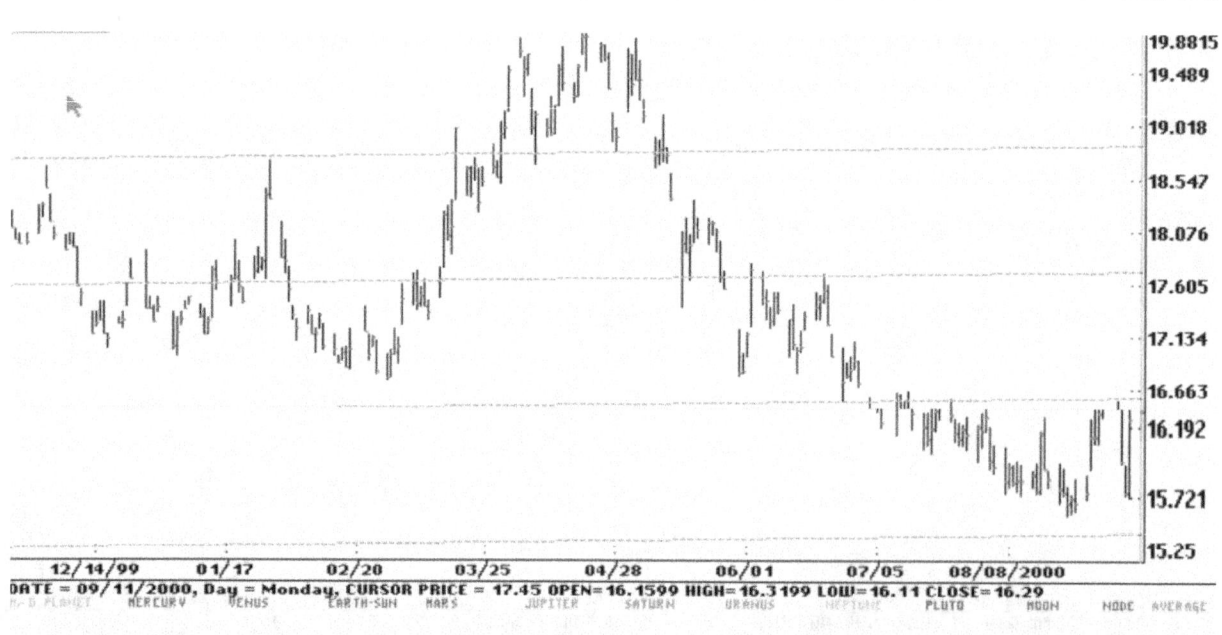

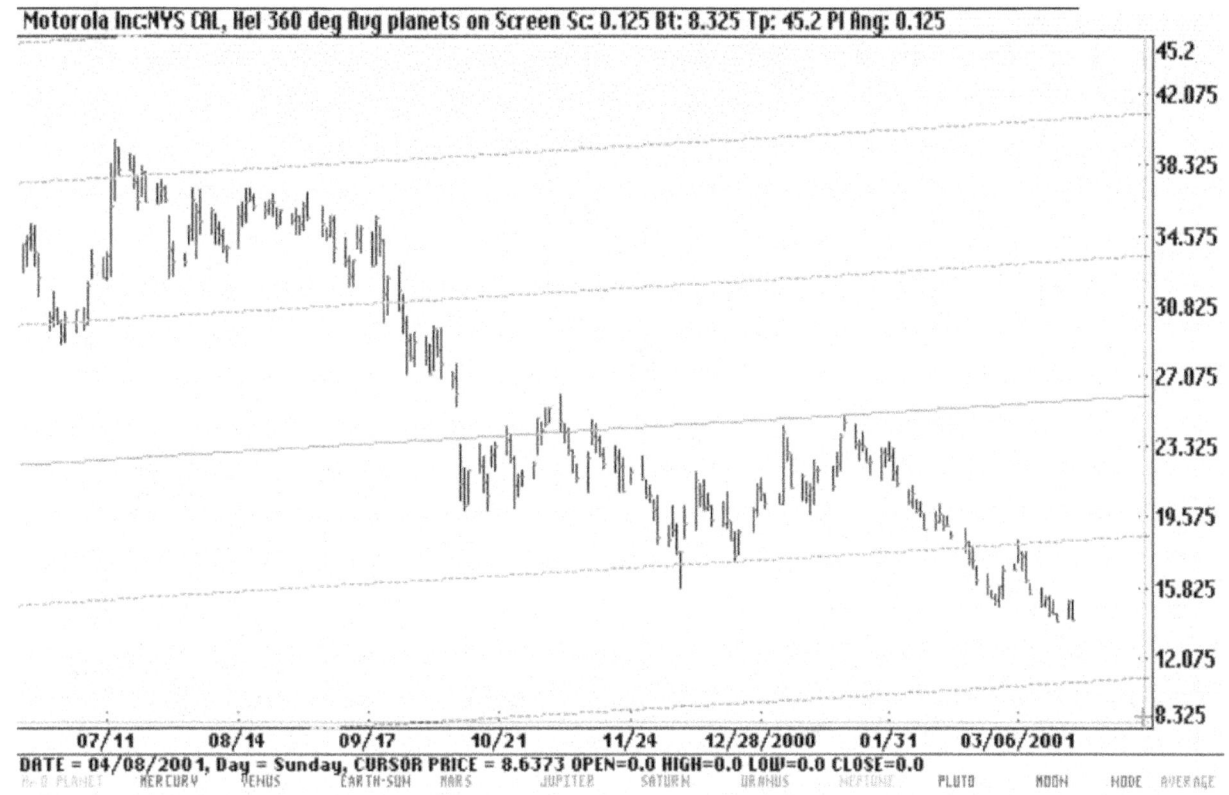

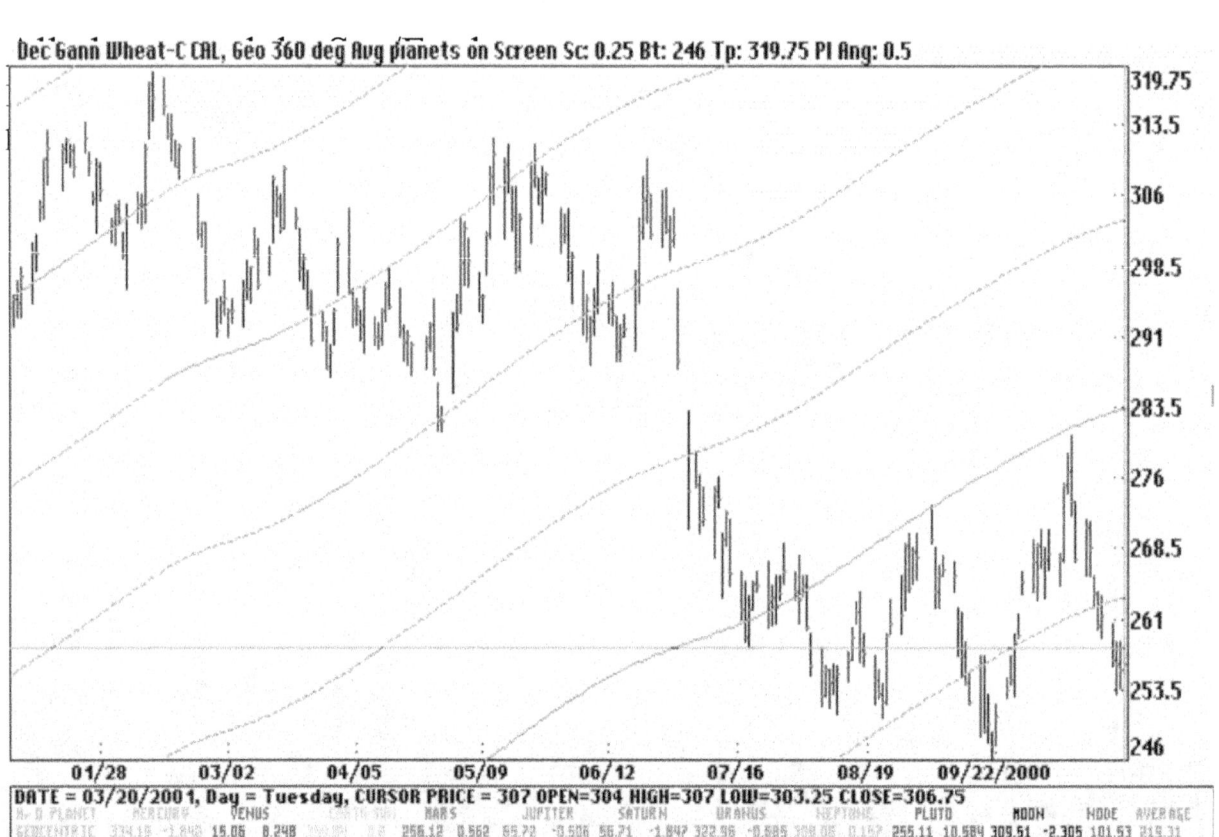

Latitude and Declination

As the Earth revolves around the Sun it's path defines an imaginary plane call the Ecliptic Plane. Other planets define their own planes as they travel around the Sun. The planet's plane is generally at some angle above or below the Earth/Sun plane. This angle is called Latitude and can be either Heliocentric or Geocentric as shown on the next drawing. It is measured in degrees North or South of the Sun/Earth plane. This example shows a planet in North Latitude

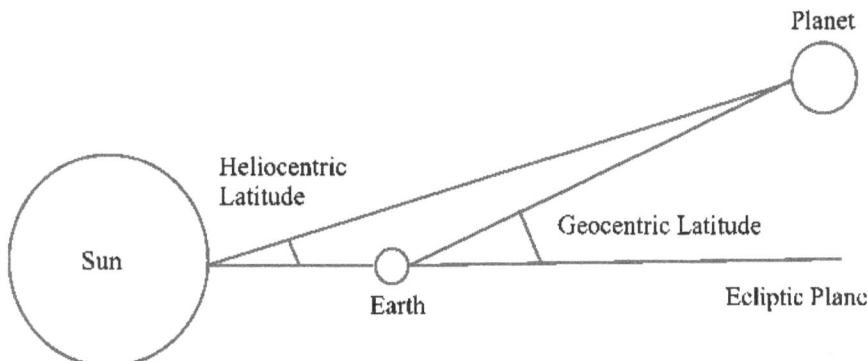

Declination is a measure of a planet's position above or below the Earth's Equatorial Plane. Imagine the Earth's equator extended in all directions out into space. This example shows a planet in South Declination.

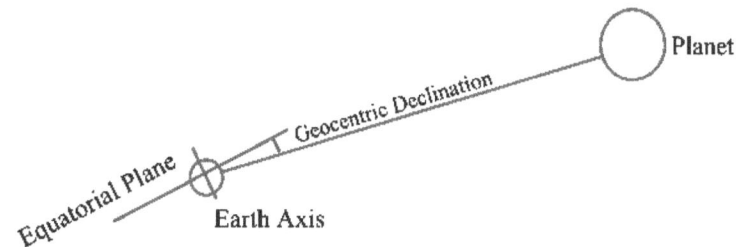

Select Latitude or Declination under the View menu or click on a Tool Bar icon.

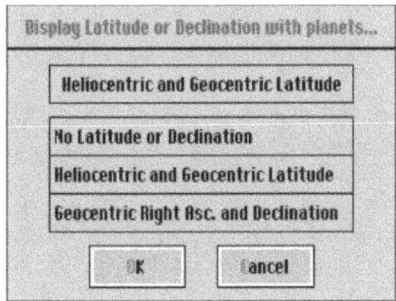

The latitude of the planets will be a maximum of about 80 North or South of the Ecliptic. The important points to watch are the maximum North and South points and the zero crossing points where the latitude goes from North to South or from South to North. The markers are activated by selecting Options Sizes, Labels & Markers.

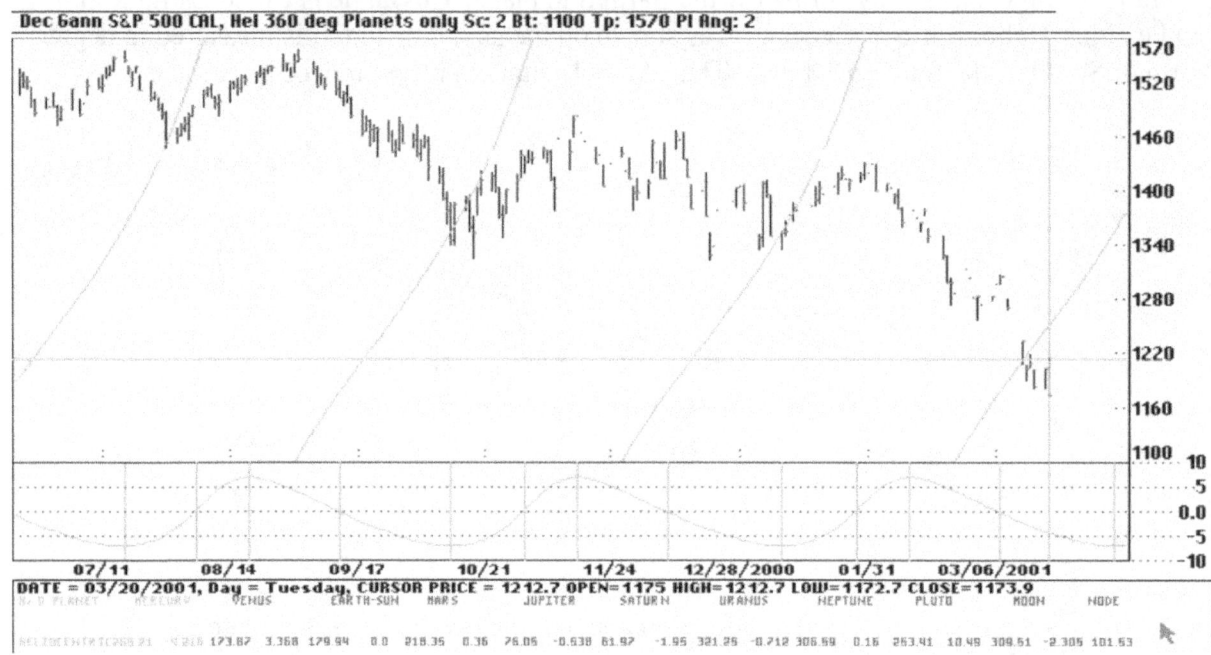

Declination should also be watched for the same maximum North and South points and zero crossings. Declination can be a maximum of about 28 degrees depending on the planet. It has a more complex shape since it is referenced to the Earth's equator and is modulated by the Earth's seasonal cycle and 23° tilt.

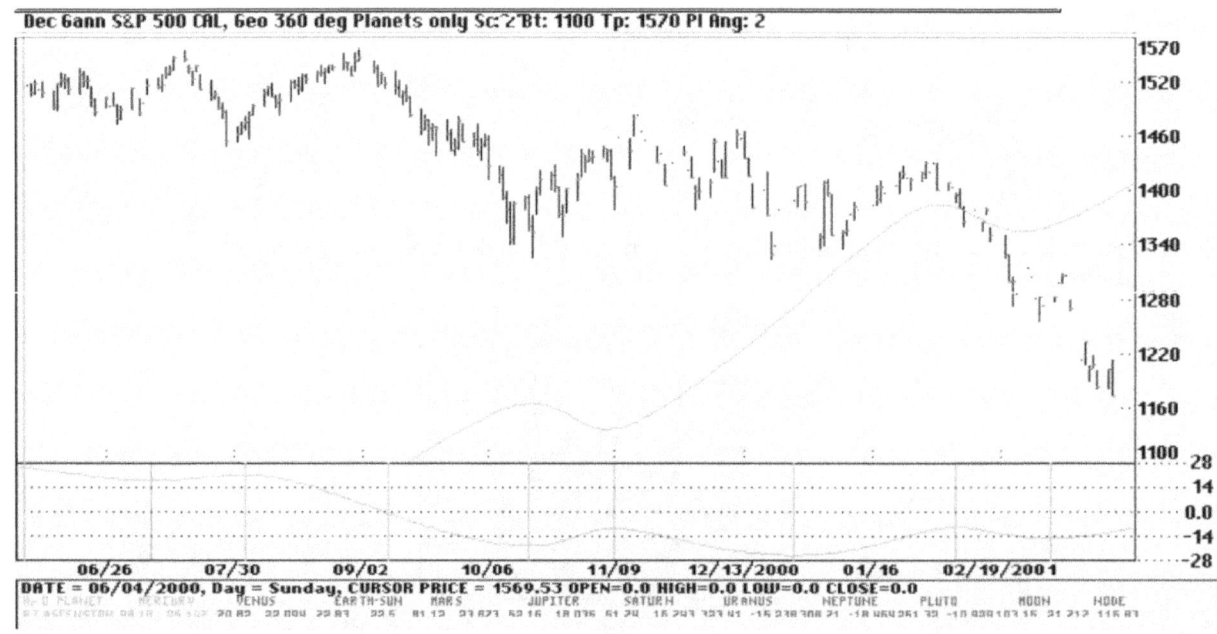

Parallels and Contra-Parallels

When two planets have the same latitude or declination they are said to be Parallel. When two planets have the same declination or latitude but one is North and the other South they are said to be Contra-Parallel. The concept of a parallel is similar to when two planets have the same longitude and are in conjunction.

To activate this feature select a planet aspect under the Time Cycles menu. The selected planet will be compared to any other planets on the screen. Here Mercury is the selected planet and the Venus parallels are marked by a dotted marker. If a planet is in parallel the dotted marker will have the same color as its planet color.

The current thinking is that a parallel is more powerful if both planets involved are of the same polarity, that is, both North or both South. Contra-Parallels appear to work better when they are nearer to zero as this example shows.

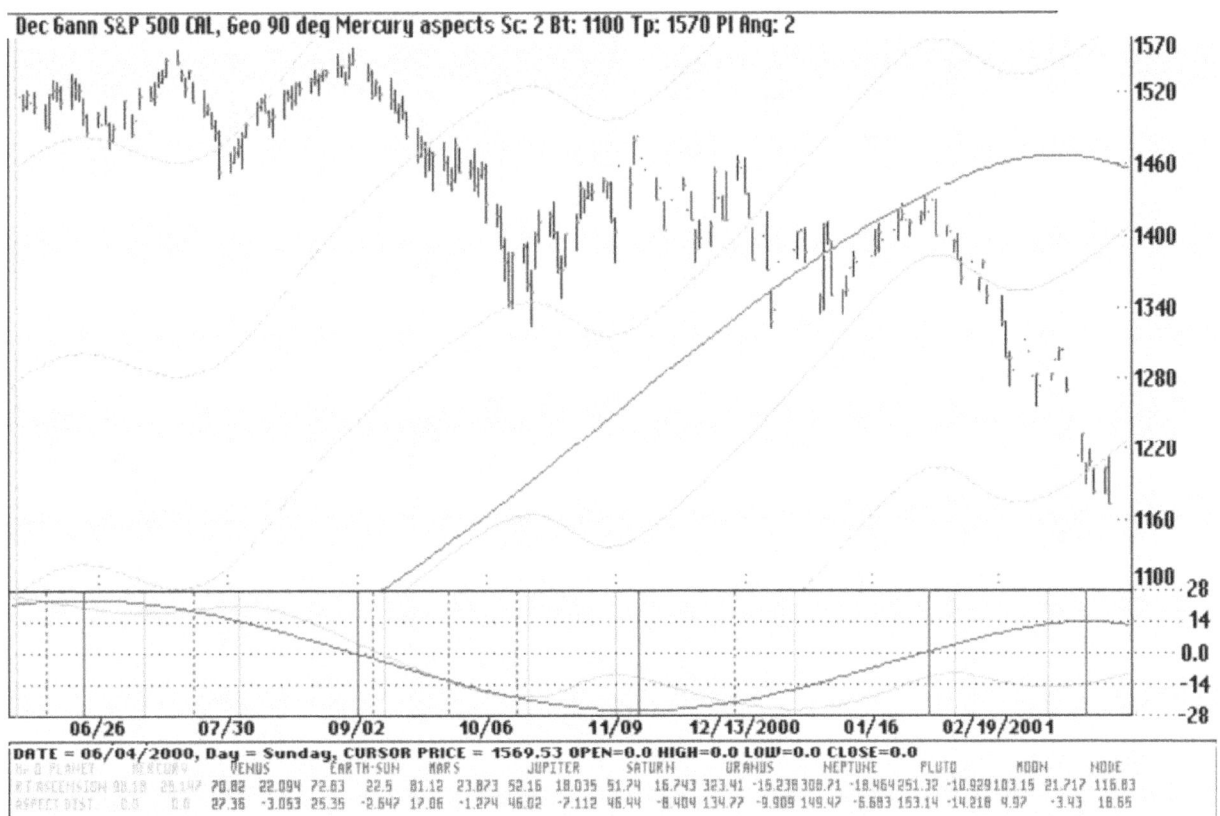

In the box at the bottom of the screen in the above chart, the exact value for the latitude or declination is displayed. The aspect distance shows the degree difference between the selected planet and any other planets on the screen. At the cursor's position at 'A' both Mercury and Venus are at 22.094 approximately. Venus has a slight difference of -.3.053.

125

Remember you have a choice of heliocentric and geocentric latitude but only geocentric declination. There can never be any Sun or Earth latitude since it is referenced to the orbital plane of Sun/Earth. There can be Sun declination which varies ± 23 degrees18' and reaches these maximums on June 21 and December 21. If you select declination and you are currently viewing heliocentric the program will automatically switch to geocentric mode. If you select latitude without the planets active the program will switch to your preference set under Options: Configure System: Preferences New Chart: Item #5 since you can display either heliocentric or geocentric latitude.

You can change the default scaling for the Latitude and Declination window by clicking the Left and Right mouse buttons inside the window.

Dimension

If supply and demand are perfectly equal markets will move sideways in very narrow ranges. Some type of energy input will cause the market price to rise or fall. These inputs can be caused by weather in the case of commodities or politics in the case of currencies, metals, stocks and bonds. Regardless of the input we need a way to predict where prices are headed.

According to basic Gann techniques a future price will be related to an important low or high in a simple arithmetic relationship. For example, a low off 100 will produce resistance points at 200, 300 etc. A high of 470 would show support points at 235 (1/2), 117.5 (1/4) or 352.5 (3/4). See drawing below.

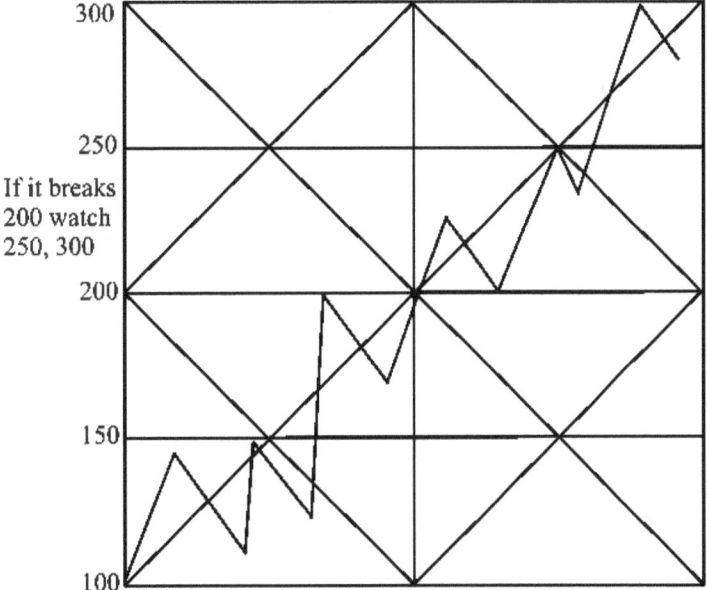

This is an example of a linear or arithmetic expansion. Every resistance point is an even multiple of the starting value. The price of 200 is 100 x 2, 300 is 100 x 3 and so on. No matter how you sub-divide it the result is always an arithmetic part of the previous part. The price of 150 is 1 ~'2 of 100, 50 x 2 is 100 and so on. This technique works over narrow ranges of price but beyond a certain point prices will break out of their range and travel to a higher level that is not an arithmetic relationship to the previous level.

This is the basis of what Gann called Natural Law. Everything in nature follows some type of non-linear expansion. If it didn't work this way flowers and leaves would be squares or rectangles, electron or planetary orbits would be evenly spaced and the stock market would be much more orderly! Of course nobody could make any money trading because it would be obvious to everyone where the price was heading.

In the latter part of the 1800's and early 1900's several books were written that explored Natural Law as it related to plant and animal growth, crystal formation and the architectural forms of the great cathedrals in Europe. In the early days a scientist was expected to me knowable about chemistry, botany, physics, astronomy, engineering and everything else of a physical nature. They were searching for a connection to Natural Law that they believed all the scientific fields contained. Unfortunately there is nothing in nature that is exact. All leaves on the same tree are similar to each other but they are never exactly the same. The orbits of the planets are elliptical, not perfect circles. This is all part of a grand plan the explanation of which is beyond the scope of this manual. The end result was that science became specialized as each group tried to fine tune their field of expertise to 18 digits of precision. Today the chemists don't talk to the botanists who don't talk to the physicists who don't talk to the pharmaceutical researchers. None of them see their common bond to Natural Law.

Gann was able to combine what he learned from these early writings with his knowledge of the secrets of Freemasonry. Since everything follows Natural Law he decided to apply this knowledge to the markets. This manual can't substitute for the hundreds of books written so a brief description of some of the principals will have to do.

Squaring a Circle

A number of Gann's charts and overlays contain both circles and squares superimposed on one another. Chart #8 shows part of Gann's Square of 144 with 2 inner circles labeled 'A' and 'B'. In the drawing below we will explore the relationship between the sides of a square, its diagonal and a circle surrounding it. From basic Geometry we know that the hypotenuse of a right triangle is equal to the square root of the sum of the squares of its two sides. In the drawing below the square root of (1x1 + Lx1) is the square root of 2 or 1.414213... This makes the length of the sides of the outer square equal to 1.414 on each side. A circle surrounding the outer square would have a diameter of 1.414 also. A square around that circle would have a length equal to 2 on a side.

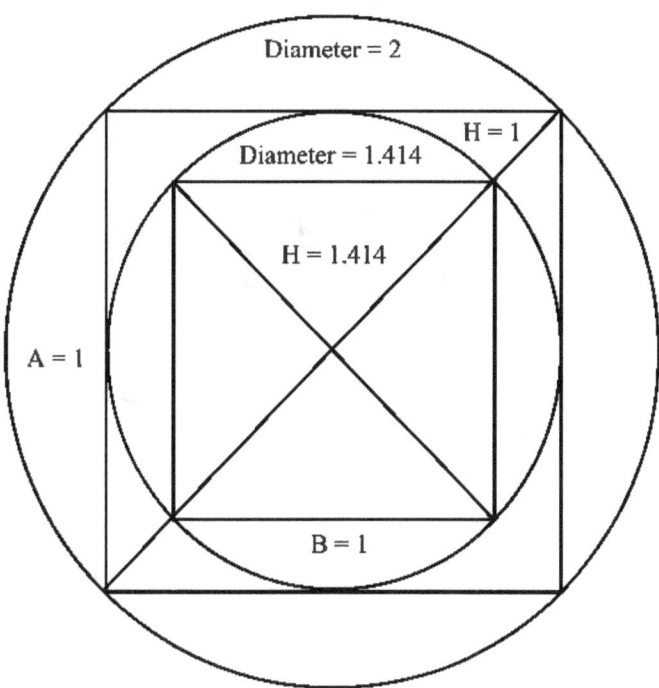

Two squares stacked on top of each other will produce the Square Root of 3.

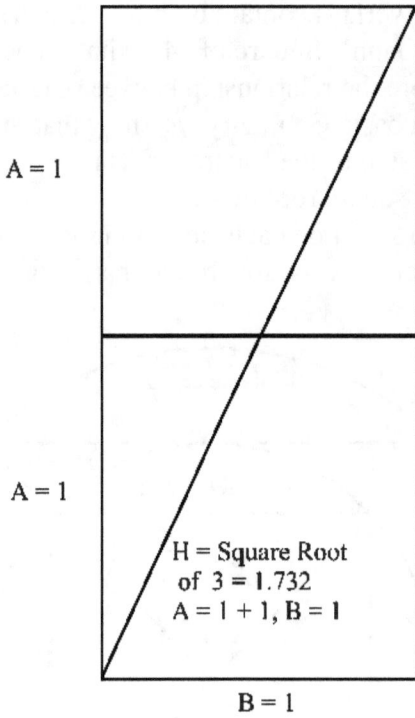

Below the familiar fibonacci ratio is derived from a radius drawn from A to B. CD and EF are both .618 and EC or FD are 1.618 The length ED is 2.236 or the Square Root of 5

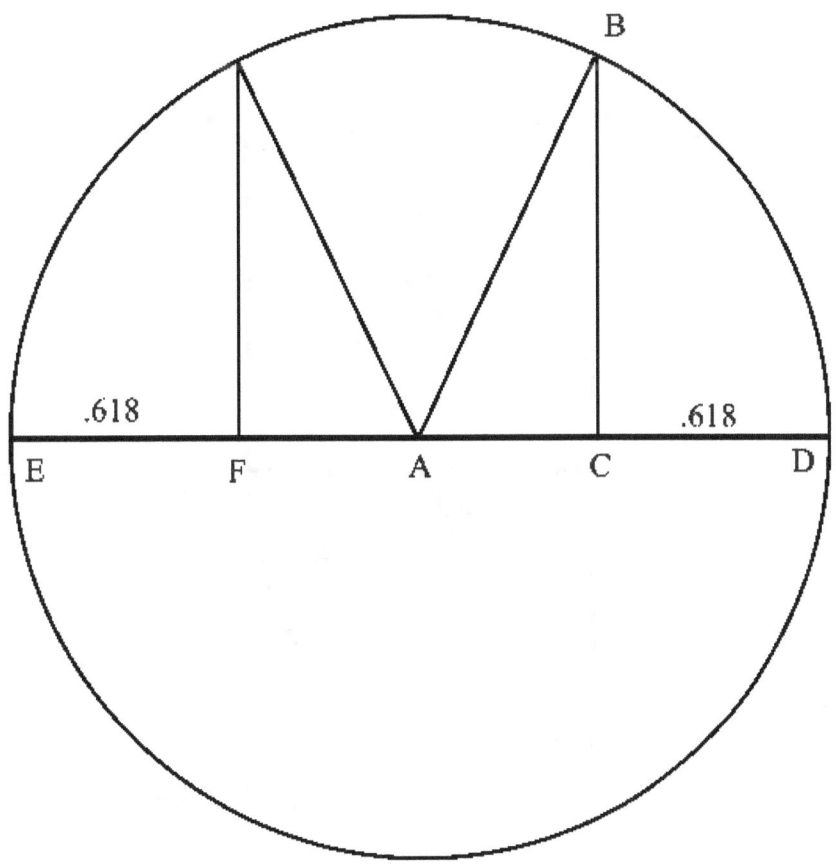

This drawing shows the relationship between two circles displaced by their radii. All of the common square root relationships can be discovered by a little experimentation with a compass and straightedge. *The Elements of Dynamic Symmetry* by Jay Hambidge (ISBN 0-486-21776-0) is an excellent book on these techniques.

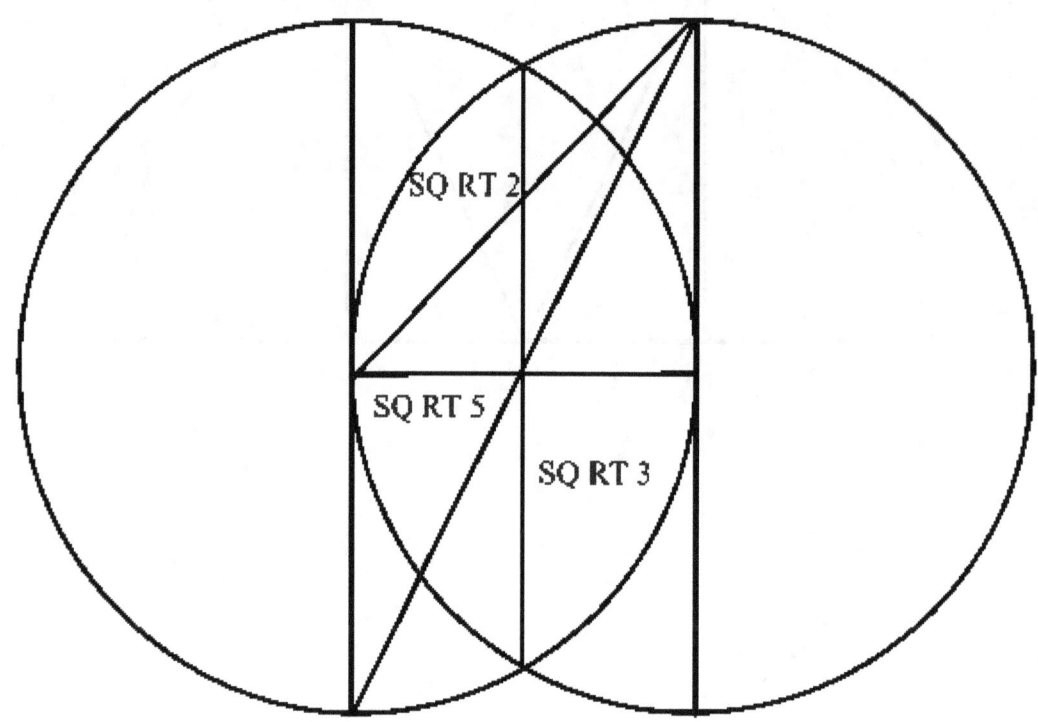

This last drawing shows a cube with its sides equal to 1 unit. The diagonal YZ at the base is equal to √ 2 as shown in the previous examples. The diagonal XY drawn from opposite corners would equal √ of 3. Since A = 1 and the base of right triangle XYZ is √ 2 the hypotenuse XY would be: XY = √ (1x1 + √ 2 x √ 2), XY = √ (1x1 + √ 2 x √ 2) XY = √ 3. The important point to realize with this example is that line XY when viewed directly from the top, bottom or sides would appear to be of the length √ 2 even though it would actually be the √ 3 in length. (SS, for example) If viewed from point X or Y it would appear to have no length at all. (CC) If the line XY were viewed at any viewing angle between SS and CC it could be any arbitrary length.

When viewing a price chart it is important to realize that the chart is a 2 dimensional representation of a 3 dimensional phenomena. At times the price bars are heading toward you out of the paper and at other times the bars are spiraling into the chart. The Third Dimension module of Ganntrader attempts to help you visualize this other dimension.

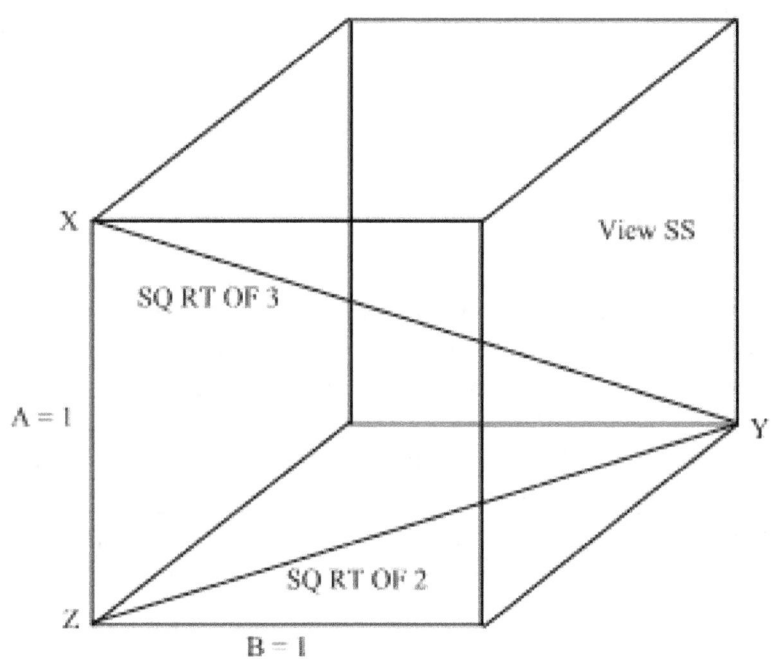

Basic Arcs and Circles

The Third Dimension portion of the program has its own menu. To activate the features select either PT Circles or PT Arcs. To explain the difference between a Price Time Circle and a Price Time Arc look at the circle drawn using a compass on next chart and the next chart after that. The point of the compass is placed at the low at 'A' and the compass is expanded to the height of the high at 'B'.

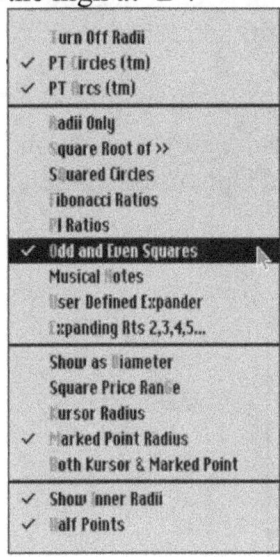

A circle as in the first chart has a time and price component. The price range from 'A' to 'B' is 34 points but the time dimension is 136. Notice the point where the arc reaches the price level of 'A' catches the low at point 'C'. This is one use for an arc or circle.

The reason that this round 'circle' has a price dimension of 34 and a time dimension of 136 has to do with the fact that the chart's scale is .25 per grid line. Drawing circles on charts has been done for years by chart readers and can be quite useful. If you use a compass on a chart you have a problem in that a chart with a different scaling would not have caught this low at 'C'. Compare the next two charts.

Apple Computer goes over $60. In order for circle AB to still hit the low at 'C' requires that the circle be redrawn as an ellipse. The solution to this problem introduced by Ganntrader is to have an independent multiplier for the price portion of a circle. Under the Setup menu you will find Third Dimension Factor. In both of the next charts this factor is set to .25, the same as the chart's scale. This feature is similar to the way the 1x1 angle value can be set independent of the chart's scale. Once you find a setting that works you can be assured that the effect of the arcs and circles will be adjusted properly if the chart scale is changed. The radius is computed using the formula $R = \sqrt{(price / factor)^2 + time^2}$, the familiar Pythagorean Theorem known to any Geometry student.

When Price Time Circles are selected the Third Dimension Factor is set equal to the chart's scale whereas Price Time Arcs permit the Factor and Scale to be independent. If you place Gann's

Square of 90 overlay on a chart with a scale of 4 cents per grid line you are effectively using a square of 360x90. If you draw a circle on a chart using a compass you are effectively using the Third Dimension Factor if your chart is scaled to anything other than 1 cent per grid line.

As you should know by now, the program also permits you to change the bar spacing using the <Z> and <Alt <Z> keys. This causes further problems since the left to right spacing of the chart is changed and a previously drawn circle has to be adjusted to compensate. Unlike other programs, Ganntrader takes care of this problem automatically.

In order to create the circle as shown on the next chart do the following:

1) Select PT Circles under the Third Dimension menu.
2) Move the cursor to the low at 'A'.
3) Press either the Enter or Insert key to mark it.
4) Hold down the Left mouse button and move the cursor to line up with the high at 'B' directly above point 'A'.
5) Select Radii Only under the Third Dimension menu. This turns off any expansions that may be active.
6) Hit Enter or Insert a second time to lock in the termination point of the radius.

Once the termination point of the radius is locked in you can move to a new point and draw additional arcs and circles using steps 2 through 6 above.

Circles and Arcs can be thought of as dynamic price and time measuring tools whereas Gann's angles are more static in nature. You know if a market breaks a 1X1 angle it is heading to the 1X2 below it. Arcs and Circles can give you all the intermediate points in between. For any given period of time it's as if people can handle a low energy activity for a long time but a high-energy activity for less time. The product of Price X Time like a circle's radius is the same anywhere on the circle. A person can handle a 2-hour walk in the park but not a 2 hour ride on a roller coaster. It is the same 2 hours but the energy levels are different.

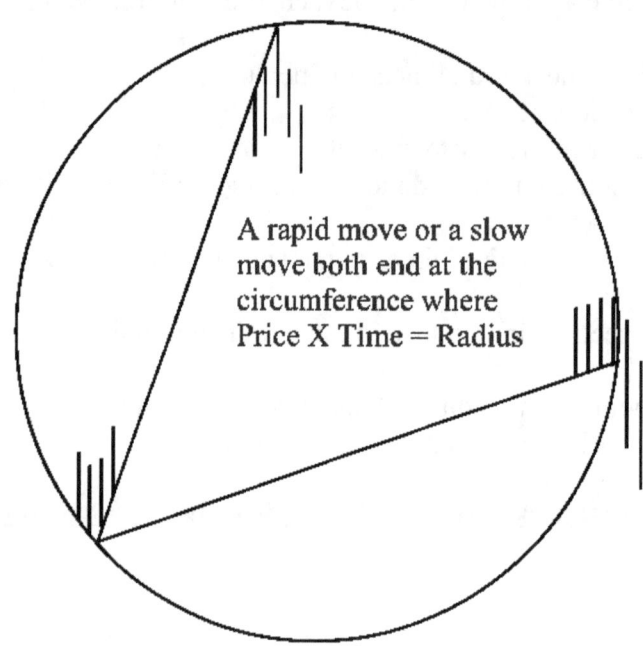

These next 2 charts of Gateway 2000 illustrate this idea well. Here the Third Dimension Factor is set to .3 which seams to work well for GTW. Simply move from origin to termination points marking both as you go using the previous instructions. These are the same setups with the screen scrolled left and right to show them all. The points where the arcs cross the price of the origin points can also produce a change in trend. They are marked with vertical lines.
In these examples radii from both the origin and termination points are drawn. Click on the Tool Bar icon, select Both Cursor & Marked Point under the Third Dimension menu or hit the <Ctrl><F5> function key.

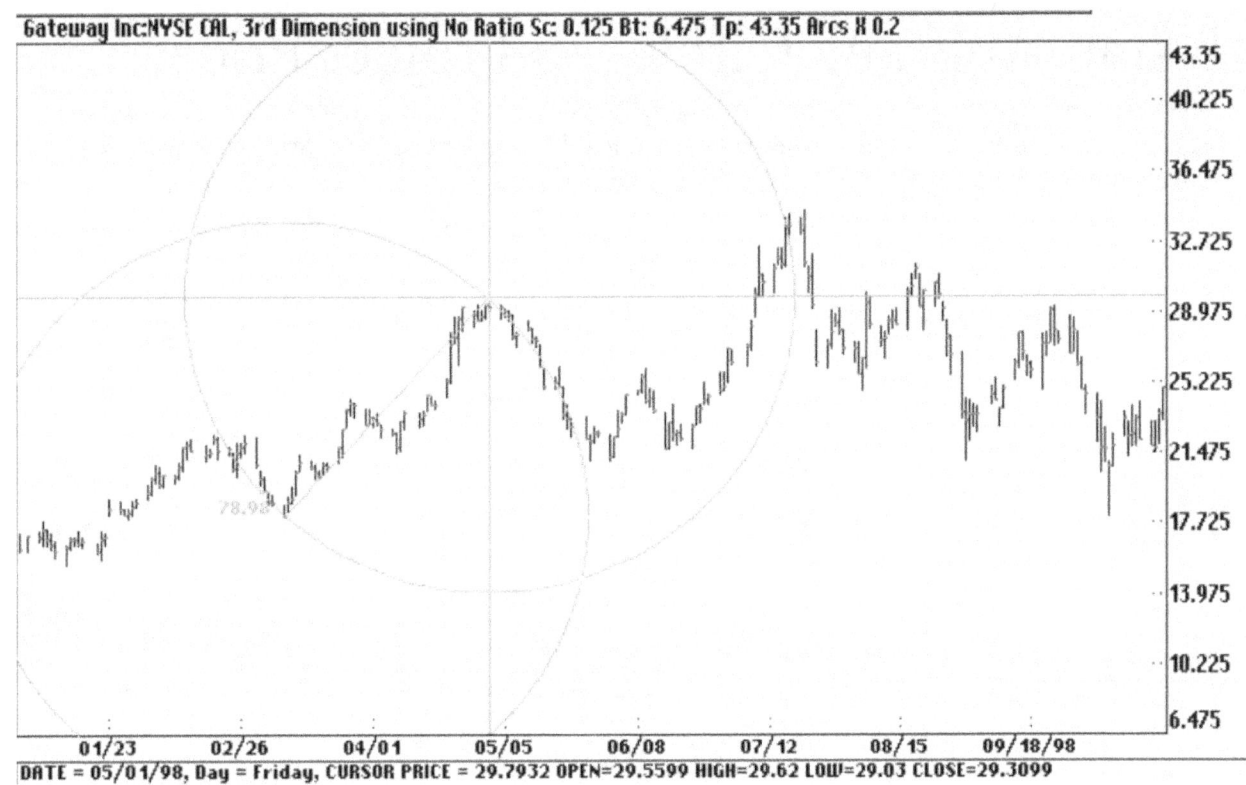

DATE = 05/01/98, Day = Friday, CURSOR PRICE = 29.7932 OPEN=29.5599 HIGH=29.62 LOW=29.03 CLOSE=29.3099

DATE = 07/21/98, Day = Tuesday, CURSOR PRICE = 34.2601 OPEN=33.65 HIGH=34.3699 LOW=31.43 CLOSE=31.59

Using Arcs and Circles to Project Price

This is a good example of using the extremes of the circle's circumference or their 1/2 points to project prices. Note that in this example the 'circles' look like ovals. The price bars were squeezed up to the maximum price bars on screen using the <Alt><Z> keys. The Third Dimension Factor is equal to the chart's scale so these ovals would actually appear as round circles if the chart were printed.

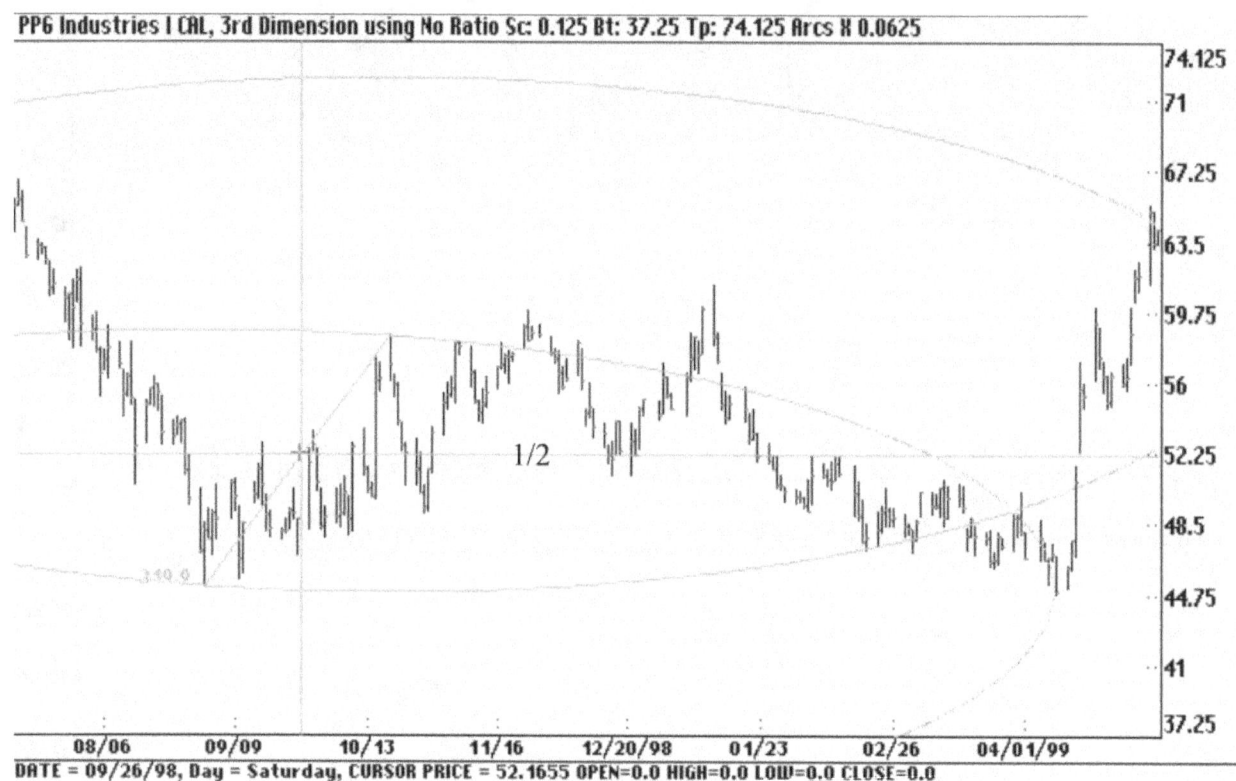

Vertical Points in Arcs Project Reactions

When you see a market moving up or down in a curved manner try placing an arc on the price bars. At least three points must touch the arc to be valid. The point the prices go vertical at the end of the arc will usually result in a major reaction.

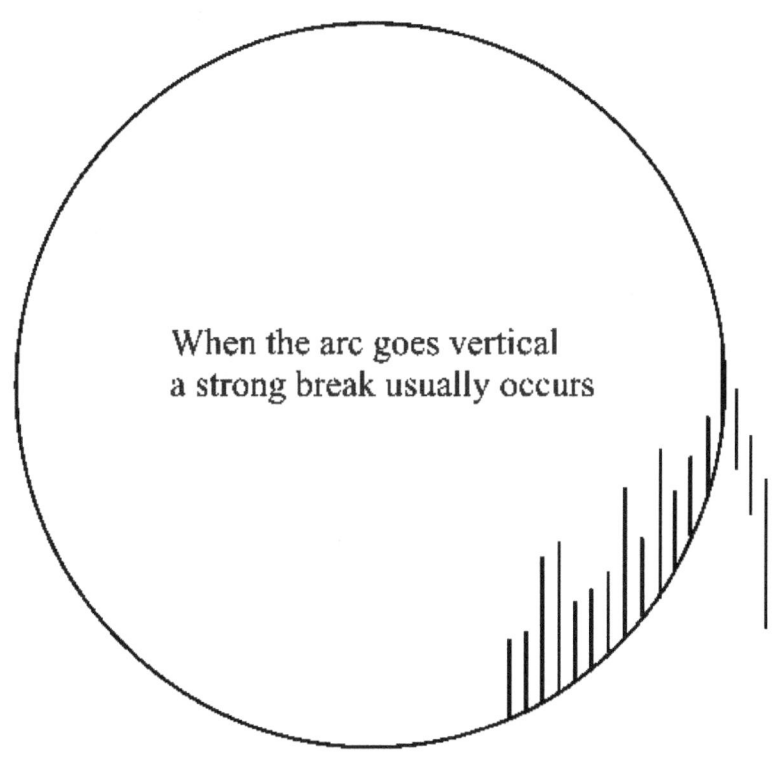

When the arc goes vertical a strong break usually occurs

The origin point was marked at 'A' but this time an arc is drawn from the cursor's cross hair rather than the origin. You should move the mouse up, down and around until at least 3 points touch the arc. If you can't get at least 3 points on the curve you can't depend on it working. At the point the arc goes vertical a break down will occur. See point 'B' You can originate an arc from the cursor, origin or both by selecting <Ctrl><F3>, <F4>, or <F5>, by selecting Cursor Radius, Marked Point Radius or Both Cursor & Marked Point under the Third Dimension menu or by clicking the appropriate Tool Bar icon.

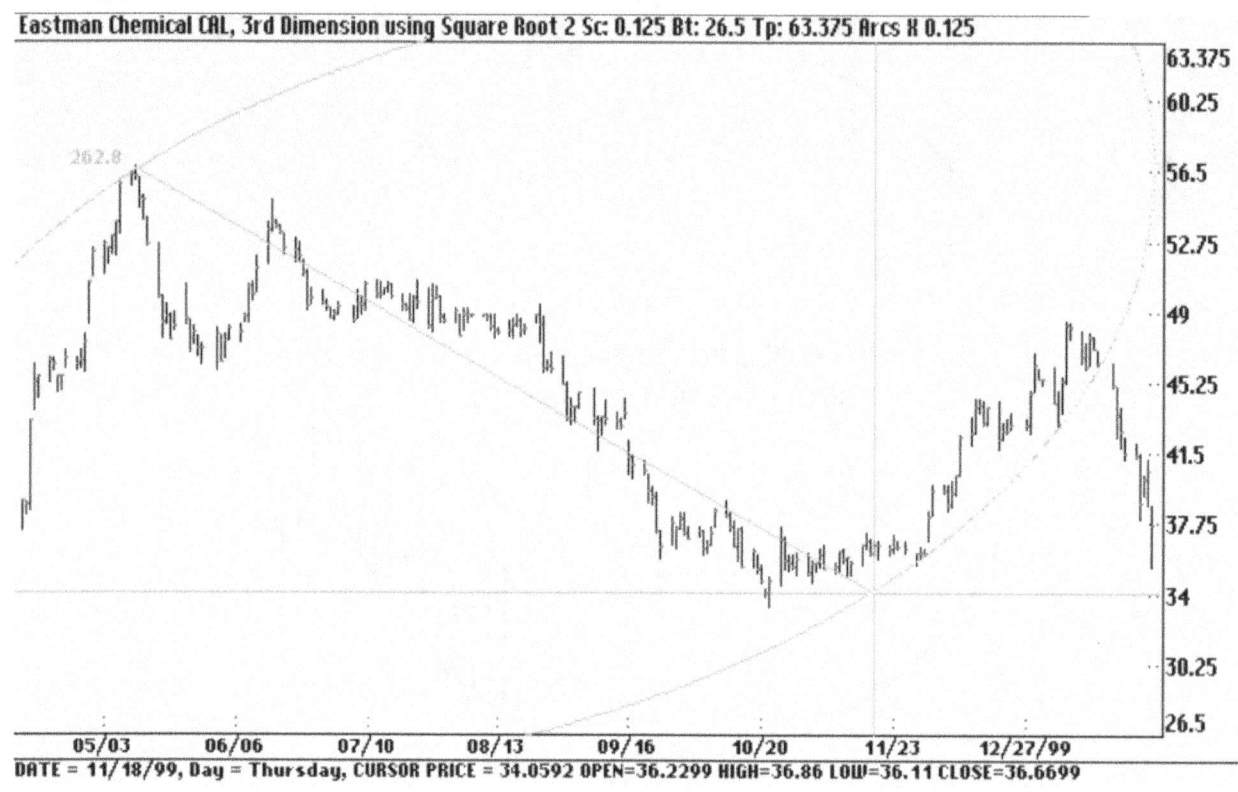

Expansions of Arcs and Circles

As we discussed at the beginning of this section, markets expand or contract into new price levels following various multiplier ratios. A square surrounded by a circle surrounded by a square expands by the √2. A triangle or pentagram surrounded by a circle would expand at a different rate. A cube or pyramid shaped solid object surrounded by a sphere is yet another expansion mode. You can consider a line between a high and low or a line directly above a low in line with a high to be one side of the surrounded object. The object is a square, triangle, cube or any other 2 or 3 dimensional shapes. These expansion arcs and circles are activated using the following steps:

1) Select PT Circles or Arcs under the Third
Dimension menu.
2) Move the cursor to the first point.
3) Press the <Enter,' or <Insert> key to mark it.
4) Hold down the Left mouse button and move the
cursor to the desired termination point.
5) Select and expansion multiplier under the Third
Dimension menu. The default is 'J_2.
6) Hit <Enter> or <Insert> a second time to lock in the termination point of the radius.

The function keys duplicate all the selections in the Third Dimension menu. See the keyboard overlay. We'll explore some square root expansions in the next section.

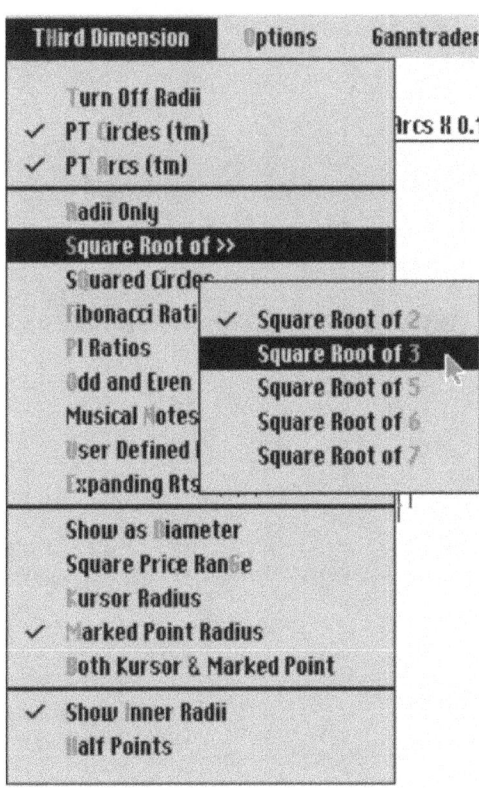

Square Root Expansions

The initial impulse waves after a low are a good place to start an arc and check for root expansions. Here a radius is drawn from 'A' to the top at 'B'. The arc was set to originate from the cursor point at 'B' rather than the origin at 'A' by clicking the Tool Bar icon. The halfway points were also activated with another Tool Bar icon. The function keys <F1> followed by <Ctrl><F3> or the menu items could have been selected as well. Gann always considered the ½ point to be very important. It can be added to most of the expansion selections.

Inside Radii Contractions – Chart #12

The next chart shows a squared circle expansion on a weekly wheat chart. The low of 234, a very important low in this market, was squared using a square of 234 units in price and time. The 1/2 points as well as the inner radii were also included by clicking the Tool Bar icons. You can see all the major highs and lows bouncing off these levels. Here's another example using the √3 and the inner radii on an RML monthly chart.

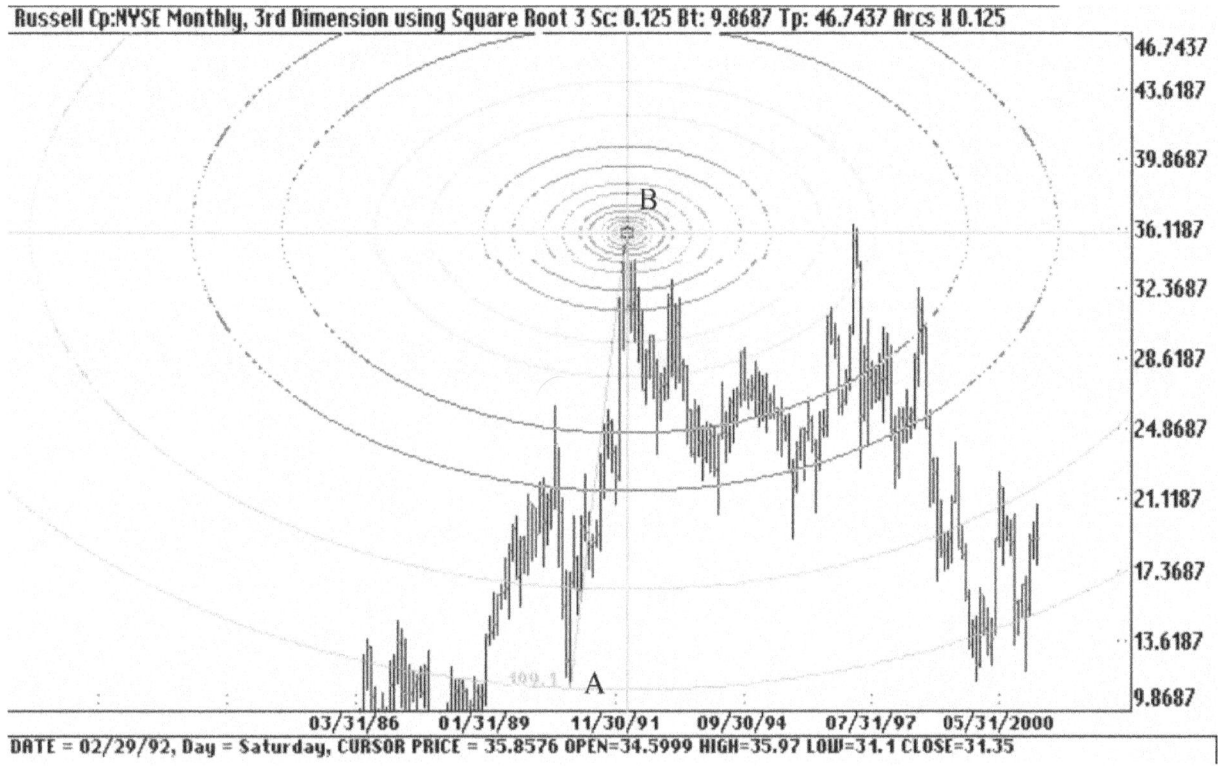

Square Root of 3 – Chart #13, Chart #14

Most examples of the Third Dimension are best seen using the large charts in the back of the manual. Chart #13 shows the DJIA monthly with an arc drawn between the 1929 high and the 1932 low using a monthly chart. It uses the √3 expansions as well as the ½ points. If a picture is worth 1000 words this chart definitely shows the power of this tool. Try the '42 and '45 from these same points.

Chart #14A and B shows a radius drawn from low to low between the 1974 and 1982 DJIA lows. This arc appeared to work well except during the hysteria of 97-99 although the prices have stopped on the '43 line as this is being written. (June 99) As the fundamental traders try to think up another story to justify the next leg up in the internet stocks the market is treading water on the '43 line! Only time will tell.

Third Dimension Factor – Chart #15, Chart #16, Chart #17

To fine-tune the swings in 1997-99 an arc was drawn from the 1982 to 1987 lows. Charts #15 has the Third Dimension Factor set to 16 and Chart #16 has it set to 28 which produces round circles instead of ellipses. The Third Dimension Factor is located under the Setup menu. These lines catch most of the price and time action.

Chart #17 is a 5 trading day chart started from the first impulse wave after the October 1997 low. Radii from both the origin and termination points were used, activated by a click on the Tool Bar icon.

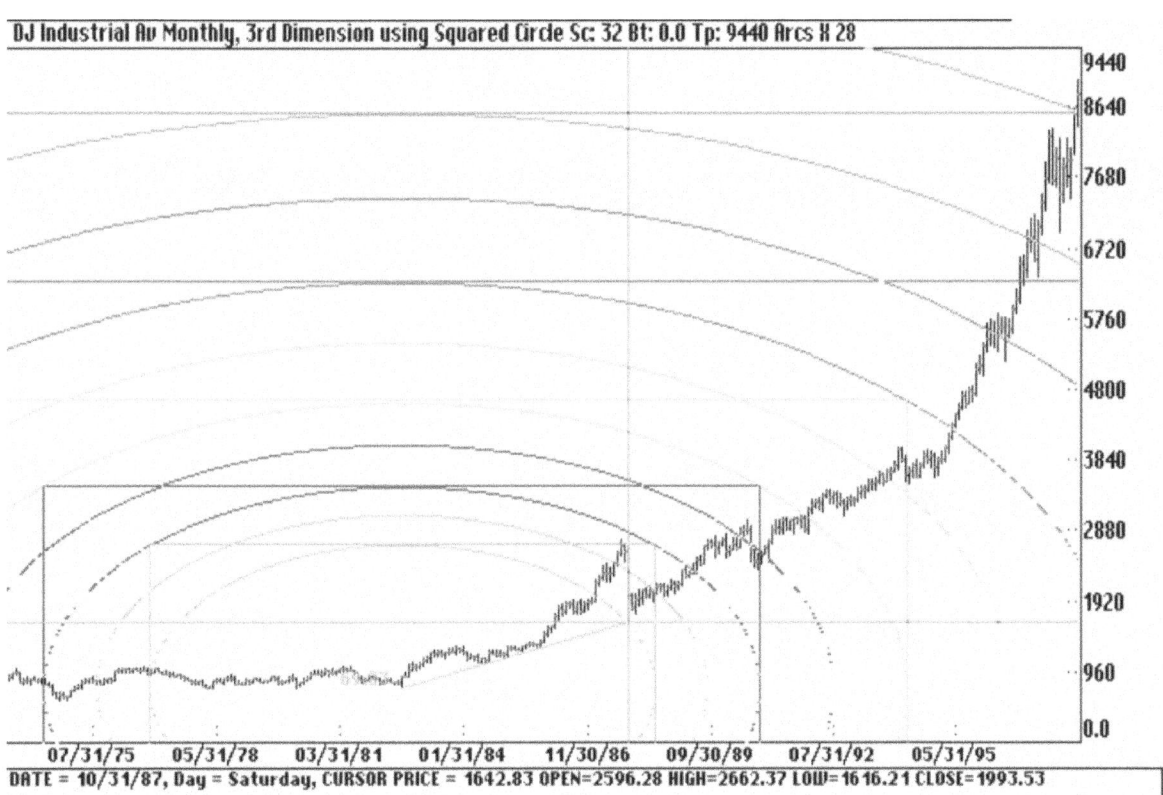

Miscellaneous Expansions

The most important expansions are √2, Squared Circles which are √2 expansions with the squares included, √3 and √4s. The √6, √7, π and Musical Note expansions are also included and can produce good results at times. The π expansions multiply the original radius by 3.14 159... and musical notes expand the original radius by the musical scale. There are 8 notes in each octave which are displayed in alternating colors.

The User Defined Expansion can be used for any expansion value of your choosing. It is entered under Setup: User Defined Expansion.

Odd & Even Squares – Chart #18

The Square of 9, discussed in a previous section, is another example of a non-linear expansion. With the Square of 9 expansion the initial price was expanded by taking its square root, adding 2 for a 3600 move and squaring the results. For example a price of 25 could be expanded by 3600 as follows: '425 = 5, (5 + 2)2 = 49, a 3600 move on the Gann Square of 9. Any other degree move can be had by using a number other than 2. Adding 1 for example would yield a 180° move.

The Odd and Even Squares expansion works on the original radius using the same formula. The program takes the square root of the original radius, adds 1 and squares the results. If the 1/2 points are active the adder is .5 instead of 1.

Chart #18 shows an S&P500 calendar day chart with an arc from the October 1997 low at 'A' to the first impulse high at 'B'.

Odd & Even Square Time Expansions – Chart #19, Chart 20

These next two charts use the Odd & Even expansions to measure time. In Chart #19 the initial day count of 34 days between points 'A' and 'B' was used as the radius. In Chart #20 an initial day count of 25, an odd square of 5 x 5, was used as the starting point and all the odd and even squares as well as their 1/2 points were plotted. On both charts the point of interest is where the arc intersects the price level of point 'A'.

On the screen below, after marking the origin point at 'A' the cursor is moved directly to the right until it is under point 'B' but still in line with the price level at 'A'. You will see a radius read out as shown in the circle. Since you are measuring time the number should always be a whole number with no decimal portion. Also the radius line will disappear when it is exactly even with the price level at 'A' making it easier to get an exact placement for the termination point.

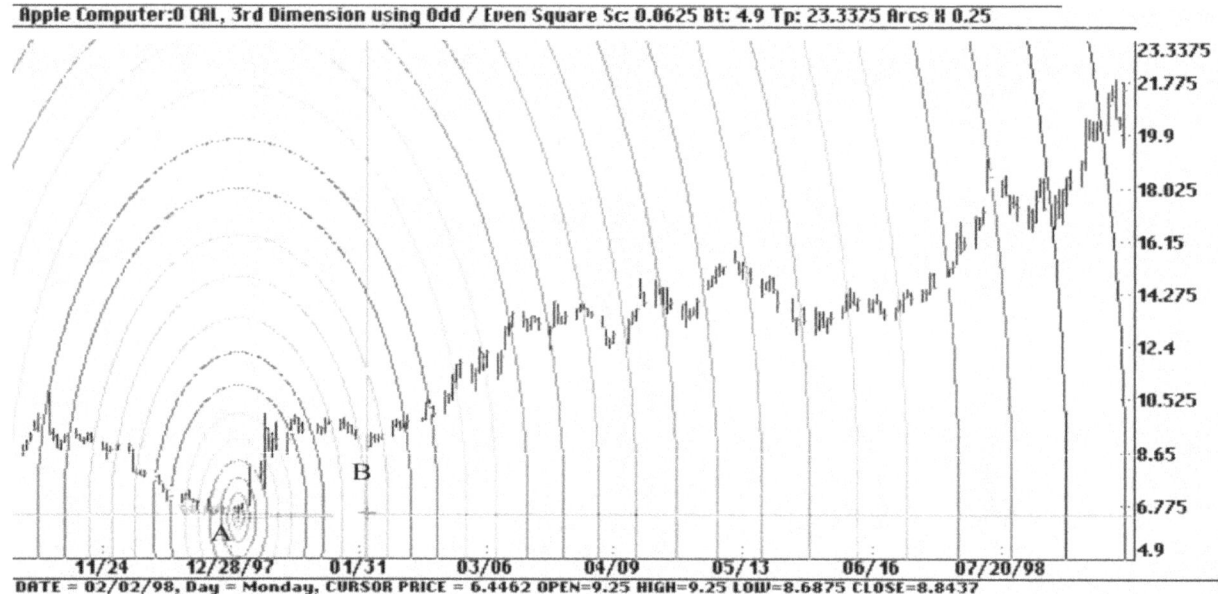

Fibonacci Expansions

The Fibonacci expansions work in a similar fashion to the Odd and Even Squares expansion. The square root of the original radius is added to .382 or .618 and the result is squared again. If you select the 1/2 points additional adders are .19 1, .500 and .809. This technique is similar to that used by Michael Jenkins in his books and course except his calculations are based on price levels instead of radius lengths.

To make a radius correspond to a price level simply start the radius from zero and extend it straight up to the desired price level or start the radius in line with a price and extend it straight up to the terminating price level. In both cases the time portion of the right triangle would be zero and the radius would consist of price only. The radius would still be a hypotenuse but the formula would be reduced to Radius = $\sqrt{(Price / Factor)^2 + 0^2}$) or Radius = Price / Factor.

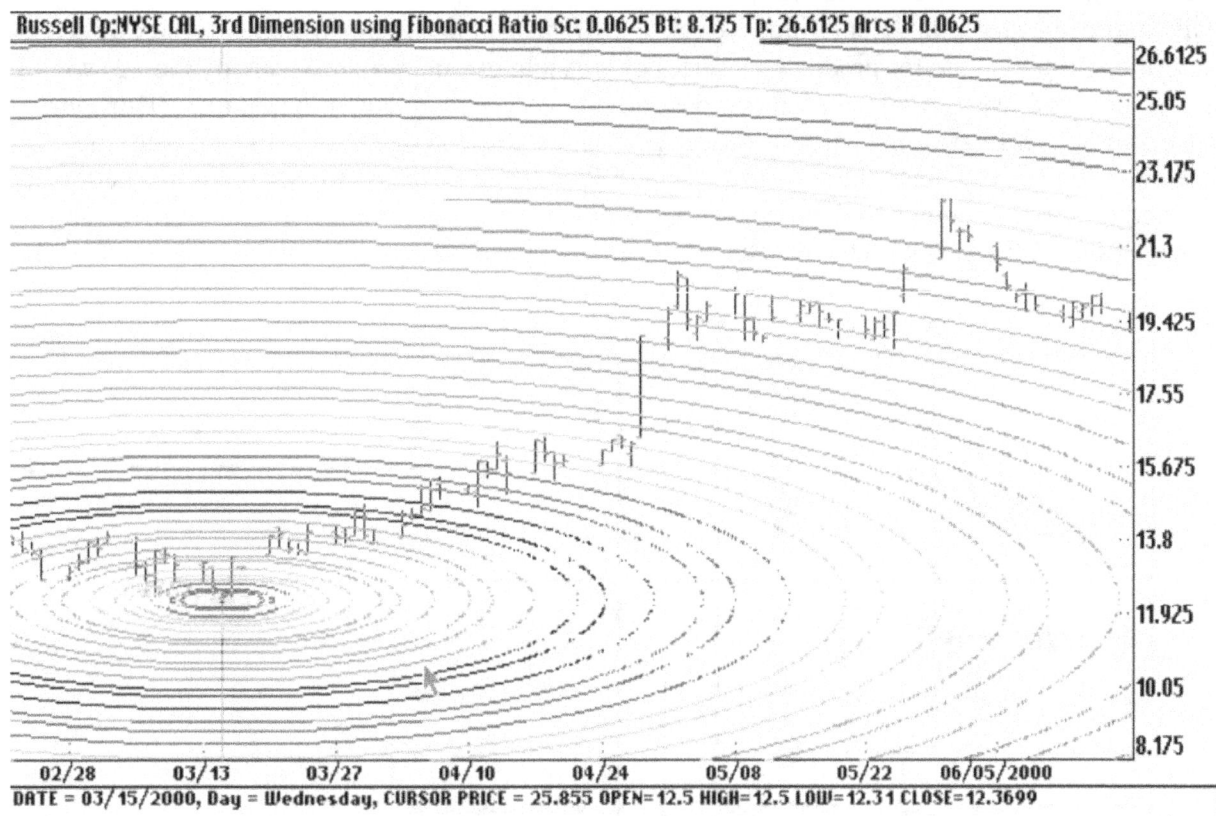

Look at the above chart and see how the price trend lines stall under the arc lines and then finally get through them and go to the next arc line. As the arcs expand the distance between the lines increases. Sometimes you will find that in the outer edges of the arcs the prices will stall under resistance for several days or even weeks until they finally break through.

Expanding Square Roots – Chart #21
This figure appears in Jay Hambridge's book *The Elements of Dynamic Symmetry,* page 18. He describes the technique for producing a series of arcs that expand progressively by the √2, √3, √4 and so on. To draw it simply place a compass on point 'A' and extend it to point 'B'. Draw an arc down until it touches the base of square AB. With a straightedge draw a line up from the intersection until you reach the top of square AB. Extend the compass to this new intersection at 'C' and draw the arc down to the base again. Continue for as many expansions as desired. The intersections of the arcs with the baseline will be the expanding square roots.

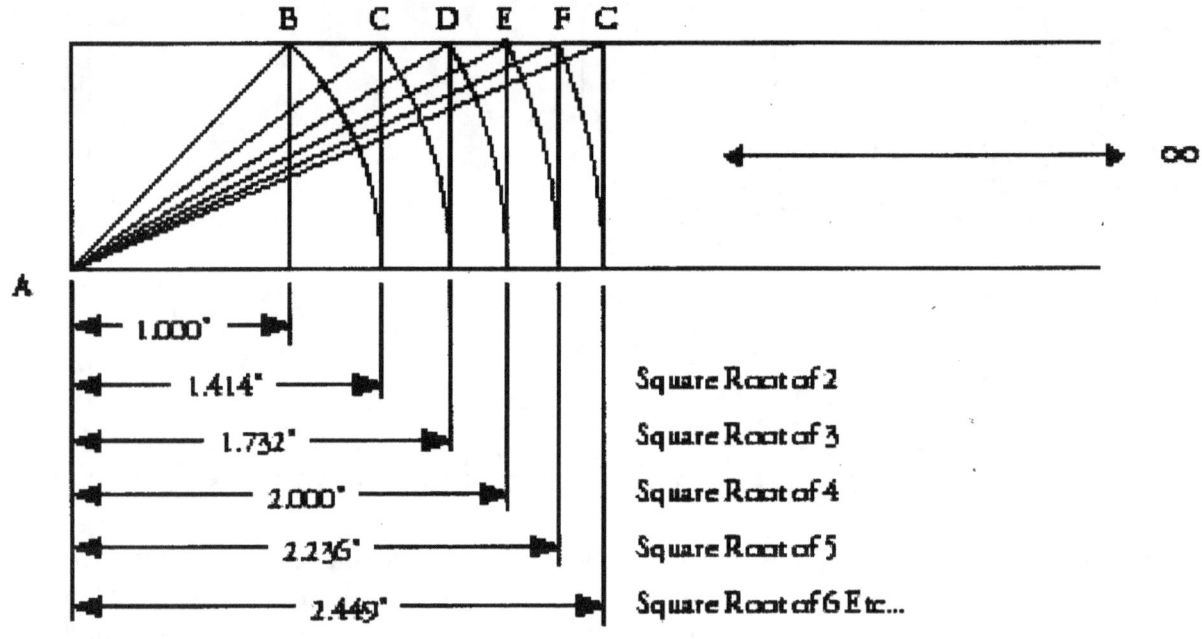

If you can imagine square AB as a square of a price range on a chart you can understand how this feature works in Ganntrader. Two items under the Third Dimension menu should be selected to use this technique: Expanding Rts 2, 3, 4, 5... and Square Price Range. Mark the first point in the usual way and move the cursor off the starting point while holding the left mouse button. Align the price portion of the cursor cross hair with the price you are trying to square. You will see a square and circle superimposed on each other. It takes a little practice to get used to using it but the object is to precisely place the circle within the square by moving the mouse around. When the circle and square are exactly centered the price and time are equal, assuming the Third Dimension Factor is equal to 1. On Chart #21 the points at which the arcs meet the baseline mark a change of trend. The program generates 7 expanding roots but generally the first 5 or 6 are the most important. In this example we adjusted the Dimension Factor to 1.1 for a better fit.

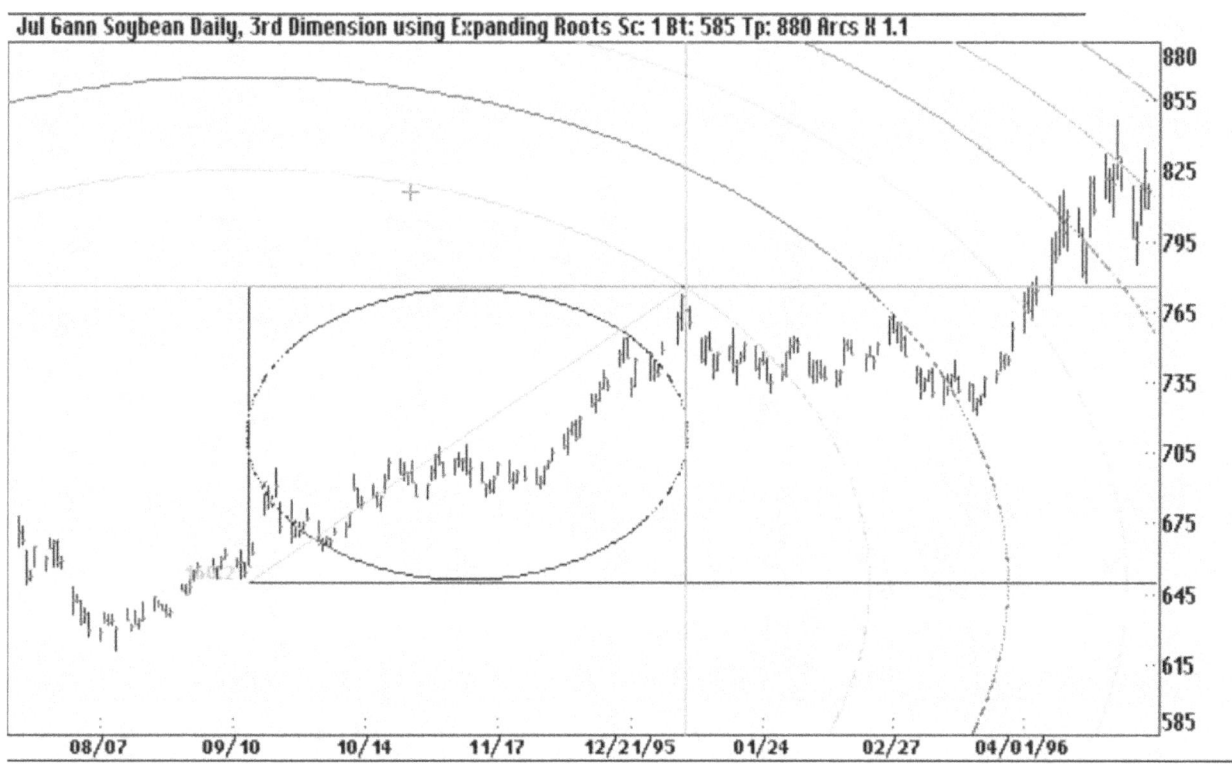

You can use diameters instead of radii for most of the Third Dimension circles and arcs. Select Show As Diameter under the menu, hit the <Ctrl><F1> key or click on the Tool Bar icon.

Modify an Existing Setup

You can modify an existing Third Dimension setup by first moving to the origin of the setup. You can use the backspace key or click on the Tool Bar icon. Once the cursor is on the origin you may see an information box if Sizes, Labels & Markers is active under the Option menu. Hit any key to clear the box and then change the setup using the function keys, selecting a different Third Dimension menu item or clicking on a Tool Bar icon. If you need to change the radius length you must delete the setup by hitting the <Delete> key and make a new setup with a new radius.

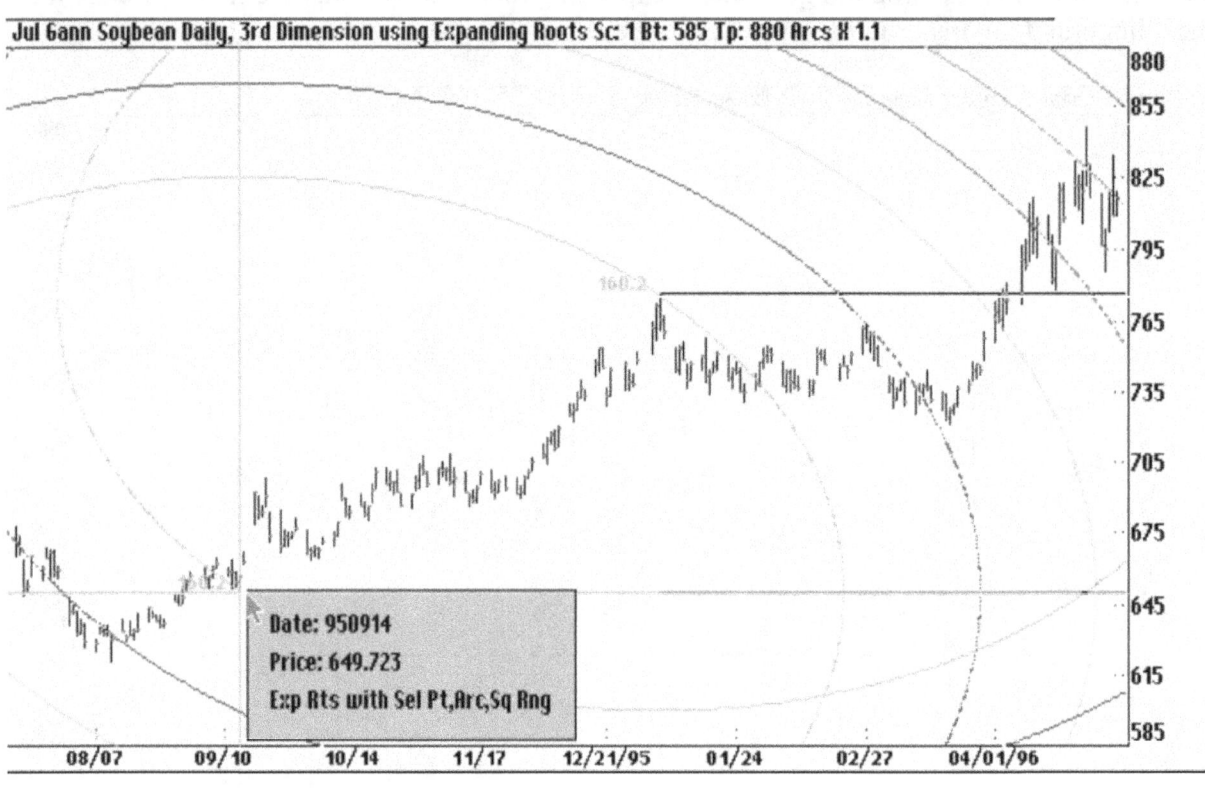

Batch Mode

In the Ganntrader once you have studied a chart and located the various square, angle, range division and 3D setups using all the features of the Ganntrader you need a way to save your work for later use. This is the function of the Default File Setup or the Batch Mode.

Under the File menu there are four related items, Default File Set-up, Include In Active Batch, Show Active Batch and Select Batch File.

Most software trading programs do not have this batch mode. It is extremely valuable to make using squares, angles, range divisions and #D setups more convenient.

Default File Setup

Default File Setup will save the present state of the chart in the Ganntrader. This function of the program is a necessity in Gann Method Trading. The chart's scale, cursor position, square setups, selected angles, 3D setups and planet aspects will be loaded along with the data the next time the file is loaded. Essentially it is a snapshot of the current chart's status.

Here this Soybean file will be saved with the Square of 9 setup from November 7, 1997, with the cursor located on the price of 11/27/98 and the scale and chart bottom as shown. The next time the file is loaded these parameters will return with the data file.
The files used for CSI Quicktrieve or MetaStock data formats are named on the disk such as FOO1.DTA, F109.DTA or F123.DAT etc. Ganntrader creates the same file name with the extension of *.GTQ for Quicktrieve or *.GTC for MetaStock or Computrac to store the setup information. For example, the CSI file F109.DTA would have a Default File Setup file created by Ganntrader called F109.GTQ It would be stored in the data file's sub-directory along with the data. Whenever the data file is loaded the setup file is loaded as well.
Your choices with this box are to save the setup or delete an existing one. If you save a setup and there is already one existing for this file the new setup will replace the old one. If you want to save a collection of setups for the same data file use the Batch Mode described in the next section.

Batch Files

In the Ganntrader in addition to having a default setting for each file you can also have a collection of setups stored in a batch file for quick reference. Select Active Batch allows for the creation, display and deletion of these batch files. The batch files can store any number of data file setups. For example you can create a batch file for Airline stocks, Grains, Metals, Long term trades, Active trades, Currencies etc. They are essentially a collection of setups while the Default File Setup discussed in the previous section is a single setup.

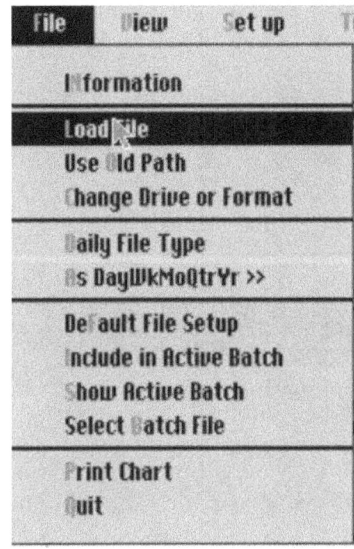

Under the File menu you will find two selections, Show Active Batch and Select Batch File. The Show Active Batch selection and the Tool Bar icon will display the most recently selected Batch file. If no Batch file is currently active you will see a list of Batch files to select from. If you had clicked on Select Batch File this same box would have appeared.

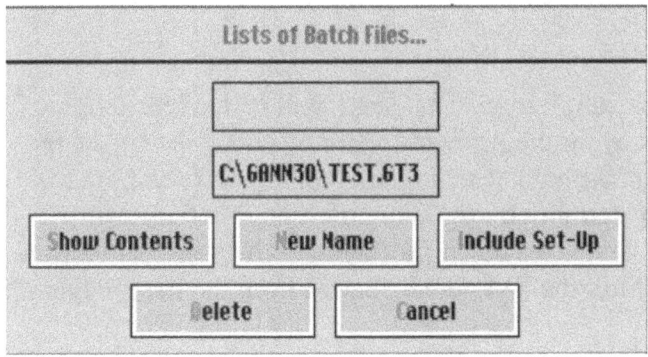

New Name

The New Name button allows you to create a new batch file and will include the present chart on the screen as its first entry. It requires that the first chart setup be displayed on the screen. The name of the file can be up to 8 characters long and will be given the extension of GT3 automatically. There can be up to 200 different batch files with up to 200 setups in each. If you are not using a mouse with the program you must indicate OK by using the <Alt> key with the <O> key. Since the letter O could be a valid letter in a file name the <Alt> key is used to distinguish them.

Include Set-Up

The Include Set-Up button allows you to include additional charts and setups in the present active batch file. Simply have the desired chart displayed on the screen and hit this button. Include In Active Batch under the File menu performs the same function as this button.

Delete

The Delete button allows for the deletion of an entire batch file.

Show Contents

The Show Contents button is pressed after selecting a batch file from the list. A list of all the setups in the selected batch file will be displayed as the next screen shows. This button produces the same results at selecting Show Active Batch under the File menu. An example of a batch list is shown on the next screen.

Show Chart

Select a setup from the list and click the Show Chart button. That setup will be loaded. To see the next setup in the list simply hit the <Tab> key on the keyboard. Hit <Shift><Tab> to see the previous setup. If you hit the Show Chart button without selecting an item the first setup on the list will be loaded by default. As you can see in the above example, different data files or the same data file with a different setup can be included in a batch file. These will all be loaded from a circular list with each hit of the <Tab> key. After the last item is loaded from the list it begins again with the first.

Include Set-Up

The Include Set-Up button allows you to include additional charts and setups in this batch file. Simply have the new setup showing on the screen the way you want it saved and hit this button. Include In Active Batch under the File menu performs the same function as this button.

Delete
The Delete button deletes the selected setup from the batch file. Use it to remove a setup you no longer need or to delete mistakes. You can also click on the Tool Bar icon to perform the same task. There will be a message displayed to confirm your decision before the delete takes place.

Show Contents
The Show Contents button is pressed after selecting a batch file from the list. A list of all the setups in the selected batch file will be displayed as the next screen shows. This button produces the same results at selecting Show Active Batch under the file menu. An example of a batch list is shown on the next screen.

Show Chart
Select a setup from the list and click the Show Chart button. That setup will be loaded. To see the next setup in the list simply hit the <Tab> key on the keyboard. Hit <Shift><Tab> to see the previous setup. If you hit the Show Chart button without selecting an item the first setup on the list will be loaded by default. As you can see in the above example, different data files or the same data file with a different setup can be included in a batch file. These will be loaded from a circular list with each hit of the <Tab> key. After the last item is loaded from the list it begins again with the first.

Include Set-Up
The Include set-Up button allows you to include additional charts and setups in the batch file. Simple have the new setup showing on the screen the way you want it saved and hit this button. Include In Active Batch under the File menu performs the same function as this button.

Delete
The Delete button deletes the selected setup from the batch file. Use it to remove a setup you no longer need or to delete mistakes. You can also click on the Tool Bar icon to perform the same task. There will be a message displayed to confirm your decision before the delete takes place.

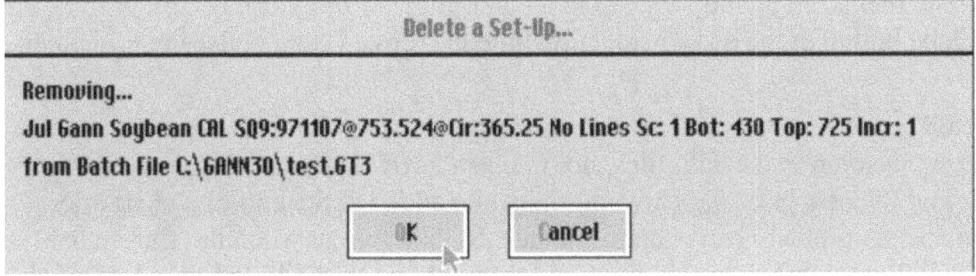

Print List
The Print List button enables automatic printing of the batch files. Three modes are possible:
Print the files from start to finish.
Print the files from a specified starting date to the end of the file.
Print a specified number of price bars to the end of the file.

Parameters Saved in a Set-Up
Whenever a chart setup is saved the following parameters will be preserved:

A) The cursor price and time position.
B) The chart bottom and scale.
C) Any of the squares available under the View menu.
D) Any selected angles.
E) A planetary aspect's degree if different from the default 900.
F) A square, angle, 3D, range division or planet chart will return to the screen with the same selected angles and lines etc.
G) A daily chart will preserve its status as to 5, 6 or 7-day chart type.
H) The printer grid pattern. Different chart densities such as 8, 12 and 24 per inch can be mixed in the same batch file.
I) The values for the 1X1, planet angles and Third Dimension Factor.
J) Any setups made to a compressed chart such as a weekly or monthly will be saved.

These parameters will be preserved whether the setup is saved under Default File Setup or as part of a batch file.

If you want one of your batch files to be your default active batch simply load the batch file and select Options : Configure System and hit the Save button. You must also have previously activated the feature under Options: Configure System: Preferences: General:
Item #2. Once the default active batch is saved you can click on the Tool Bar icon or select Show Active Batch under the File menu and not have to select the batch to open.

Don't be confused about the purpose of Default File Setup under the File menu. It is intended to be used to save only a single chart setup. When you save the default setup it is saved with the data file and is reloaded every time you load that data file.

If you want a group of these setups then use the Select Batch File or Show Active Batch selections under the File menu. To include a setup in a batch file you should select either of these items and hit the Include button in the box or select Include In Active Batch under the File menu.

Some Limitations
The Batch files save the location to the data files, not the data itself. This way the batch files are much smaller in size and the new price bars are automatically added to the end of a chart after you download new prices. A problem can occur with the CSI data format when the files in the sub-directory are sorted. Each subdirectory in the CSI format has a QMASTER file in it. The first entry in the QMASTER corresponds to file number F001.DAT, the second entry corresponds to file number F002.DTA and so on. When the sub-directory is sorted the QMASTER entries are sorted and then the file numbers are changed to match their new positions in the QMASTER. Unfortunately the entry in the Ganntrader batch file will still be pointing to the old location so you might see a setup for a corn file being placed on a gold chart. If you

experience any problems such as this the only fix is to delete the batch file entry and re-insert it after making any corrections.

The MetaStock and Computrac formats generally do not have this problem since the file number is a separate entry in the MASTER file and does not necessarily correspond to its position in the MASTER file so sorting doesn't affect it.

The printer configuration is also saved in the batch file. This way you can have a mixture of grid densities in the same batch file. You may experience some difficulties if you begin using a new printer and attempt to use a batch file that might contain your old printer's settings. Installing 8-inch paper when the printer was set to print at ii or 13 inches when the file was inserted in the batch could also be a problem. The solution is to delete and re-insert the offending entry.

Putting It All Together

1) Setup your charts - daily, weekly, monthly. Determine which type of daily chart is most effective for the market you are trading (5 day trading chart or a 7 day calendar chart or both).

2) Are you going to use screen charts or printed charts or a combination of both? Do you need to make plastic overlays for your chart grid?

3) If you are going to use printed charts what is the grid per inch you are going to use. Most prefer the 10x10 to the inch. Some real Gann traders prefer the 8x8 to the inch. How much blank space to you need at the end of the charts for forecasting purposes?

4) First study the volume and open interest of the chart. Remember that Gann always said technical analysis works best in markets with big volume. Use the rules of volume and open interest. For a market to be bullish, it must have rising volume and open interest when the price rises. If it does not have that characteristic, then the market is neutral or bearish.

5) Study the close on charts. Draw the angles to to determine the main trend of the market and the beginning and end of the counter trends.

6) Invert the price of the screen for psychological purposes. Does it look bullish or bearish both ways?

7) Check out the long-term 10 year cycles. Go back at least 6 - 10 cycles. Compare the patterns. Was the market rising or falling during the same time periods of the previous cycles.

8) Are the swing charts and main trend swing charts bullish or bearish. Are they both in the same direction. Check out the daily, weekly and monthly charts.

9) Check out the Back 360 trend angles. Are they bullish or bearish?

10) Check the selected angles. Are they bullish or bearish? Which ones work best with the market you are trading with?

11) Find the true trend angles and determine the trend of the market using these.

12) Find the timing of the market using the intersecting angles.

13) Find the channels of the market drawing selected angles and true trend angles off of prior tops and bottoms.

14) Use the dimension lines and find the time and price differences of all important tops and bottoms. Use the circle numbers (360, 180, 90, 45, 22 1/2, 11 1/4, 144, 72, 36 etc.) and the top

and bottom numbers (if a market topped at 360 it will square out time and price 360 days, weeks or months from that point).

15) Use the 1x1 angles off of all important tops and bottoms on all the charts - daily, weekly and monthly.

16) Find the Live 1x1 angle and determine if that works more effectively on the market you are working with.

17) Using the Mirror Image Foldback to determine timing in the markets you are working with. This works on all time frames.

18) Draw the Zero Angles from all major tops and bottoms on the daily, weekly and monthly charts to determine timing.

19) Set up your squares on the charts according to the circle numbers and the top and bottom numbers. These can be drawn by the program and used on the screen or on the printed charts. Plastic overlays can be substituted for these squares. Use overlays that are setup to your chart grid.

20) Divide the range to find the important support, resistance and target points from every prior range.

21) Determine the price targets using 7 Times the base. Again this techniques can be used on all time frames.

22) Square the price ranges with the mouse and plot the adjacent squares to determine trend.

23) Square the time range and plot the adjacent square to determine trend.

24) Use the Square of 9 off of every top and bottom to determine time and price objectives.

25) Determine if your market works best with Geocentric or Heliocentric Planets.

26) Find the planets or combinations that work with your market (Mercury, Venue, Mars, Jupiter, Saturn, Uranus, Neptune, Pluto, or the Moon, Sun or Earth).

27) Find the time and price supports with these planets.

28) Use the Averages of the planets to determine support and resistance (Average of 7, Mean of 5, Average of 6, Circle of 8, Average of 9, Mars thru Neptune, Jupiter through Pluto, etc).

29) Use Planetary Parallels and Contra-Parallels to determine support and resistance.

30) Use the basic arcs and circles of the market to determine support, resistance and timing points.

31) Use the arcs to project prices on charts.

32) Use Square Root Expansions to determine time, support and resistance points.

33) Use Inside Radii Contractions for support and resistance.

34) Use Odd and Even Square time Expansions to determine support and resistance.

35) Use Expanding Square Roots to determine time, support and resistance.

36) Use Pattern Recognition - use double and triple tops, double and triple bottoms, wave formations to determine changes in trend.

37) Determine which of the above techniques works best with the market you are trading in.

38) Look at all of the above and find clusters of time and price points. These will be the points that turn the markets. Usually the more clusters are at each point the more important it is.

39) Develop your sixth sense with all of the above. You will find that after you work with all of the above indicators you will develop a sixth sense with using them. You'll know which indicators, support points, timing points, angles and planet lines to trust. Stick with this method of trading until you fully understand how it works and its limitations. Don't jump to a new system, keep this method of trading and fully master it.

Appendix A

Degree Assignments for Zodiac Signs

Aries	0-30°
Taurus	30-60°
Gemini	60-90°
Cancer	90-120°
Leo	120-150°
Virgo	150-180°
Libra	180-210°
Scorpio	210-240°
Sagittarius	240-270°
Capricorn	270-300°
Aquarius	300-330°
Pisces	330-360°

Planetary Cycles

Mercury	88 Days
Venus	225 Days
Sun-Earth	365 Days
Mars	1 Year, 322 Days
Jupiter	11 Years, 322 Days
Saturn	29 Years, 167 Days
Uranus	84 Years
Neptune	164 Years, 167 Days
Pluto	248 Years, 242 Days

Appendix B

These two letters were written by W.D. Gann to one of his clients. Gann wrote very little about Astrology preferring to pass this knowledge along verbally. The following letters are the basis of the Ganntrader's planet mode. They are reproduced verbatim including what appear to be typographical errors.

For example, line one of the first paragraph below says that 8663 equals 28° of Aries. This should probably be 23 Aries. (8663 360 has a remainder of 23) or else the high on March 19, 1954 had to be 8668 not 8663. If you are interested enough in the subject you should verify these figures for yourself.

May Coffee Santos D

March 19, 1954
High 8729
Using a scale of one point to 10, 8729 equals 29° Gemini.
Using a scale of 30 points to 10, equals 21° Capricorn.
Using the Jupiter scale of 12 points to 10, equals **7°** 30' Aries.
Using one cent to 1°, equals 27° 16' Gemini.
The dollar value is $28,171.00, which equals 11° 45' Capricorn.

The average price of 5 options on March 19, 1954 was 8663, which equals 280 Aries, or 600 from the Heliocentric Jupiter. Heliocentric Jupiter is 200 35 Gemini, which means that the price of 8729 was at this degree. Heliocentric Uranus is 210 52' Cancer and the price at 210 Capricorn is opposite to this.

April 16, 1954 is 276 months from April 16, 1931, low 435. Using 50 points per month, the 450° angle crossed 8715 on March 19, 1954, and the Sun has moved 82530 from April 16, 1931. Add this to 435 and it gives 8688 as the resistance angle.

March Coffee

October 1, 1936 low 300. Time to April 1, 1954, 210 months at 30 points per month, the 45° angle crosses at 5600, and at 40 points per months, it crosses at 8700.

1931, April 16 to March 19, 1954 — Geocentric Saturn moved 285° 38'. This would be a price of 8572.

1936, October 1 to March 19, 1954 — Geocentric Saturn moved 231°, which would equal a price of 7230.

1940, May 15 to March 19, 1954 Saturn moved 181° 35', which gives a price of 6990 and using 45 points to 1° would give 8715.

1940, August 19 Saturn moved 173° 23'. At 45 points to 1°, this equals 8760 price.

Heliocentric Saturn

1931, April 16 to March 19, 1954, Saturn moved 2870 15' which equals 17° 13' Capricorn, price 8632.

1936, October 1, Saturn moved 225°, which gives a price of 7150.

1940, May 15, Saturn gained 179° 44', price 5940.

1940, August 19, Saturn gained 176° 14', price 5842.

Heliocentric Planets
March 19, 1954

The average of these 6 planets is 164.17 or 14° 17' Virgo

The average of the 6 Geocentric planets is 173.26 or 25° 26' Virgo.

Jupiter 89° 35' equals 29° 35' Gemini   Saturn 214.44 equals 4044w Scorpio
Uranus 111.52 equals 21° 52' Cancer   Neptune 204.35 equals 24° 35' Libra
Pluto 144 equals 24° Leo   Mars 221 equals 11° Scorpio

One half of Jupiter to Saturn Helio is 152.09 or 2° 9' Virgo.

The average of Saturn, Jupiter, Uranus and Neptune is 155.10, equals 50 10' Virgo.

One half of this average is 170 35' Gemini. Jupiter, Uranus one half is 100.43, equals 100 43'

Cancer Heliocentric. One half of Geocentric Jupiter to Uranus is 93.48 or 30 48' Cancer.

Important Dates Each Month
1st, 15th, 18th, and 19th. The present market is running close to these dates.

May Coffee
1953

June 19	low	5050	July 17	low	5555
August 17	high	5765	September 15	low	5565
Sept 21	high	5710	October 9	last low	5470
October 19	high	5660	December 9	high	6240

1954

January 13	high	7470	January 19	low	6560

This was 7 months from June 19.

March 15	high	5625			
March 18	low	5465	March 19	high	8729

This extreme high was 9 months from June 19/ow, 2 months from January 19/ow, 6 months from September 15, 1953/ow and 5 months from October 19 high at 5860.

Heliocentric and Geocentric Aspects

1954	March 24	Heliocentric Jupiter enters Cancer
	June 24	Heliocentric Jupiter 120° of Saturn
	April 12	Sun 60° of Jupiter Geocentric
	April 15	Sun 180° of Neptune Geocentric
	April 13	Jupiter 135° of Saturn Geocentric
	April 16	Jupiter 60° of Pluto Geocentric
	April 26	Jupiter 120° of Neptune Geocentric
	April 26	Sun 180° of Saturn Geocentric

The month of April is very important. There should be great activity and wide swings in prices due to these aspects.

Geocentric Maps Movement

From low prices on Coffee

1931, April 16, to August 7, 1953 - Mars has made 12 round trips.

1954, October 29 - Mars will be opposite or 180° from its place on April 16, 1931.

1936, October 1 to September 19, 1953 - Mars made 9 round trips of 360° each.

1954, December 9 - Mars will be 9 1/2 round trips or opposite its place October 1, 1936.

1940, May 15 to June 12, 1953 - Mars made 7 round trips or complete cycles.

1954, April 9 - Mars is 7 1/2 cycles or opposite its place on May 15, 1940. Due to the retrograde position of Mars, it will again be 7 1/2 on July 7 and on August 17, 1954, or the third time in opposition to its own place, which is very important.

1940, August 19 to September 15, 1953 - Mars had completed 7 round trips. Note low on Coffee on that date.

1954, December 4 - Mars 7 1/2 round trips or opposite its own place on August 19, 1940.

If Coffee starts to decline between March 22 and 24, 1954, it would continue down to around April 15, when the adverse aspects of Jupiter to Saturn and the Sun to Neptune are completed. From these dates, you should watch for the possibility of a rally up to April 16, 1954, when Jupiter is 120 of Neptune and the Sun 130 of Saturn. This might cause a quick rally followed by a sharp quick decline. By studying all of the data outlined above and applying it to Coffee, you will be able to learn more about what causes the changes in trend.

Soybean Price Resistance Levels

The one half point of the highest selling price and one half between the high and low are very great because these equal the 45° angle or the gravity center. For May Beans these prices are 218 3/8, 240 3/8, 251 7/8, and 319 1/8.

On the weekly or monthly chart, use the date when the extreme high or extreme low is made and draw a 450 angle up and down starting from the above halfway points. These angles are very important for determining highs and lows and a change in trend.

From the extreme lows or extreme highs, you add or subtract the proportionate parts of the circle, as given below.

44 added to 360 gives 404. From 404 subtract 90 gives 314, and the degree in the sign is 14° Aquarius. 90° or square from this is 234 or 160 Scorpio.

436 3/4 minus 360 gives 76 3/4, or 16° 45' in the sign Gemini. Subtract 120 gives 16° 45' Aquarius or a price of 316 3/4. A square or 90° from this is 16° 45' Scorpio, price 226 3/4.

The lows of 67, 68 and 69 equal 7, 8 and 9° in Gemini. 120° subtracted gives 307, 308 and 309, the triangle points, which are 7, 8 and 9° Aquarius. Subtract 90° from these prices gives 217, 218 and 219 or 7, 8 and 9° in Pisces. 131 high, add 180, gives 311 or 11° Aquarius. Subtract 90 gives 221 or 110 Scorpio.

October 5, 1936, futures trading started in Soybeans. The first sale was 120. Add 180 gives 300 or 30° in Capricorn. 218 3/8 is 8° 22' Scorpio. Add 90 gives 308 3/8 or 8 1/2° in Aquarius. 240 3/8 is 0° 22' in Sagittarius. Add 60 gives 3003/8. Add 90 gives 330 3/8. 251 7/8 is 12° in Sagittarius. Add 60 gives 311 7/8 or 12° Aquarius. Add 90 gives 348 or 12° Pisces.
1930, June high 216. Equals 6° Scorpio. Add 90 gives 306 or 6° Aquarius. Add 225 gives 441, which is the square of 21, and 441 is 21° in the sign Gemini, which is 81 more than 360, the square of 9.

4363/4, subtract 135, gives 20 13/4 or 1° 45' Aquarius. Subtract 180 gives 256 3/4 or 16° 45' Sagittarius. Subtract 225 gives 221 3/4 or 1° 45 Sagittarius. Subtract 236 1/4 gives 200 1/4 or 20° 15' Libra. The low on May Beans in Feb. 1949 was 201 1/2.

344'/2, subtract 33 3/4 gives 310 3/4 or 10° 45' Aquarius. Subtract 45 gives 2991/2 or 29° 30' Capricorn. 120, add 90 gives 210 or 30° Scorpio. Add 125 gives 255 or 15° Sagittarius. Add 180 gives 300 or 30° Capricorn.

67, add 90 gives 157 or 7° Virgo. Add 135 gives 202 or 22° Libra. Add 120 gives 127 or 7° Libra. Add 180 gives 247 or 7° Sagittarius. Add 225 gives 292 or 22° Capricorn. Add 240 gives 307 or 7° Aquarius. Add 270 gives 337 or 7° Pisces. Add 315 gives 382 or 22° Aries. Add 360 gives 427 of 7° Gemini. Add 271 1/4 gives 438 1/4. High on May beans was 436 3/4. After that high the next extreme low was 201 1/2. Note that 67 plus 125 gives 202, and that one half of 405 is 202 1/2, and 180 plus 22 1/2 is 202 1/2, which are the mathematical reasons why May Soybeans made bottom at 201 1/2.

All of the above price levels can be measured in Time Periods of days, weeks and months, and when the time periods come out at these prices, it is important for a change in trend, especially if confirmed by the geometrical angles from highs and lows.

Active Angles and Degrees

By live or active angles is meant Prices and Time Periods where the longitude of the major planets are or where the squares, triangles, oppositions are to these planets.

The averages of the six major planets Heliocentric and Geocentric are the most powerful points for Time and Price resistance. Also the Geocentric and Heliocentric average of the five major planets with Mars left out, is of great importance and should be watched.
You should also calculate the averages of eight planets, which move around the Sun as this is the first most important odd square. The square of '1' is one, and '1' is the Sun. 8 added to '1' gives 9, the square of 3 and completes the first important odd square, which is important for Time and Price.

Examples of live, active angles: At the present writing, January 18, 1954, Saturn Geocentric is 8 to 9° Scorpio. Add the square or 90° gives 8 to 9° Aquarius and equals the price 309 for May Beans.

The planet Jupiter is at 21° Gemini, which is 81° in longitude from "0" the square of 9. Subtract 135° from Jupiter gives 306 or 6° Aquarius. This is why Soybeans have met resistance so many times between 306 and 311 1/4. The Price Resistance Levels come out strong around these degrees and prices and the Geometrical angles come out on daily, weekly and monthly, but the power of Saturn and Jupiter aspects, working out time to these Price Resistance Levels, is what halts the advance in Soybeans.

24 Revolutions of Time and Price

The earth makes one revolution on its axis in 24 hours, moving 360° in longitude. One hour of time equals 15° in longitude, and for one hour of time, we use one cent of Price. This is for daily active markets but can be used for weekly and monthly time periods, as you can see by the Master Charts.

The longitude of the planets and the longitude of the average of the planets determine the Resistance Levels as the price moves around each cycle of 24 cents per bushel. You mark on the Master Chart all low prices with a red circle around them and place around all high prices a green circle. Then note the Angles of 45, 60, 90, 120, 135, 180, 225, 240, 270, 300, 315 and 360 from each high and low. Then check the longitude of the planets and the longitude of the average of the planets to see when the Price reaches these degrees or aspects and meets resistance.

Example: December 2, 1953, May Soybeans high 311 1/4. This equaled 18° 45' in Pisces, close square or 90° of Jupiter, 135° to Saturn and 180° of the averages, and 120° of Uranus. 300 price equals 30° Virgo. 302 equals 30° Libra. 304 equals 30° Scorpio. On January 18, 1954, the planet Saturn Geocentric is 8° 30' Scorpio, and 15° Scorpio gives a price of 303, therefore when May Beans decline to 302, they will be below the body or longitude of Saturn and will indicate lower. At the same time, using the Earth's annual revolution of 365 1/4 days to move around the Sun, a price of 308 1/2 is 90° or square to Saturn. As long as the price is below 308 1/2 it is within the square and in position to go lower. But by the 24 revolution, when the price breaks below 304, it is in the bear sign Scorpio, a fixed sign and will indicate lower prices.

Study and analyze all options of all commodities in the same way as we have analyzed May Beans. Remember, when these Resistance Points are met you must give the market time to show that it is making tops or bottoms and getting ready to make a change in trend. Do not guess; wait until you get a definite indication of a change in trend before deciding that the main trend has changed. You can buy or sell against these resistance levels and place a stop loss order. Having before you all the information outlined above, you would certainly have gone short of May Soybeans on December 2, 1953 and cover your shorts on December 17 at 296 because the price was down to the 45° angle from 44 on the monthly high and low chart.

24 Cent Moves or More

It is very important to watch the action on the daily and weekly chart when the price is up or down 24 cents from any high or low 48 cents, 72 cents most important because three times 24, 96 cents, 120 or 5 times 24; 144 of great importance because 6 times 24 and the square of 12, 168 which is 7 times 24 very important. You can also use one half of 24, which is 12, and watch 36, 60, 84, etc., which equals 180° or half the circle or cycle.

In the following example from A to B is 24 calendar days. The market topped out and took a large drop. The market also rallied from 194.25 to 243.50 which was 49.25 which is close to 2 x 24.

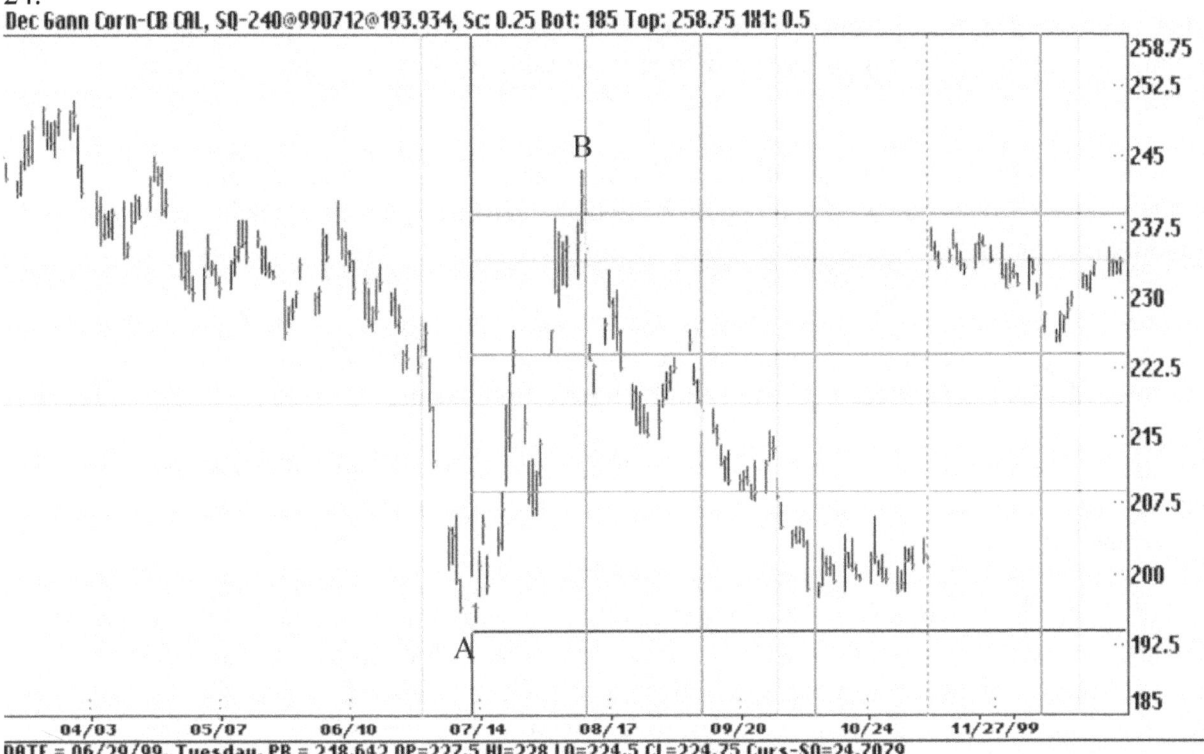

Appendix C

This section describes each item in the tool bar and pull-down menus. Page references for more information are given for each item.

Load File tells the program to search the current hard drive for the default file format. A list of Master files will be presented.

Use Old Path will immediately display the most recently selected sub-directory of data. If you know the desired file is in the same directory you just used this selection is faster than Load File.

Change Drive or Format permits you to temporarily change to a different default data drive or default data format. These items are permanently set under the miscellaneous button in System Configuration.

Daily File Type permits selection between a 5 trading day or a 7-calendar day file. Other formats are also available. This item would be disabled if you happened to load a weekly or monthly file. See page 18.

As DayWkMoQtrYr » produces a sub-menu that permits you to select a compressed data format. These compressed files are built from the file that is loaded. Here a daily file was used to automatically create the weekly, monthly and longer-term formats.

Default File Setup is used to save a snap shot of the current file's setup. The chart scale, active angles, squares and other items will be saved so that the next time the same file is loaded the setups will return.

Include in Active Batch, Show Active Batch and Select Batch File are related to the program's batch file capabilities. Essentially a batch file is a grouping of file setups. The groupings can be different setups on the same data file or a mixture of different files and setups. Print Chart activates Ganntraders high quality chart printing capabilities. Quit is selected to exit Ganntrader.

View Menu

Volume & Open Interest displays a separate window showing the files volume and open interest. If planetary declination or latitude is active this item will be disabled.

#1-#5 SQ Not Set Up will display the settings for any squares that were setup under the setup menu. In this case none have been setup so they are all grayed out.

List Squares... becomes active if there are more than 5 square setups. It opens a box that permits you to activate or deactivate any square setup.

Geocentric, Earth View displays the planet's longitude as viewed from the Earth.

Heliocentric, Sun View displays the planet's longitude as viewed from the Sun.

Latitude and Declination

Swings, Trend line Indicator activates Gann's price swing indicator.

Main Trend Indicator activates Gann's time swing indicator. Square of 9 will activate any square of 9 setups. A box will display that will permit you to activate or deactivate and setup. If a Square of 9 is already displayed on the screen this selection will turn it off.

All Swing Angles are angles drawn from the swing points produced by the Swings, Trend line Indicator selection.

Main Trend Angles are angles drawn from the swing points produced by the Main Trend Indicator selection.

Selected Angles are angles marked by the user. Any number of angles from any price and time point can be marked. This selection turns them on and off.

Back 360 Hi / Lo Angles are angles drawn from origin points that are some division of a circle of 360 back from the current set point, usually the last price bar on the screen. Gann considered counts of 45, 90 and 180 to be important for changes in trend. The angles drawn from the same points are also important.

Setup Menu

Chart Scale is mainly used just prior to doing a screen dump of a chart. It is useful when you want to set a specific chart scale for appearance reasons before capturing the screen by hitting the Print Screen key. Since the chart will usually be automatically rescaled the first time you scroll through the data this item has a limited use. This is the same dialog box available under File: Print Chart.

1x1 Angles sets the rate of rise of the 1x1 angle. This setting is used by the angle modes and the squares.

Live 1x1 Angle allows for a dynamic setting of the 1x1 angle that will match the chart's high and low ranges. It is used with the Selected Angles mode.

Planet Angle set the multiplier value for the plotting of the planet longitude lines. If set to 1 the planet's longitude would be displayed so that 1° = 1 cents or 1° = $1.

Planet Hour sets the time of day offset for the planet calculations. By default the program uses 12 noon at Greenwich, England (0° Longitude). This corresponds to 7 AM in New York City. To calculate the planet's positions for 9 AM NYC time you would enter + 2. Positive or negative numbers may be entered. Fractions of an hour should be entered as decimals. 3:15 would be entered as 3.25 (15/60 = .25)

Third Dimension Factor is used by the arcs and circles. The price portion of the radius is divided by this value prior to calculating the radius.

User Defined Expansion can be used to specify and expansion ratio for an arc or circle. The program has many built in expansions such as $\sqrt{2}$, $\sqrt{3}$ π etc. This permits you to enter your own 'secret' value.

Swing Charts is an entry point for the price and time threshold points used by the swing chart feature, the default values are 1/4 of the default scale for the price swing and 3 time periods for the time swing.

Square of 9 Increment Value multiplies the price divisions of the square of 9 display by this number. Most of the time it should be set equal to 1. It is provided here for experimental purposes.

Back 360 Angles resets the reference point for the back 360 angles. The reference point defaults to the last price bar on the screen but you may want to move it out into the future to see when the 360 multiples come in.

Automatic Setups will scan your data seeking the highest high and lowest low beginning with the daily and working to the yearly. It will then set up a square of the high, low and range between them and also mark a selected angle from the high and low. Since these points are important to watch in all markets this feature is a time saver.

Sq 9 Setup is used to enter the setup parameters for a Square of 9 display.

Square Setup is used to enter the setup parameters for a Square display.

Change Any Setup works with setups for Selected Angles, Squares and Squares of 9. It is a single dialog box that allows for activation/inactivation and deletions of any setup.

Time Cycle Menu

The Aspect selections permit you to display a planet of interest and any number of degree displacements or aspects to it. The point where any other planet crosses these lines is the point of 'Aspect'. You can activate more than one aspect by holding down the Alt key and press the appropriate red hot keys for the Time cycle menu and the individual selection. For example, to display Jupiter and Saturn aspects at once type <Alt><T><J, followed by <Alt><T><T>. That is, T for Time Cycle and J for Jupiter's selection.

Planets only turns off the aspects and returns the display to planet longitude only.
Gann used several average positions of the planet's longitude. There were used for Time measurement as well as support and resistance. The Average of 5 through the Average of 9 were the ones he used. The last two selections, Avg Planets on Scr, ALT 'A' and Keep Planets & Avg. ALT 'K' permit you to average any combination of 2 or more planets for experimental purposes. The <Alt>.<A> and <Alt><K> are the keyboard shortcuts for these selections.

Third Dimension Menu

PT Circles and PT Arcs turn on the Third Dimension features of the program and Turn Off Radii turns the feature off.

The only difference between circles and arcs is that circles have the Third Dimension Multiplier set to the chart's scale. With this setting the arcs will be circles when printed on the printer.

The basic radius can be expanded to the four corners of the chart using any number of expansion ratios.

The Square Root of >> produces a sub-menu with the following selections:

User Defined Expander activates the value entered under Setup: User Defined Expansion.

Show as Diameter changes the arc or circle size from a radius to a diameter.

Square Price Range is used to surround a range from a high to a low and convert that dimension into a radius. It is generally used in conjunction with Expanding Rts *2,3,4,5...*

Cursor Radius draws an arc or circle from the cursor's cross hair point. Marked Point Radius draws an arc or circle from the initial marked origin point and Both Kursor & Marked Point draws from both.

Show Inner Radii draws radii from the original radius inwardly to a very small size.

Half Points draws an arc or circle expansion radii halfway between the normal expansion radii.

Options Menu

The first 4 items in this menu affect the spacing between the price bars on the screen.

Divide Range activates the divide range feature of the program. Two points should be marked, usually a high to a low.

7 Times the Base is used in conjunction with Divide Range. Essentially it assumes that the initial price range is one of eight divisions in a much larger range.

Auto Center attempts to keep the price bars centered on the screen, equally space above the bottom and below the top.

Scale Screen causes the program to rescale only the price bars that are visible on the screen. When turned off the program scales the entire file including that portion that is off the screen.

Grids turns the screen's background grid lines off and on

Snap to Hi / Lo causes the cursor to jump to the price bars high or low whenever the cursor is either side of the halfway point of the bar. It is useful when you need to precisely place the cursor on the high or low when you want to square a high or low or mark an origin point for a selected angle.

Sizes, Labels & Markers activates the program's labeling of price and time points, setup values and other markings. At times you will want less screen clutter.

Shade Swings draws a colored box around the time and price swings.

Close Only displays the price bars as a line connecting only the closing price for each bar. This feature is only used on the screen display, not the printed charts.

Gob Date, Price 'G' activates the Goto feature. The letter G is the keyboard equivalent.

Configure System opens up the program's system configuration settings.

Tool Bar

The Tool Bar icons duplicates the more common program features. Here is a rundown from left to right

Same as Print Chart under the File menu.

Same as Show Active Batch under the File menu.

This item will delete an existing batch entry. If you display a batch entry on the screen that you no longer need simply click this button. It is the same as selecting File: Show Active Batch, selecting an entry and clicking on the Delete button.

This icon will move you to the origin points of all selected angles. You need to have the cursor on the origin point before you can modify or delete a setup.

This icon will move you to the origin points of all Third Dimension Setups. You need to have the cursor on the origin point before you can modify or delete a setup.

This icon will move you to the origin points of all Square Setups. You need to have the cursor on the origin point before you can modify or delete a setup.

This icon will move you to the origin points of all Square of 9 Setups. You need to have the cursor on the origin point before you can modify or delete a setup.

This icon will move you to the origin points of all Division of the Range Setups. You need to have the cursor on the origin point before you can modify or delete a setup.

Same as Geocentric, Earth View under the View menu.

Same as Heliocentric, Sun View under the View menu.

Same as Latitude and Declination under the View menu. Activates geocentric or heliocentric latitude.

Same as Latitude and Declination under the View menu. Activates geocentric declination.

Same as Avg Planets on Screen ALT 'A' under the Time Cycles menu.

Activates the Main Trend Indicator. Same as Main Trend Indicator under the View menu.

Activates the Trend Line Indicator. Same as Swings, I/L Indicator under the View menu.

Inverts the prices on the screen. No menu equivalent. Keyboard equivalent is Shift 6 (^).

Displays Arcs and Circles using diameter. Same as Show as Diameter under the Third Dimension menu.

Displays Arcs and Circles using radius. Same as turning off Show as Diameter under the Third Dimension menu.

Draw Arcs and Circles from cursor. Same as Kursor Radius under the Third Dimension menu.

Draw Arcs and Circles from origin point. Same as Marked Point Radius under the Third Dimension menu.

Draw Arcs and Circles from both points. Same as Both Kursor & Marked Point under the Third Dimension menu.

Draw Arcs and Circles inside the original radius. Same as Show Inner Radii under the Third Dimension menu.

Draw Arcs and Circles halfway expansion radii. Same as Haff Points under the Third Dimension menu.

Clears the screen of all special setups and returns to a regular price chart. This doesn't delete the setups, it simply turns them off. Keyboard equivalent is <C>. for clear.

Appendix D

The Setup program will install a Ganntrader 3.0 program folder under the start menu. The Ganntrader 3.0 icon can be used to start the program. The rest of the list will be described here.

SVGA Video Configuration

The Setup program automatically ran this utility when the program was installed. The utility will check the type of video system in your computer and create the correct driver. If you install a new video card in your computer you should rerun this program. Machines running NT or Windows 2000 can't use this utility so the Setup program would not have installed it in the Ganntrader 3.0 program folder.

Authorization Manager

Authorization Manager is used to install or remove the program's authorized installation. It was run automatically when the Setup program installed the program. If you select the item you will see the following menu. You can use it to install or remove the authorization and also check the number of remaining installations on your original Disk #1.

A special modify section is only used when there is a problem getting your program to install. Gannsoft technical support will explain it's function should there be a need for it.

Remaining Installations

This utility simply calls Authorization Manager and displays the remaining installations on your original Disk #1. To use the feature simply insert Disk #1 in the A: drive, select this item and click OK.

Ganntrader Program Folder

Move Authorization Back To Disk #1
This utility is the most important in the Ganntrader program folder. It will remove the authorization file and return it to the Disk #1 in the A: drive. The available installations will be increased by 1 count in the process. Your total allotment of installations will always be maintained either with a count on Disk #1 or a count on your hard disks. To run the utility simply insert Ganntrader Disk #1 in the A: drive and select this item in the menu. If your Ganntrader was installed on the C: drive you can simply click OK. If installed on another drive make sure you select it in the 'Drive' window on the left.

You may have noticed a Ganntrader 3.0 selection in the Add / Remove programs utilityin the Control Panel. That selection will remove the Ganntrader support files, icons and menu items but you must run this utility first since this utility is removed along with the other Ganntrader menu items and you won't be able to remove the authorization!

There are a few reasons why you will want to remove the authorization.

1) If you purchase a new machine you will probably want to remove Ganntrader from the old machine and install it on the new.

2) If you install a new operating system such as updating from windows 95 to 98 or NT4 to Windows 2000.

3) If you convert the file system from FAT16 to FAT32
in Windows 95/98.

4) Any type of low-level hard disk repairs or formatting.

5) Certain disk optimizers can move the hidden files around which can cause trouble. See the Norton instructions below.

Norton Utilities Error [301.2]
If you should ever start the Ganntrader program and see an error 301:2 this indicates that the authorization file is still on the hard disk but it has been moved from its original location. A backup and restore from a tape drive can cause this problem as well as disk optimizers such as the one supplied with the Norton utilities. The fix is fairly simple. Move the authorization back to the floppy using the above menu selection and then select Authorization Manager to reinstall it. You can't simply try to reinstall because Authorization Manager will find the authorization on the disk and not put on another copy.

To fix Norton so it won't move the Ganntrader authorization start up Norton and enter *EKB as a type of file that is fixed or non-relocatable. Norton will leave the file where it was originally placed and both programs will work fine together.

Error [001.2]
The only other common error is [001:2]. This indicates a missing authorization. Run the Authorization Manager and select install. Our authorization system has been trouble free for most users. Should you have a hard disk failure or other difficulty please contact us. We can arrange for a reset of your lost installation via telephone, FAX or E-Mail.

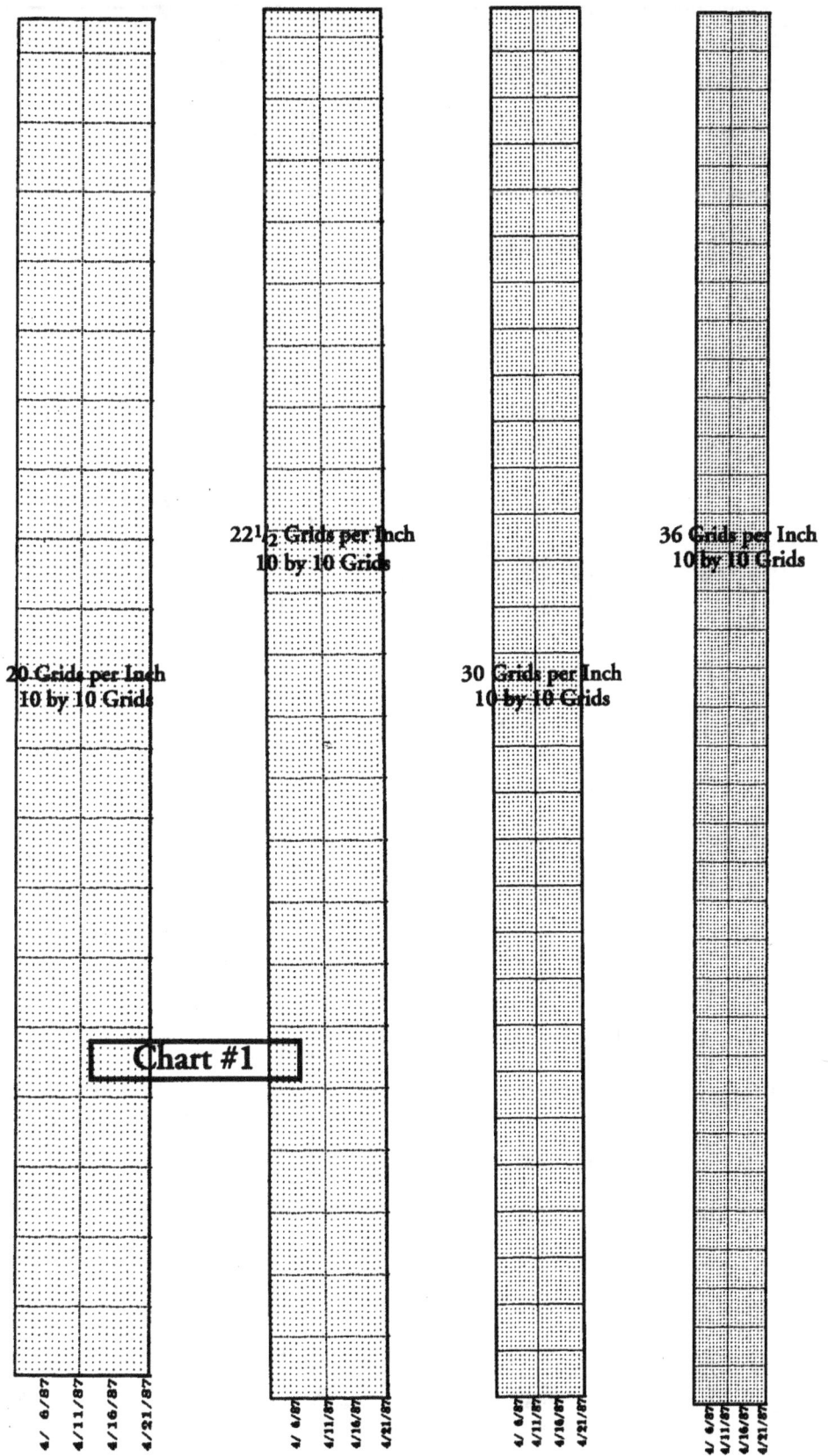

Chart #1

8 Grids per Inch Density
8 by 8 Grids

10 Grids per Inch Density
8 by 10 Grids

8 Grids per Inch Density
10 by 10 Grids

190

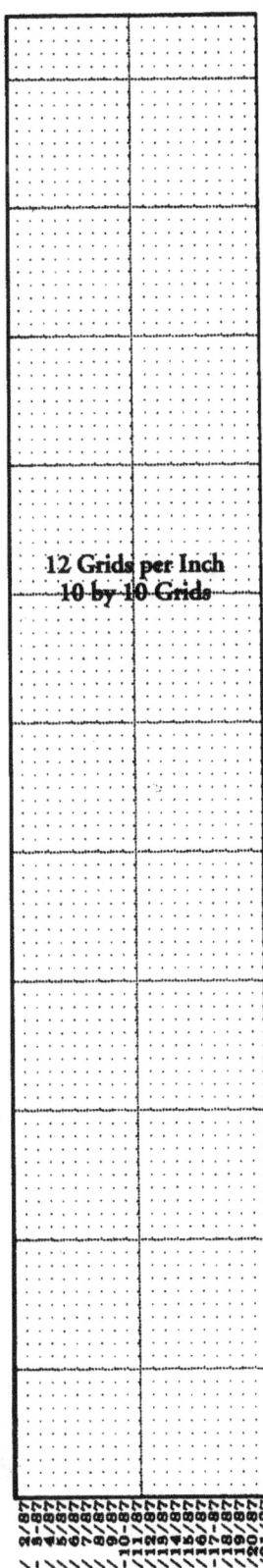
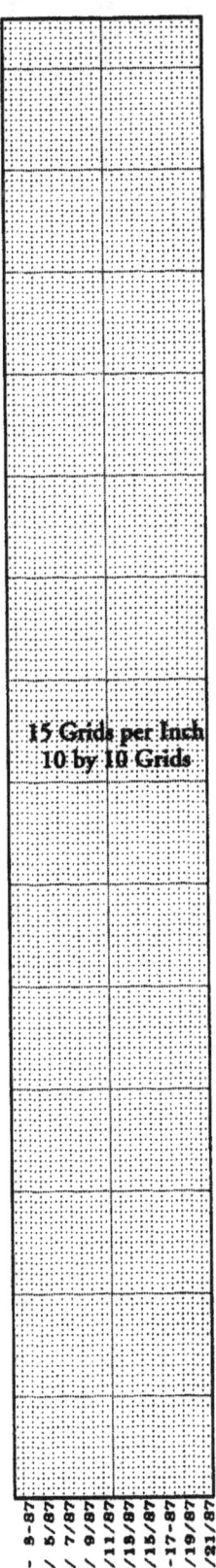
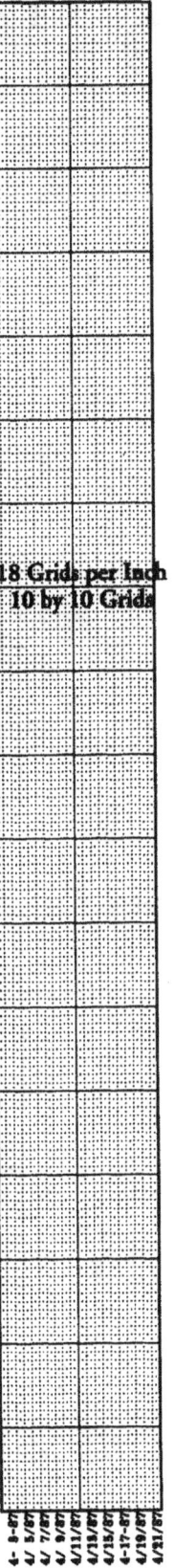

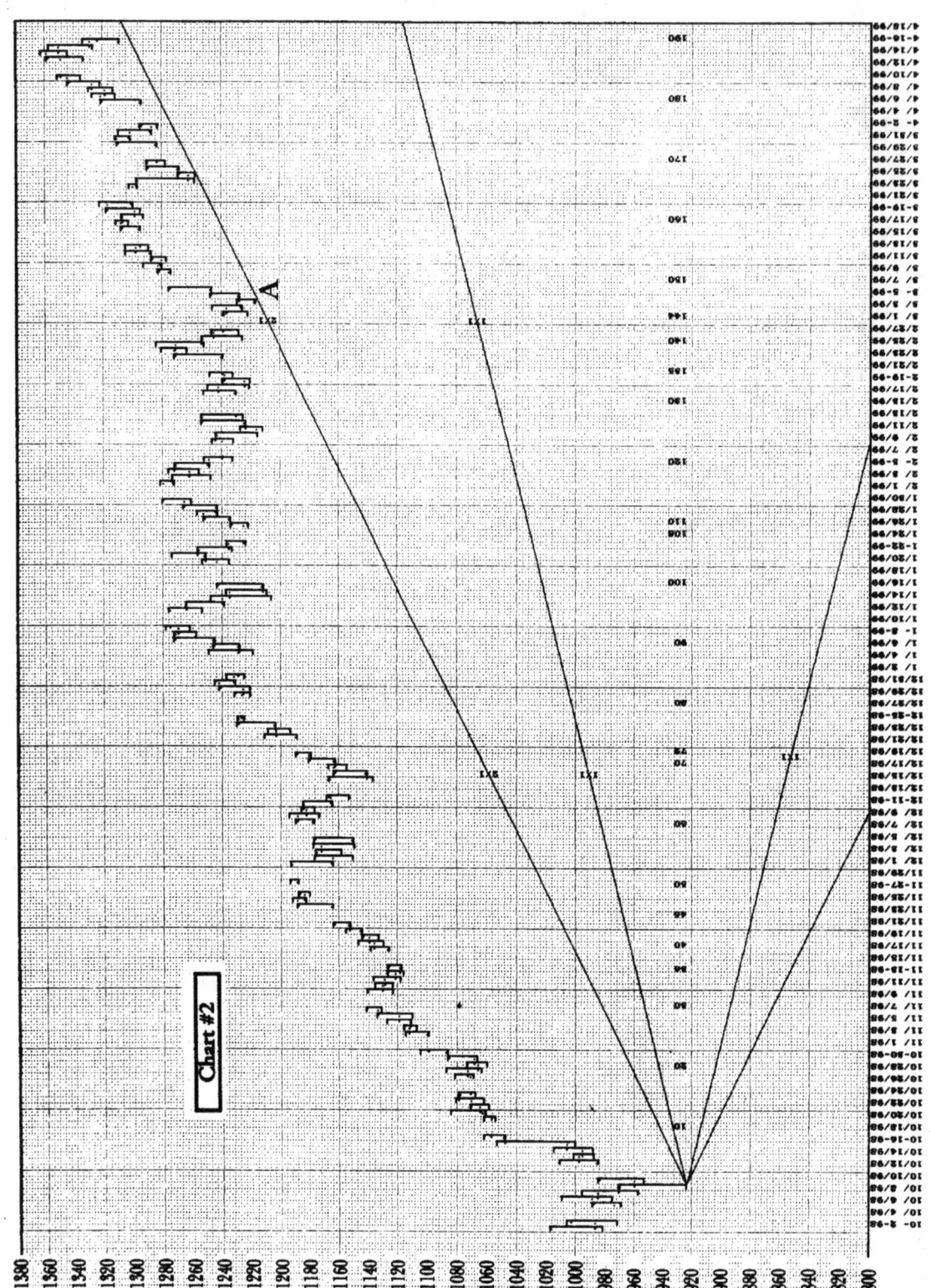

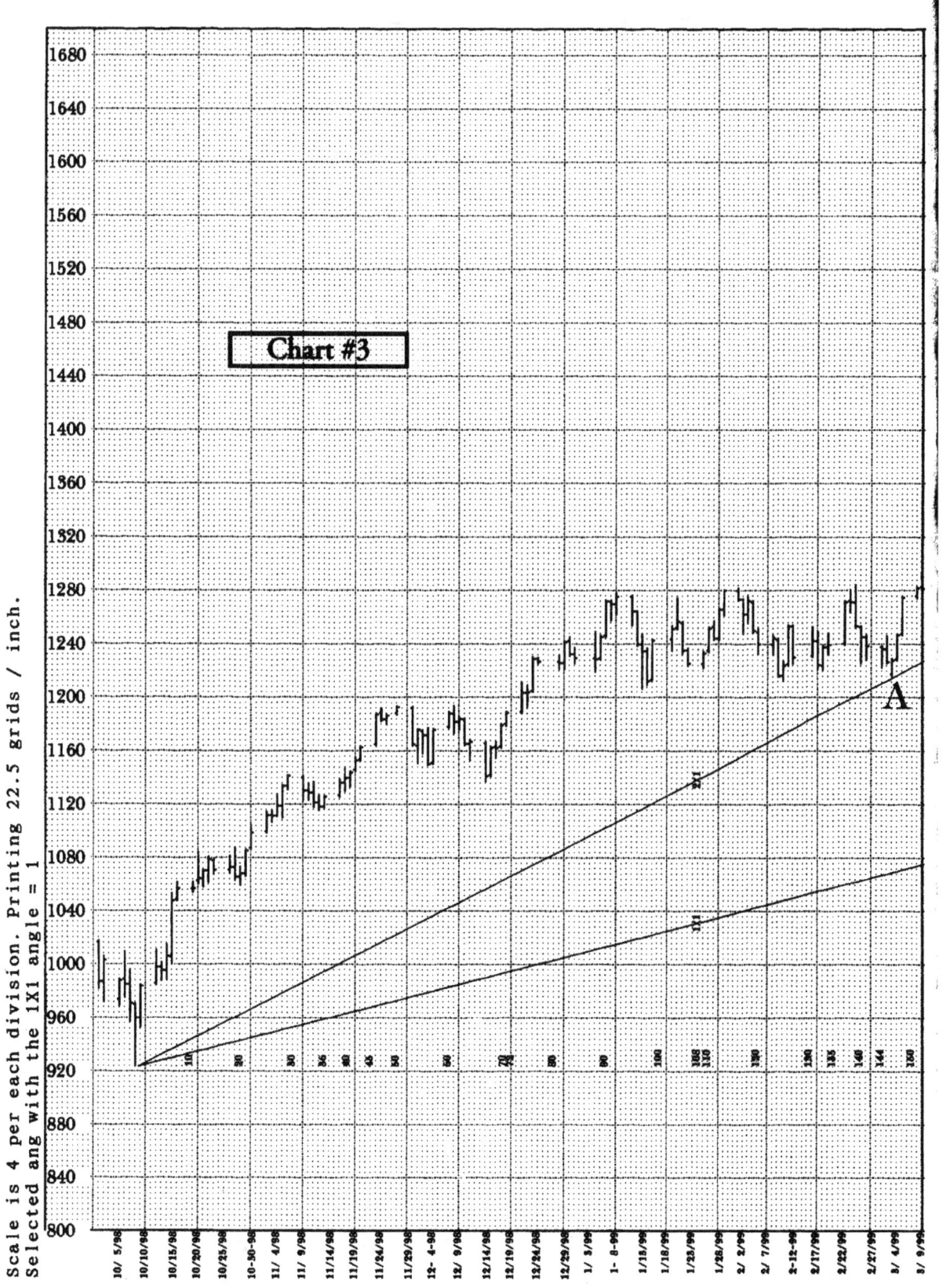

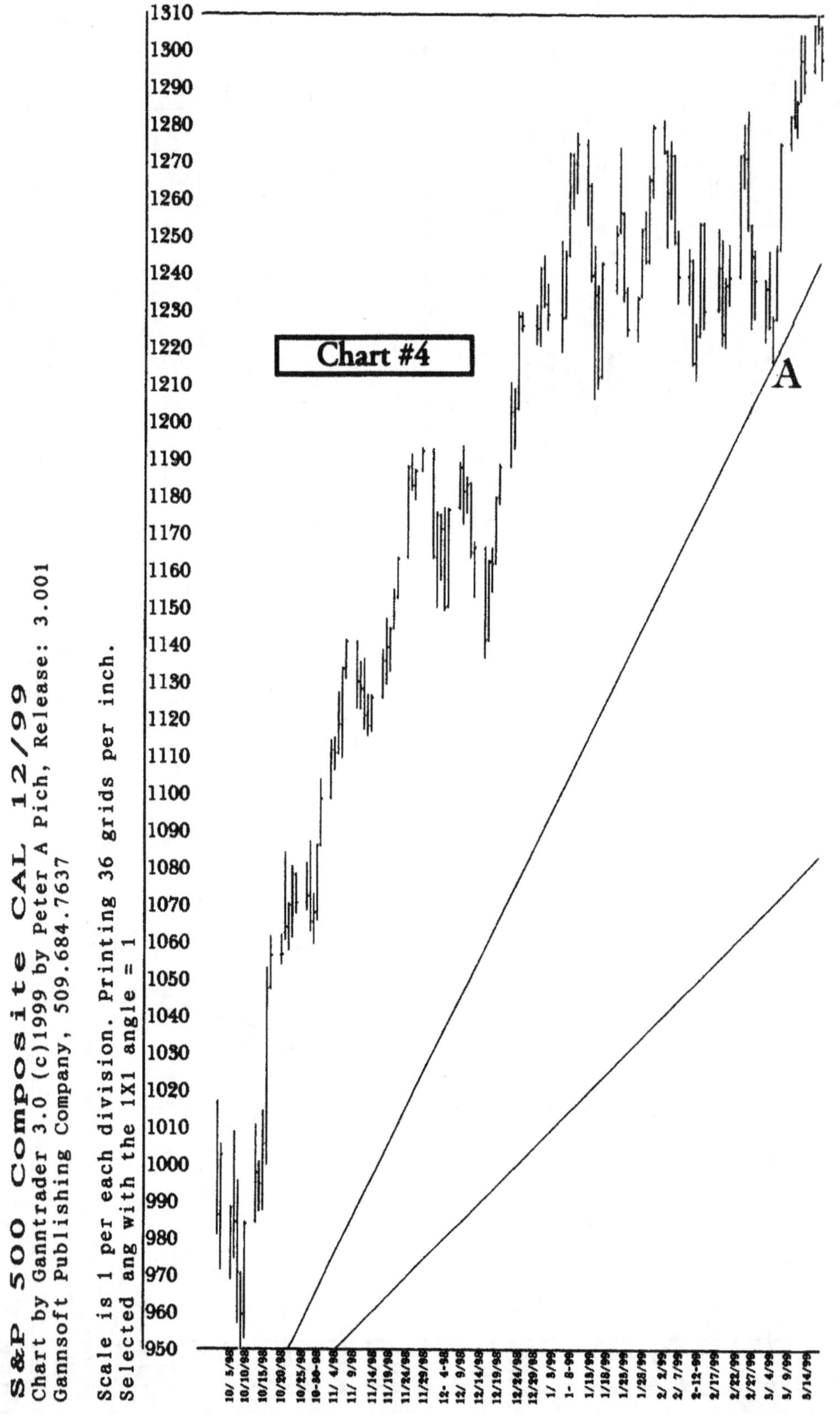

S&P 500 Composite CAL 12/99
Chart by Ganntrader 3.0 (c)1999 by Peter A Pich, Release: 3.001
Gannsoft Publishing Company, 509.684.7637

Scale is 1 per each division. Printing 36 grids per inch.
Selected ang with the 1X1 angle = 1

Chart #4

A

194

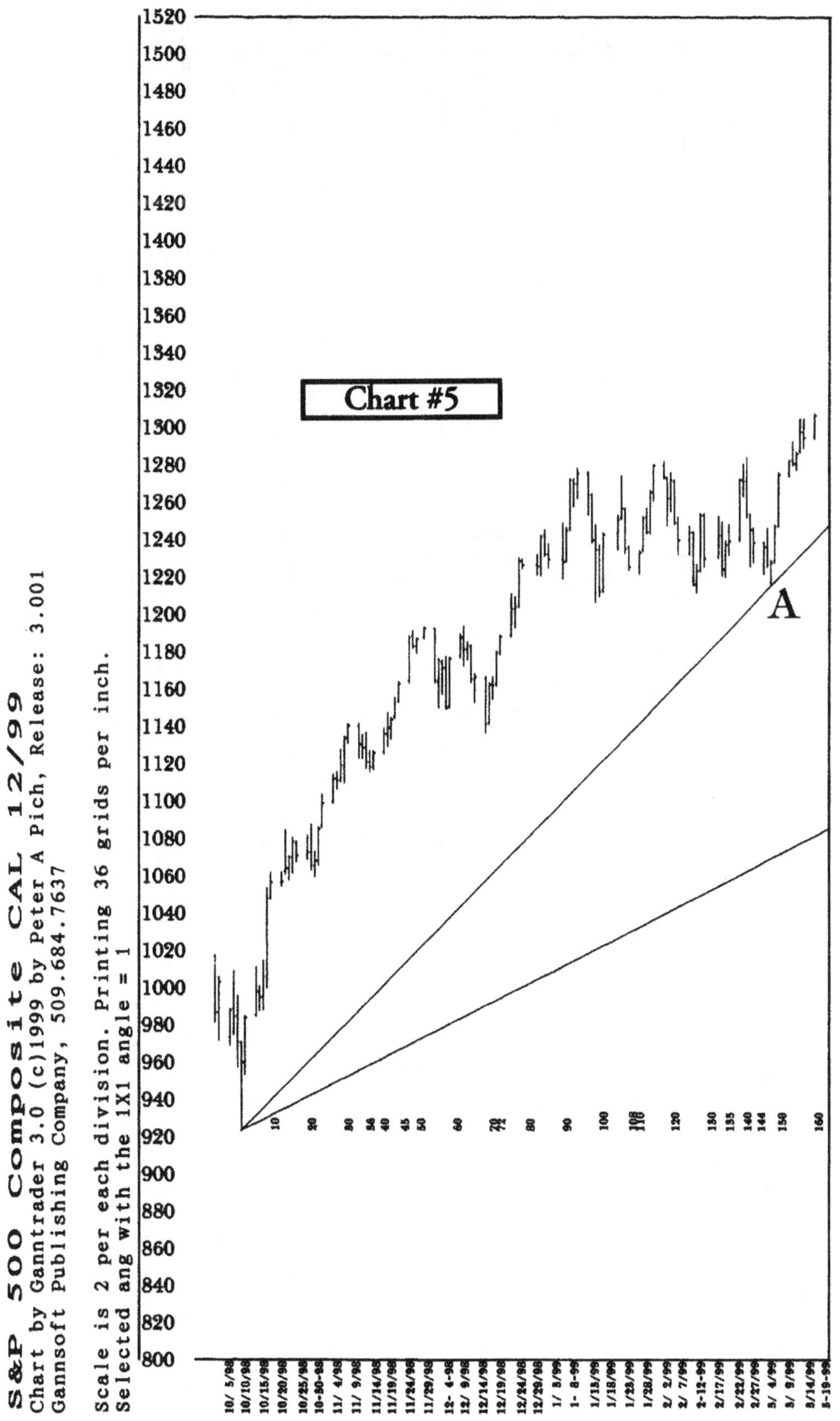

S&P 500 Composite CAL 12/99
Chart by Ganntrader 3.0 (c)1999 by Peter A Pich, Release: 3.001
Gannsoft Publishing Company, 509.684.7637

Scale is 2 per each division. Printing 36 grids per inch.
Selected ang with the 1X1 angle = 1

Chart #5

A

IBM Weekly 12/99
Chart by Ganntrader 3.0 (c)1999 by Peter A Pich, Release: 3.000
Gannsoft Publishing Company, 509.684.7637

Scale is 1 per each division. Printing 30 grids per inch.
Square of 113.5 from Date: 971212, Price: 113.5, 1st Angle: 1

IBM Weekly 12/99
Chart by Ganntrader 3.0 (c)1999 by Peter A Pich, Release: 3.000
Gannsoft Publishing Company, 509.684.7637

Scale is 1 per each division. Printing 30 grids per inch.
Square of 113.5 from Date: 971212, Price: 113.5, 1X, Angle: 2

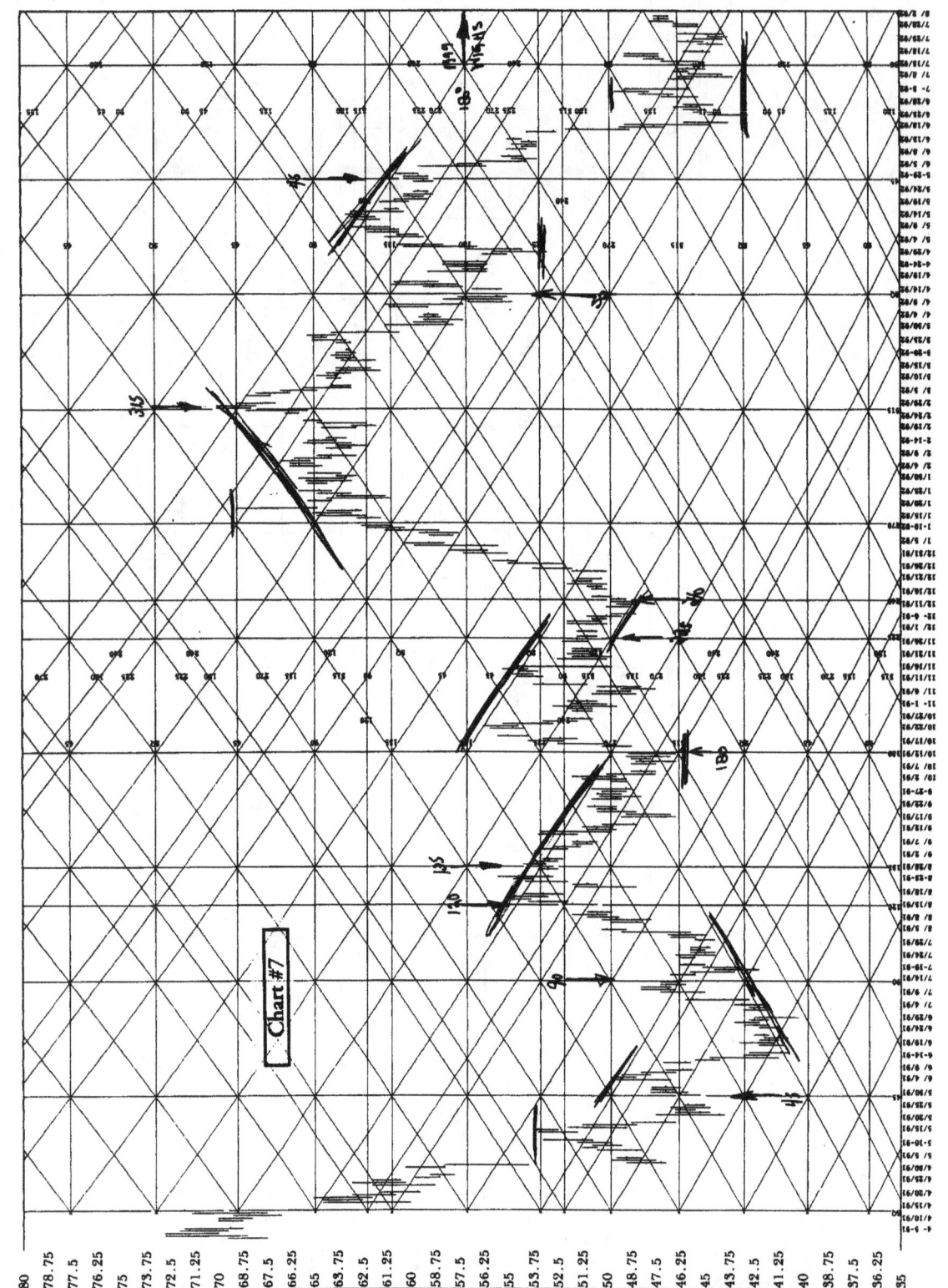

198

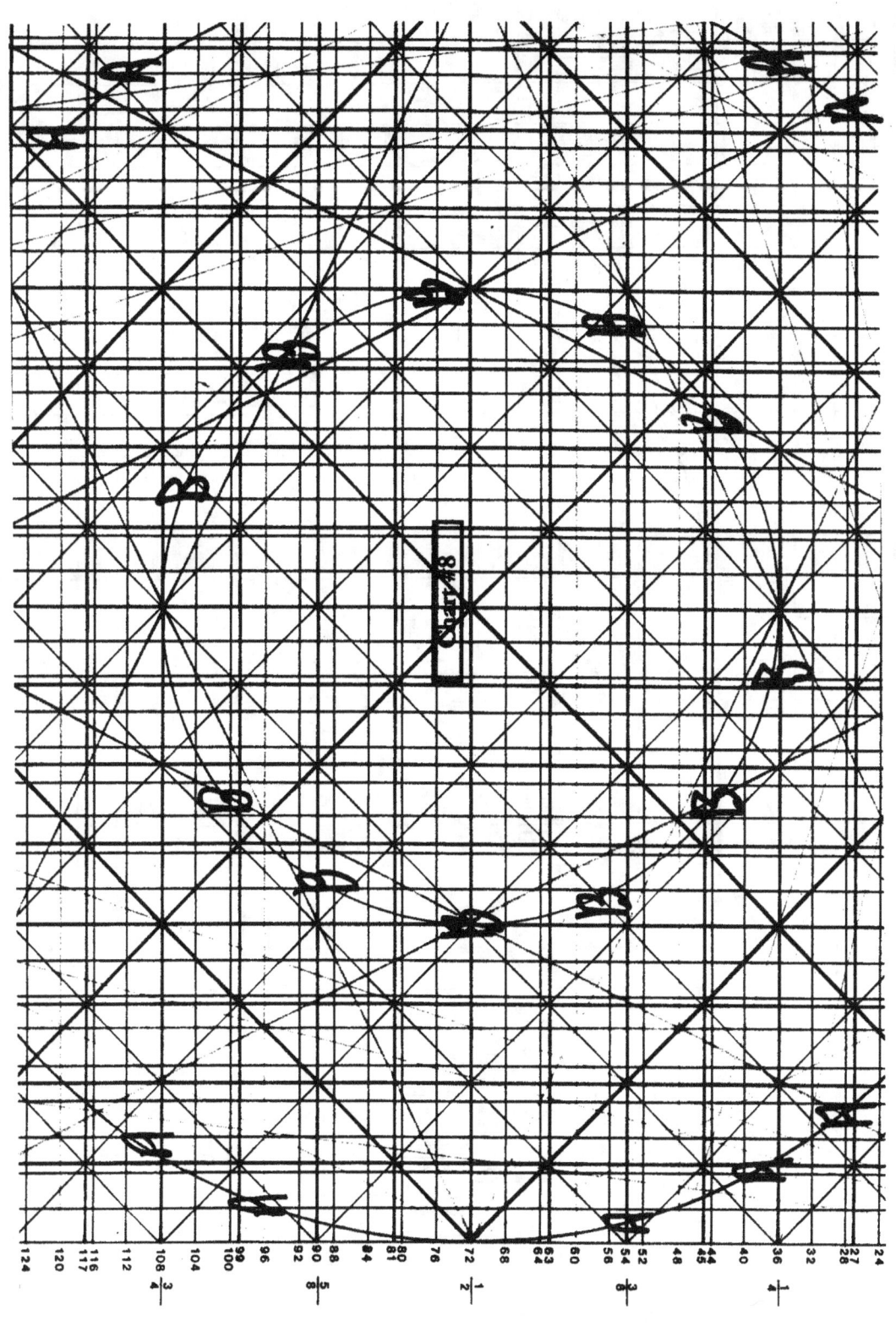

W.D. GANN PRICE TIME TREND CALCULATOR —— 1952

Apple Computer Inc Weekly 12/99
Chart by Ganntrader 3.0 (c)1999 by Peter A Pich, Release: 3.001
Gannsoft Publishing Company, 509.684.7637

Scale is 0.25 per each division. Printing 22.5 grids / inch.
3D Arc from Date of 960719 and Price of 16, using No Ratio multiplied by 0.25

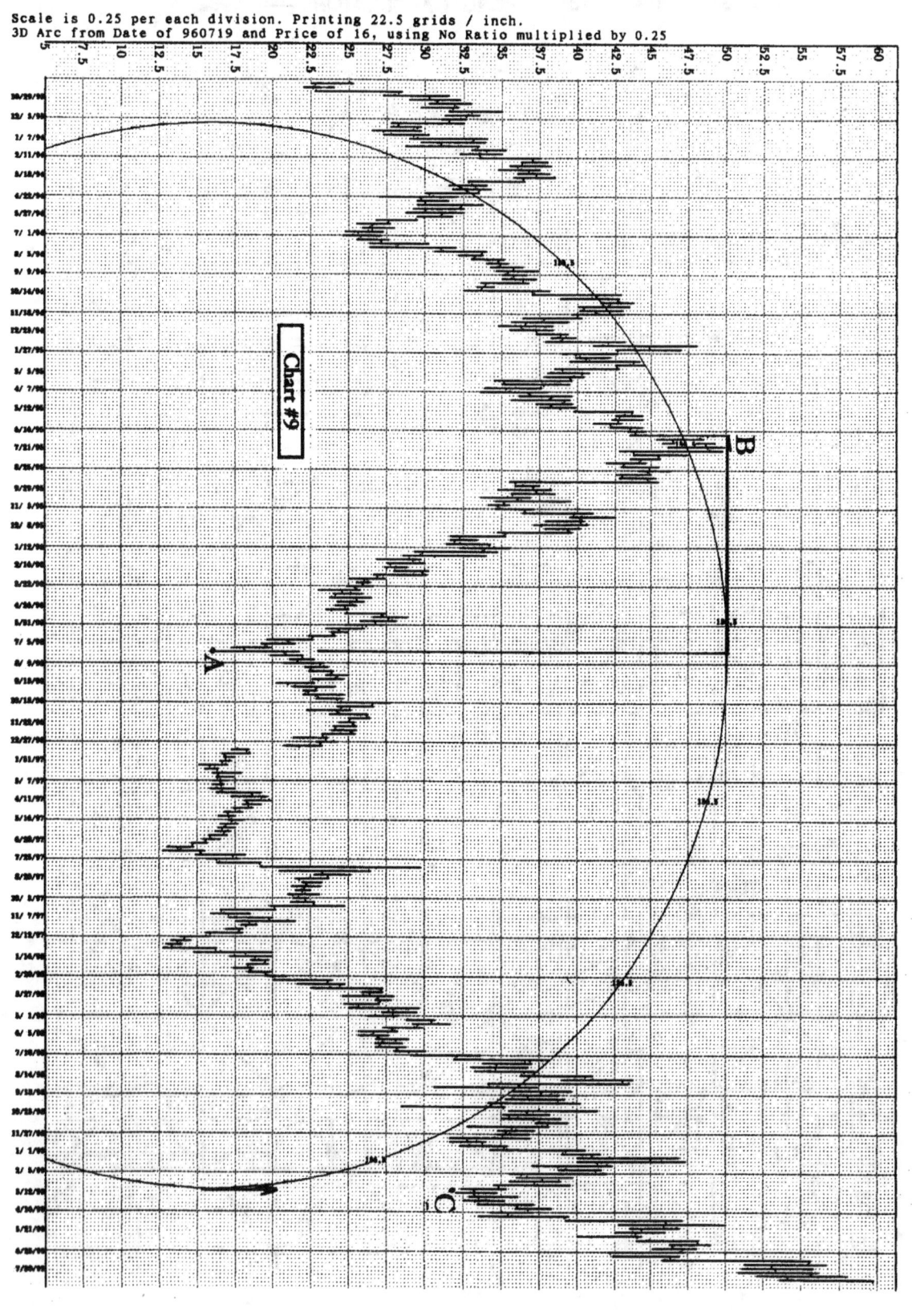

Apple Computer Inc Weekly 12/99
Chart by Ganntrader 3.0 (c)1999 by Peter A Pich, Release: 3.001
Gannsoft Publishing Company, 509.684.7637

Scale is 0.5 per each division. Printing 22.5 grids / inch.
3D Arc from Date of 960719 and Price of 16, using No Ratio multiplied by 0.25

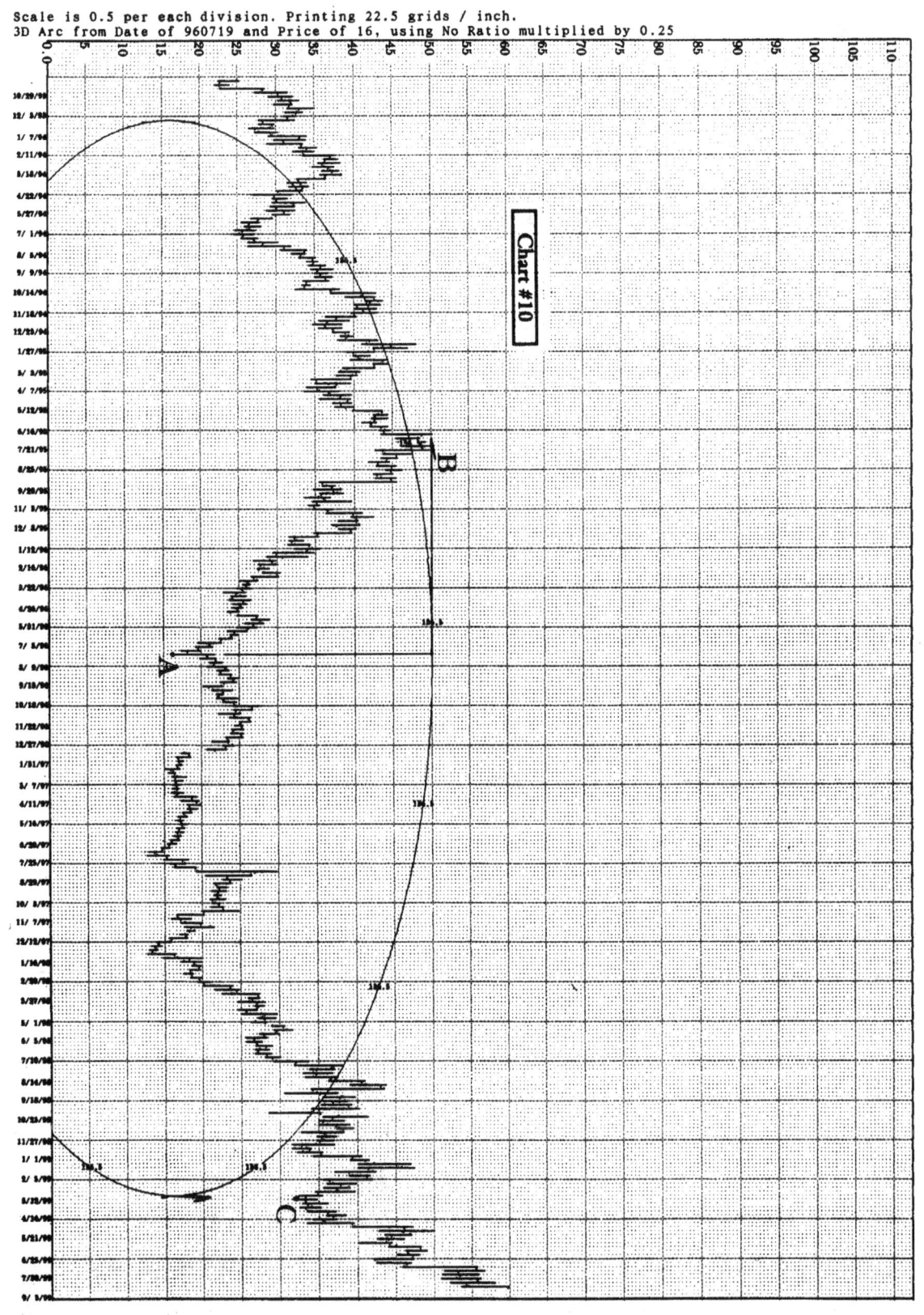

Chart #10

Apple Computer Inc Weekly 12/99
Chart by Ganntrader 3.0 (c)1999 by Peter A Pich, Release: 3.001
Gannsoft Publishing Company, 509.684.7637

Scale is 0.25 per each division. Printing 22.5 grids / inch.
3D Arc from Date of 960719 and Price of 16, using No Ratio multiplied by 1

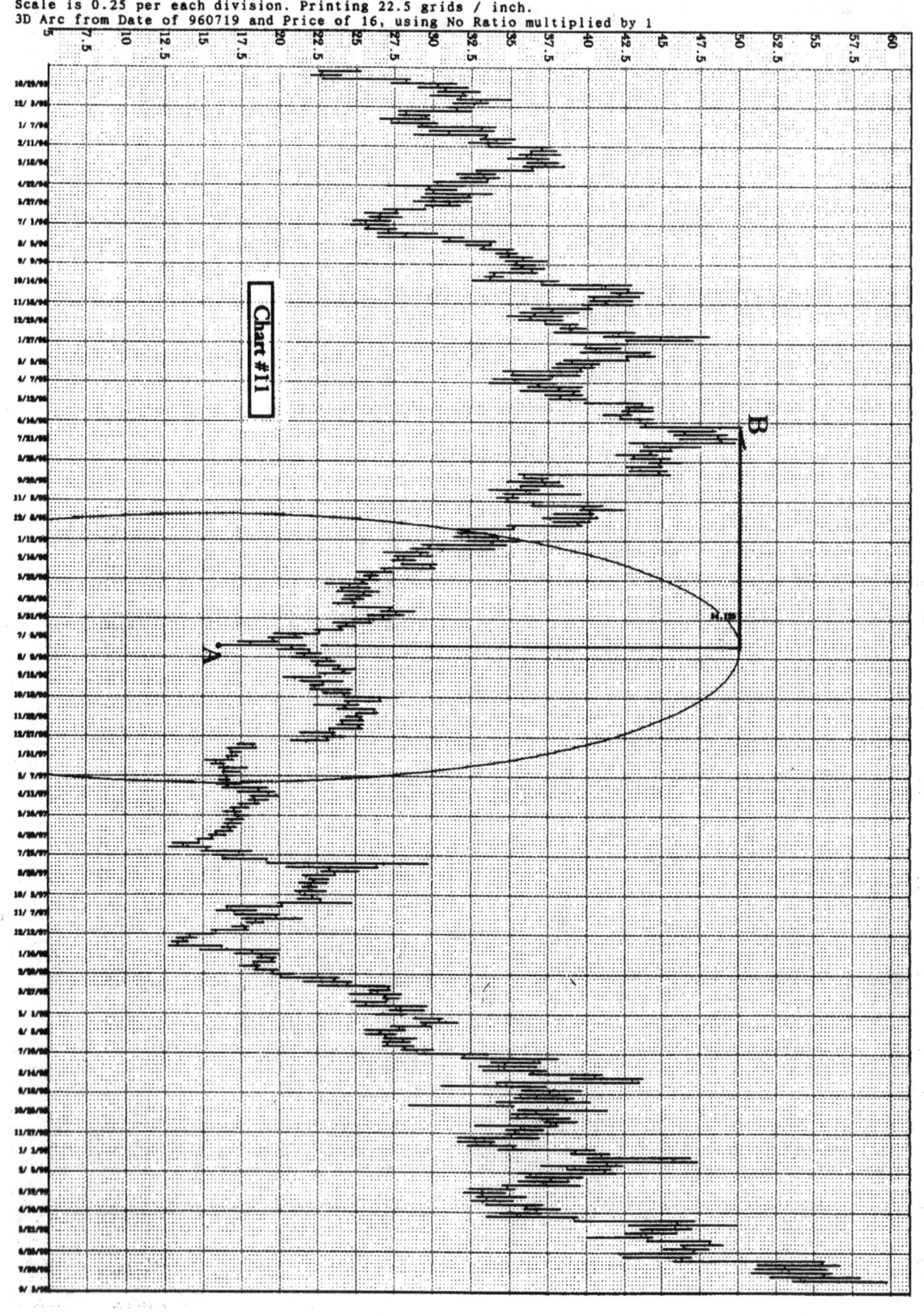

Chart #11

CBT WHEAT Weekly 23/99
Chart by Ganntrader 3.0 (c)1999 by Peter A Pich, Release: 3.000
Gannsoft Publishing Company, 509.684.7637

Scale is 1 per each division. Printing 36 grids per inch.
Selected ang with the 1X1 angle = 4
3D Arc from Date of 770826 and Price of 234, using Squared Circle multiplied by 1

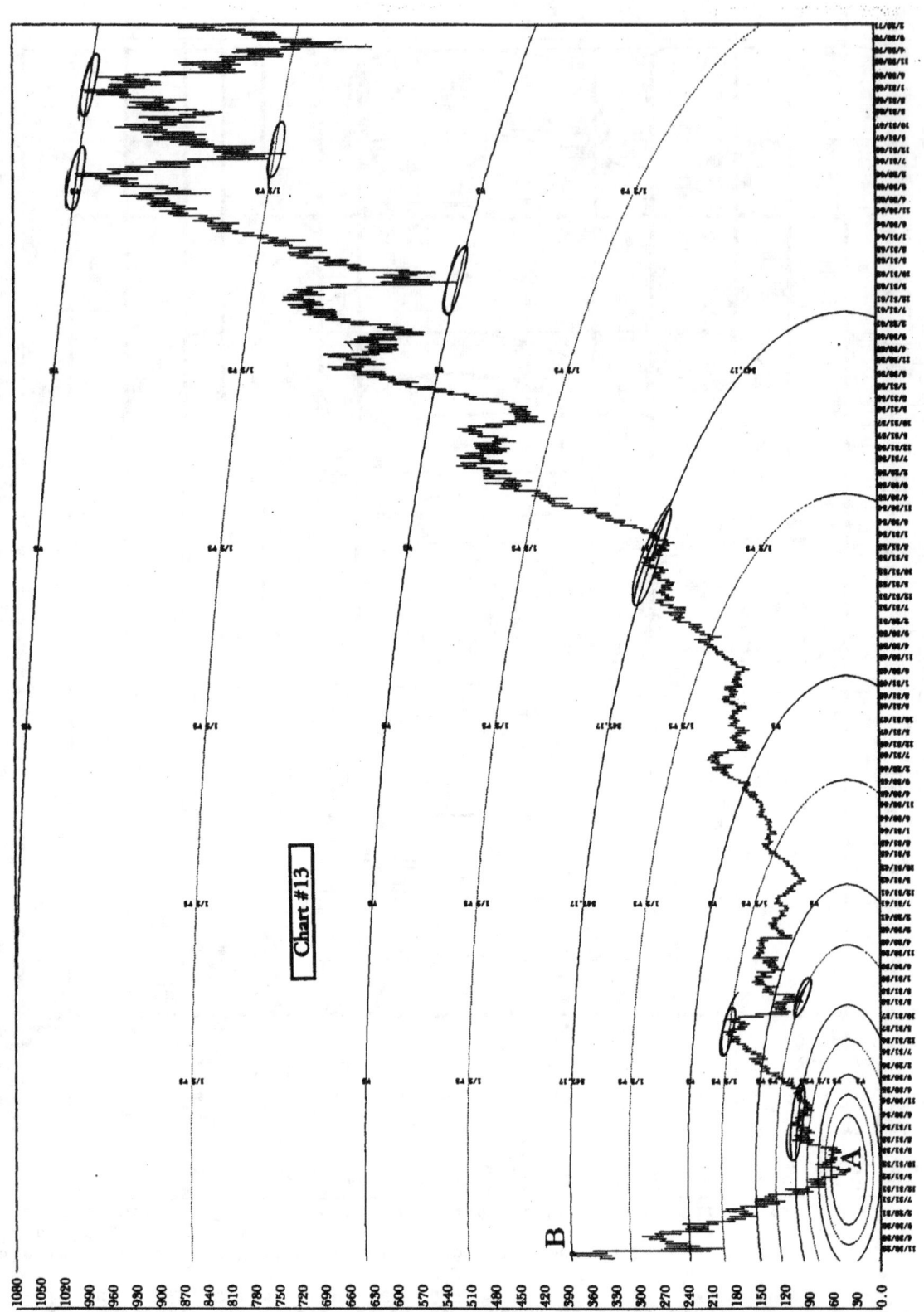

DJIA Monthly 12/99
Chart by Ganntrader 3.0 (c)1999 by Peter A Pich, Release: 3.001
Gannsoft Publishing Company, 509.684.7637

Scale is 16 per each division. Printing 36 grids per inch.
3D Arc from Date of 820831 and Price of 770, using Square Root 3 multiplied by 1

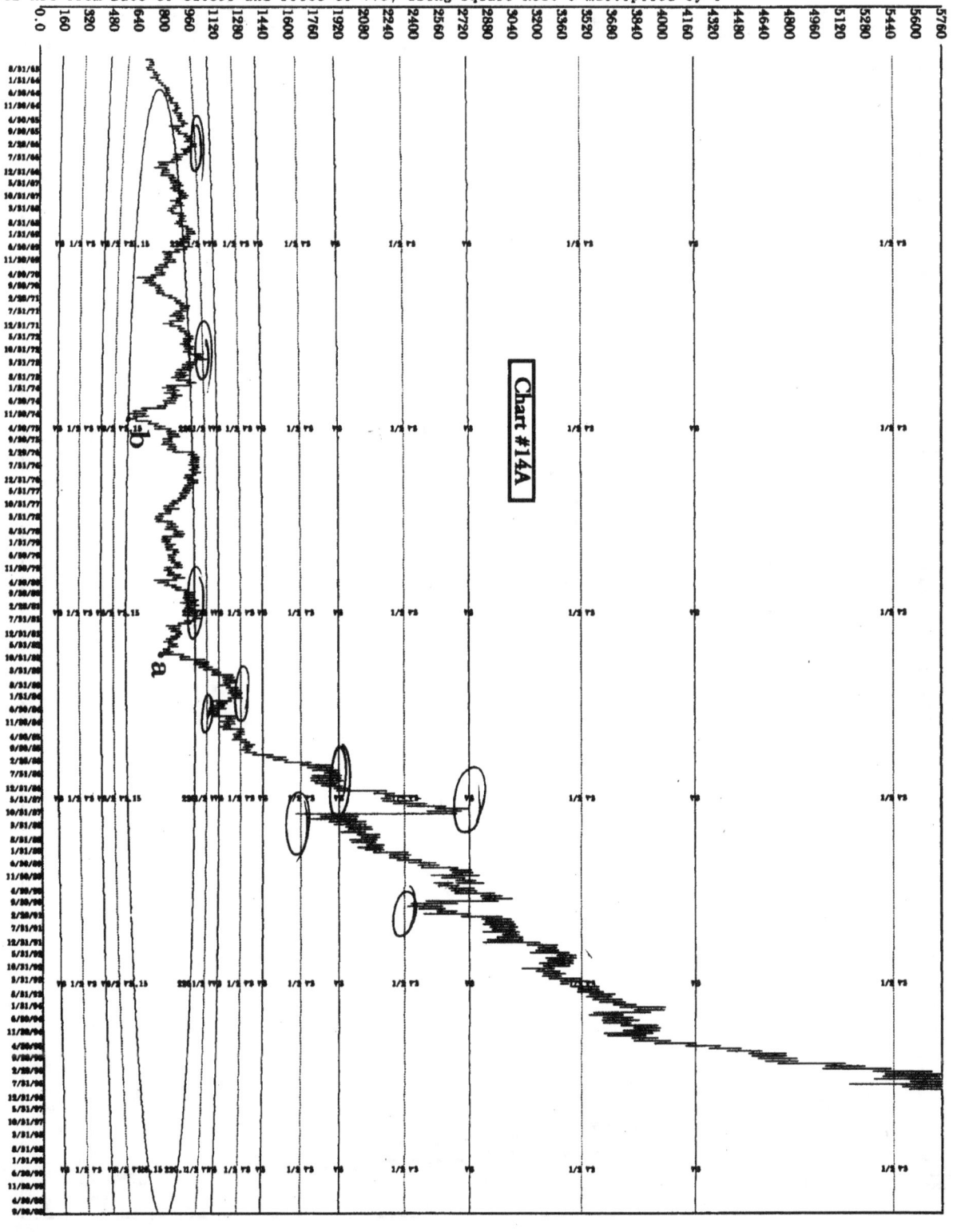

Chart #14A

DJIA Monthly 12/99
Chart by Ganntrader 3.0 (c)1999 by Peter A Pich, Release: 3.001
Gannsoft Publishing Company, 509.684.7637

Scale is 16 per each division. Printing 36 grids per inch.
3D Arc from Date of 820831 and Price of 770, using Square Root 3 multiplied by 1

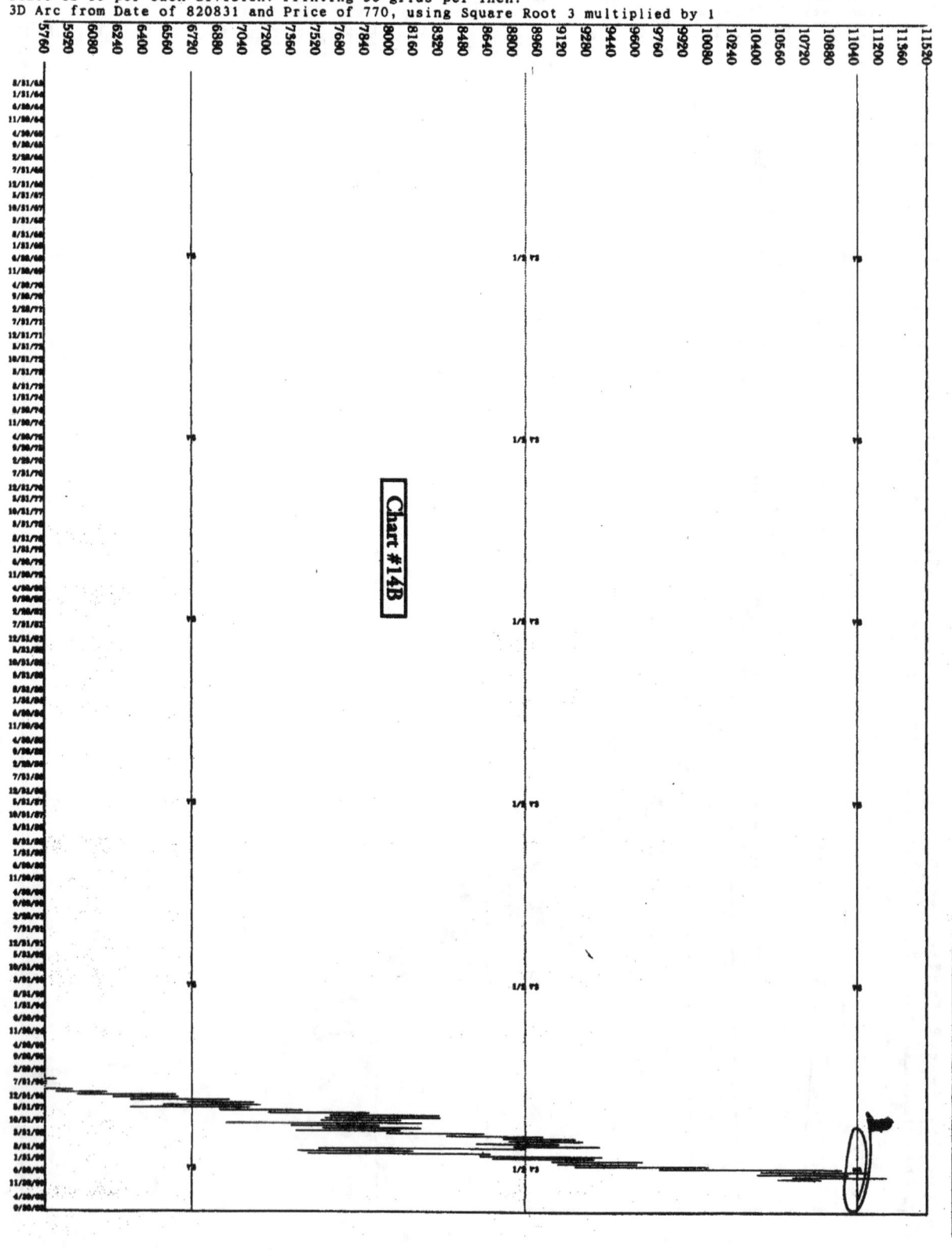

Chart #14B

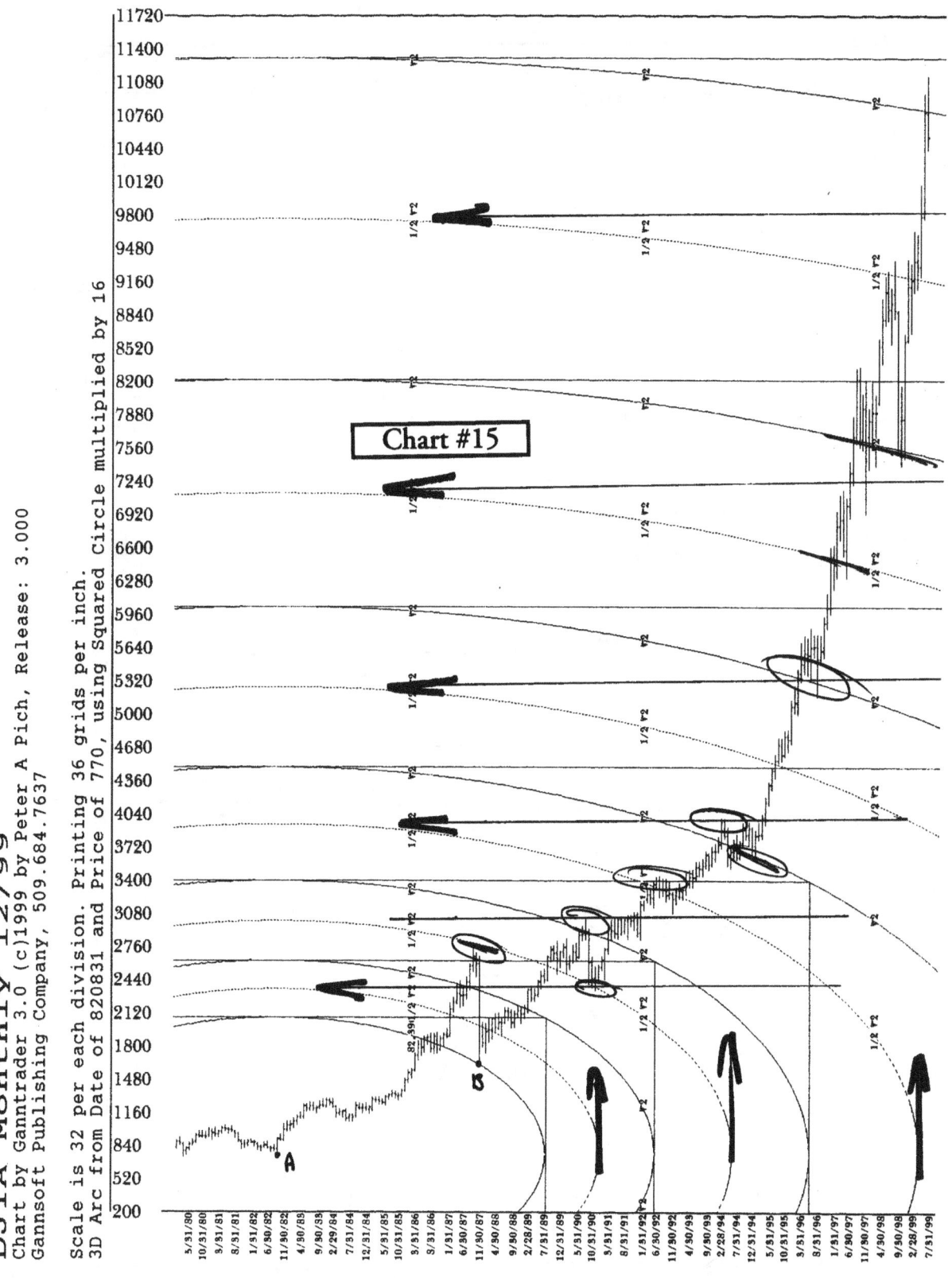

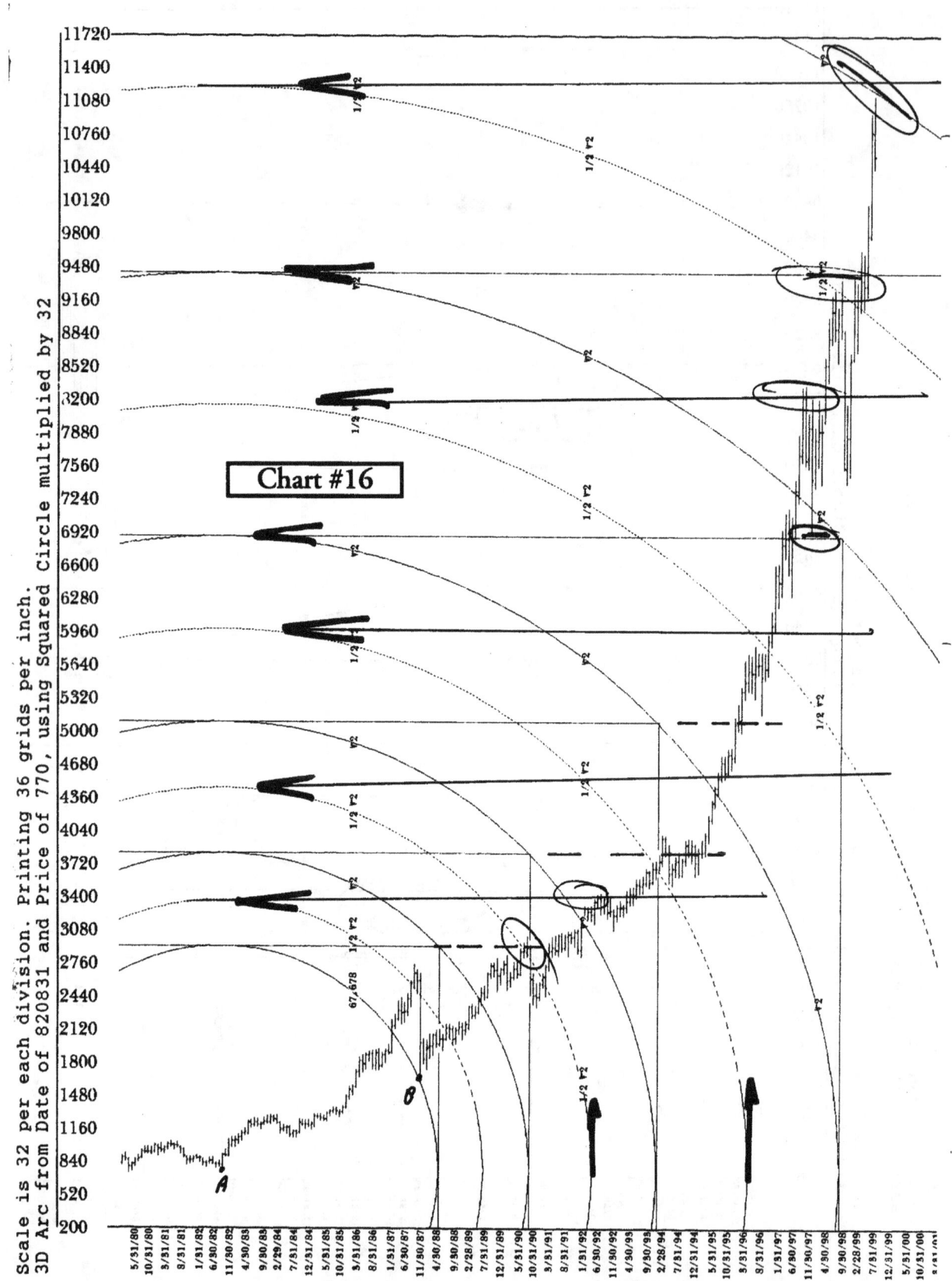

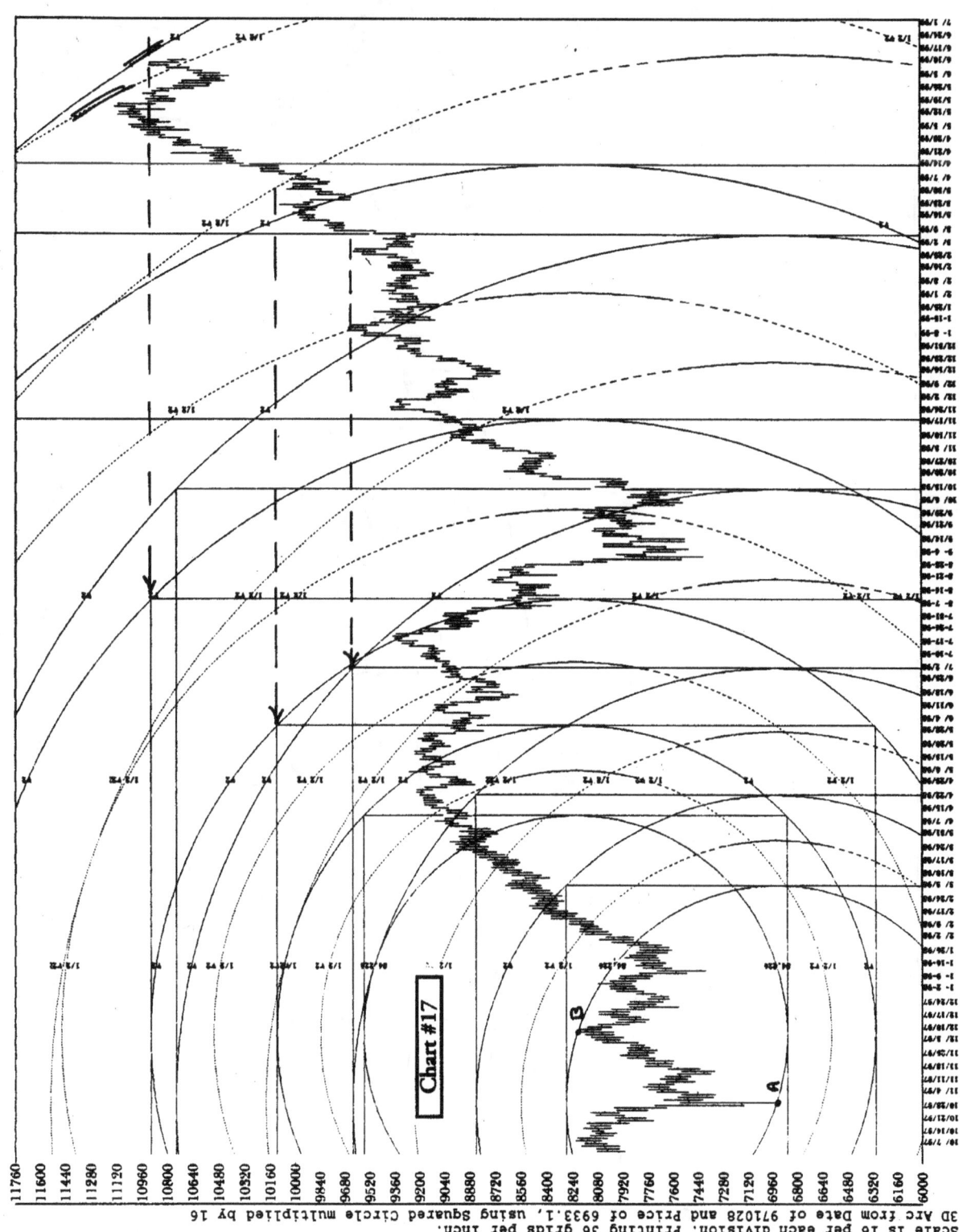

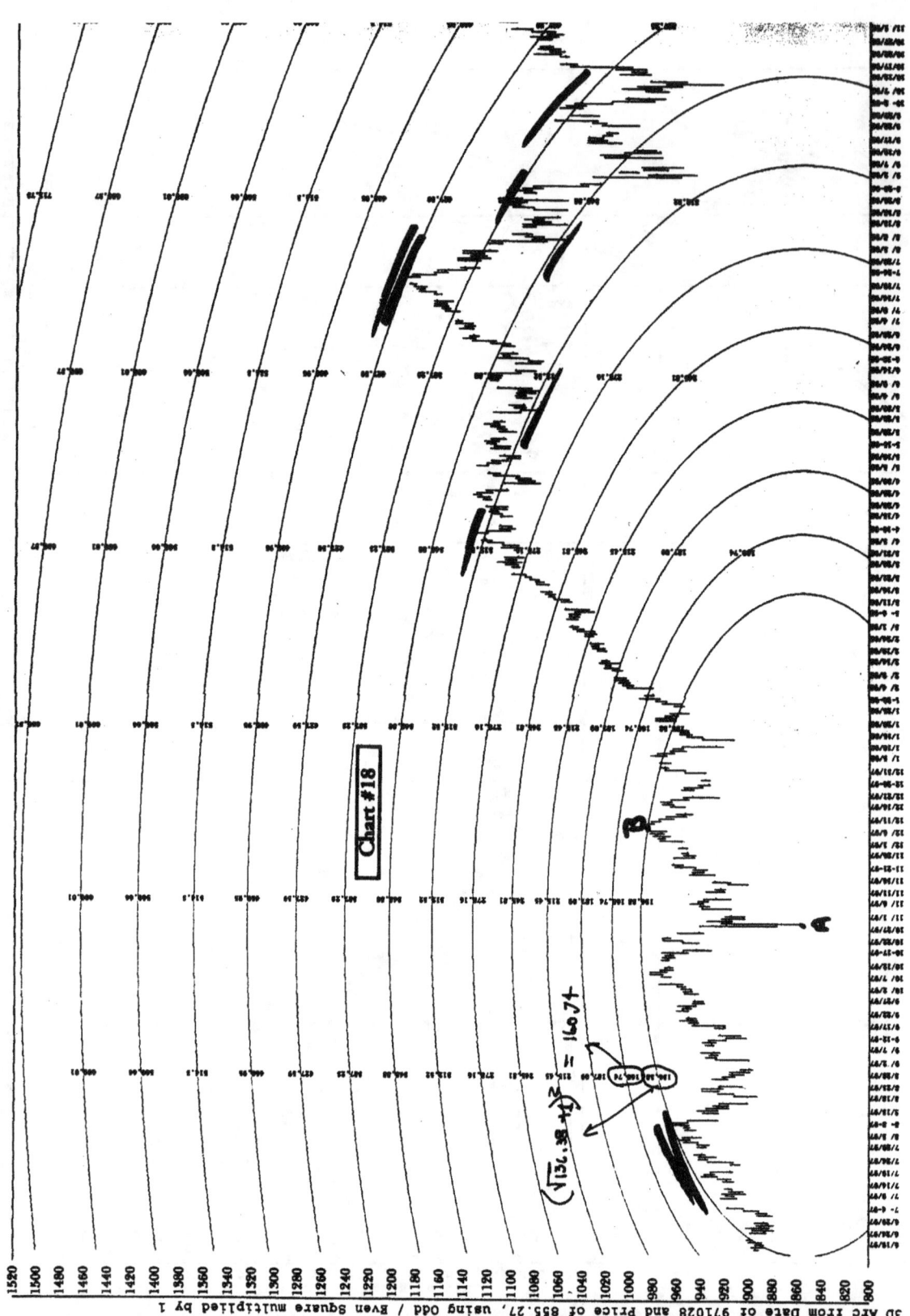

210

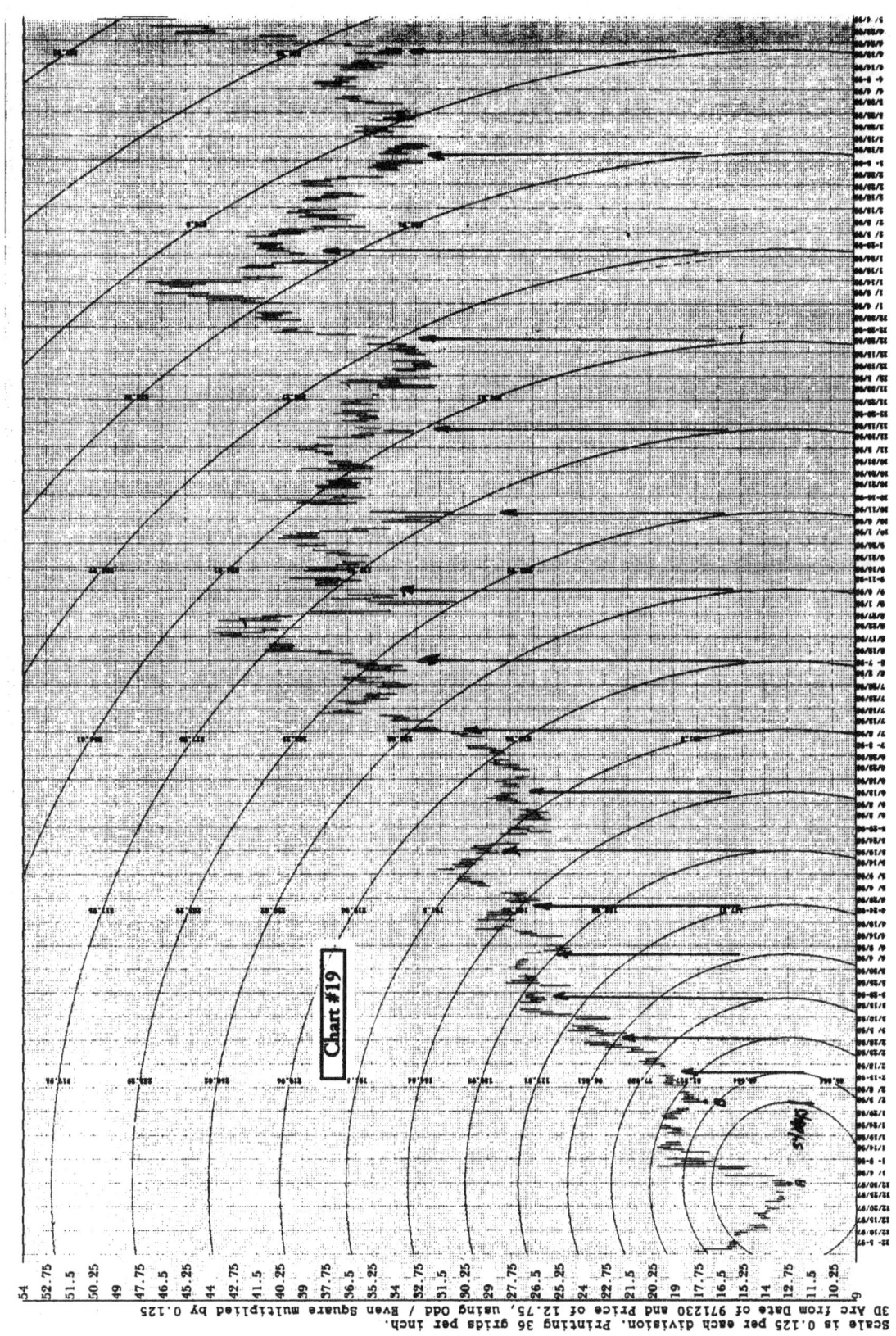

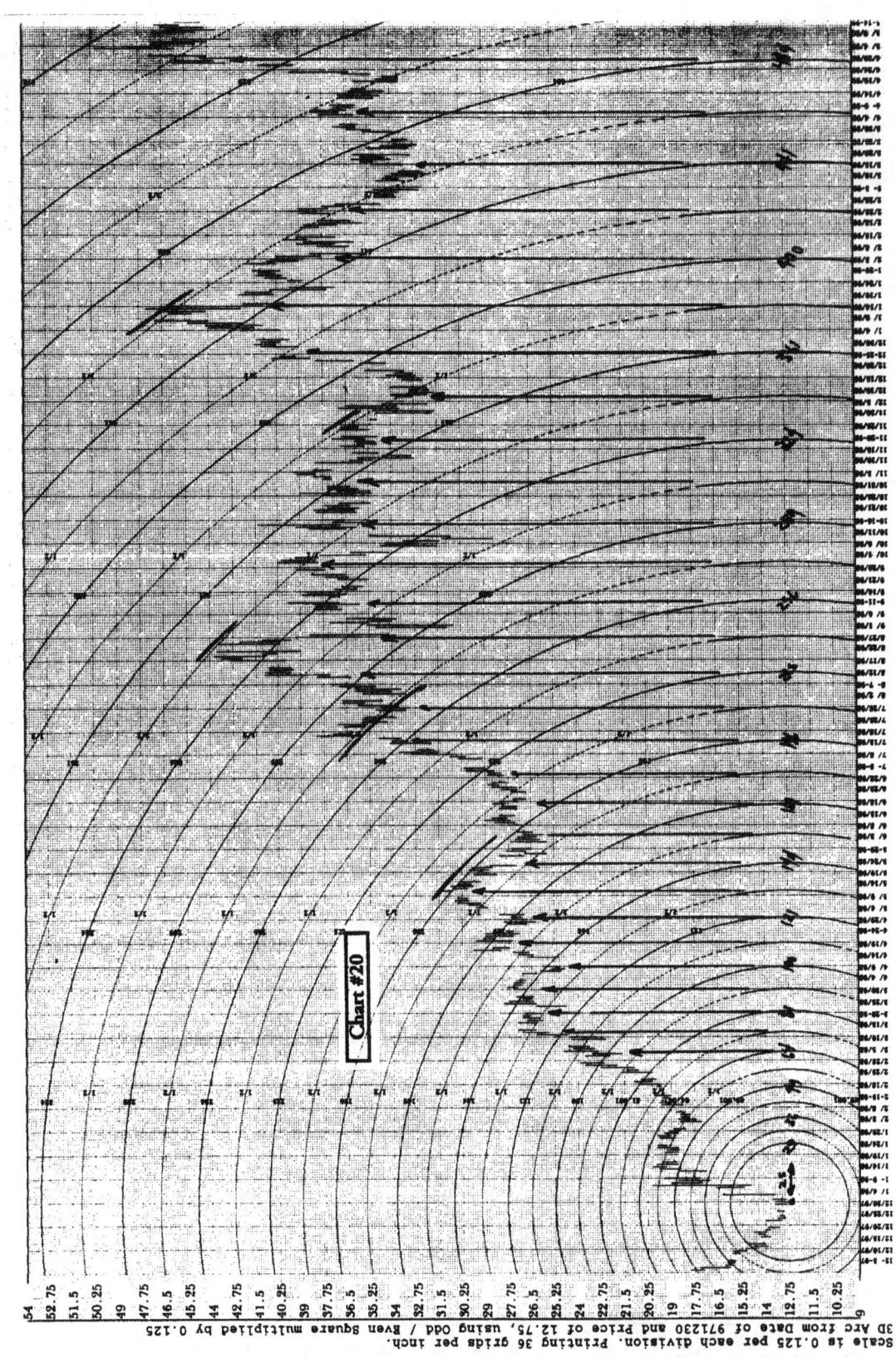

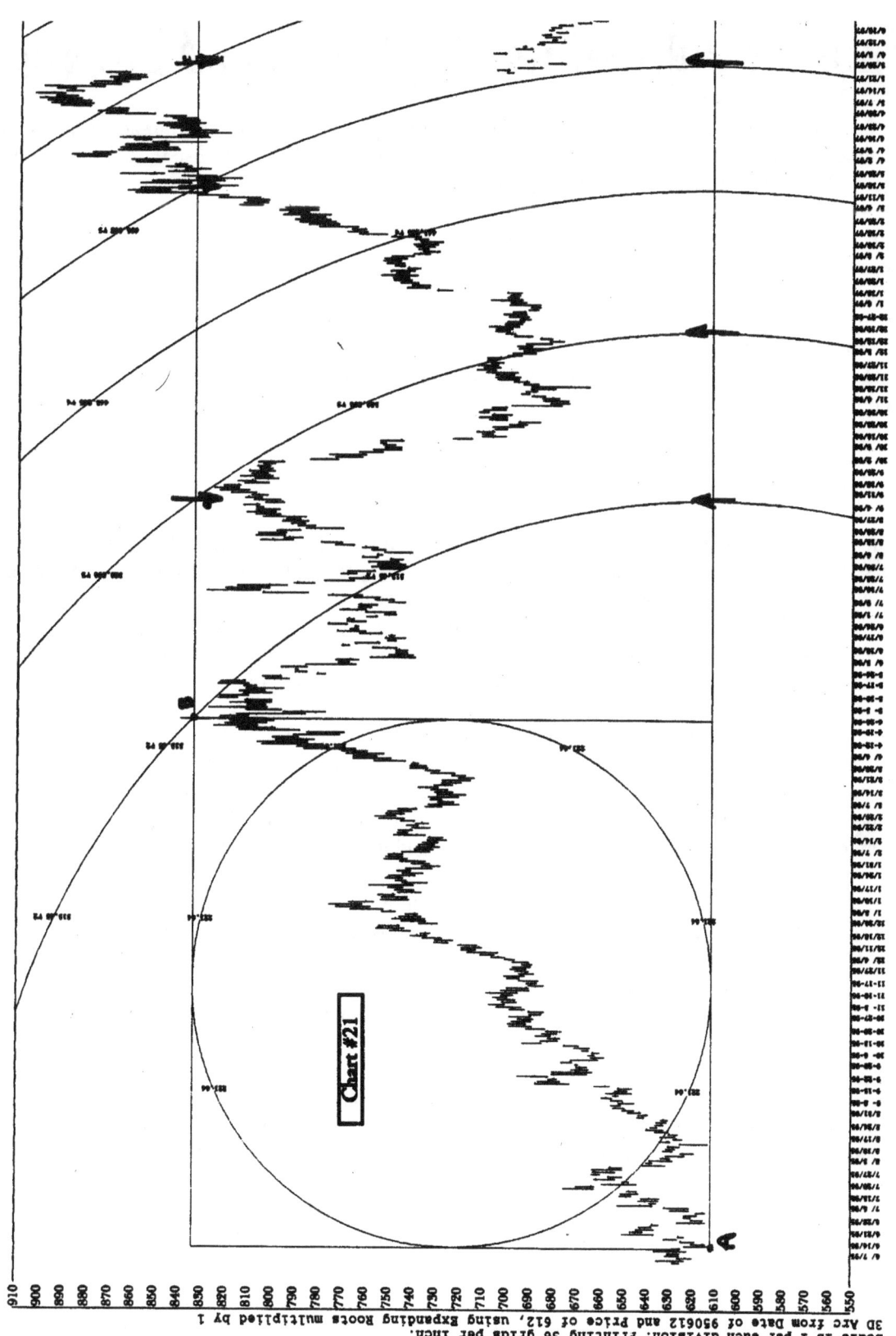

213

Gannsoft Publishing Co. License Agreement

If you purchase the Ganntrader 3.0 software, your use of the program constitutes your acceptance of the following terms and conditions. You will be granted a non-exclusive license to use the software entitled Ganntrader 3.0, subject to your compliance with the following:

You will receive a software disk that enables you to make two installation copies of the software as long as only one copy is used at a time. You may transfer the Software to another party provided that all copies of the Software are removed from your computer. The new user may apply for the rights under this agreement by paying a $495 license transfer fee. The original disk with 2 installations in place should be returned to Gannsoft Publishing Company. Upon receipt of the transfer fee and verification that all installations were removed the new party will receive the current version of the Ganntrader 3.0 by return mail and be granted all rights and privileges under this agreement.

If your original disks are found to be defective under normal use within 90 days of date of purchase, they will be replaced free of charge when received by Gannsoft Publishing Company.

Under no circumstances, and under no legal theory, tort, contract or otherwise, will Gannsoft or its licensors, be liable to you for any damages, including any lost profits, lost data or other indirect, special, incidental or consequential damages, arising out of the use or inability to use the software, any data or information supplied, even if Gannsoft, its licensors or authorized dealer advised of the possibility of such damages, or for any claim by any other party. Some states do not ally the exclusion or limitation of incidental or consequential damages so this limitation may not apply to you.

Your sole and exclusive remedy for breach of warranty is that Gannsoft Publishing Company will at its option either refund you or replace your Software so long as you return the Software along with your dated proof of purchase. Except for the express warranty of the original disk set forth above, this software is provided 'As-Is' and you accept the entire risk as to the quality and performance of the software. To the maximum extent permitted by applicable law Gannsoft and its licensors, disclaim all other warranties, express or implied, by statute or otherwise, regarding the software, including the fitness for a particular purpose, quality, merchantability, or their noninfrngement. No oral or written information or advise give by Gannsoft or its licensors, their respective employees, distributors, dealers or agents shall increase the scope of the above warranties or create new warranties. The liability of Gannsoft or its licensors under the warranty set fourth above it limited to the amount paid by the customer for the product. Some states do not allow this exclusion of implied warranties, so the exclusion may not apply to you. In that event, any implied warranties are limited in duration to 90 days from the date of your purchase of the software.

You the purchaser understand the risk of stock and commodity speculation and assume all the risk of your activities in any investments. Any examples used in this book of past performance of the market, the software or Gann's methods shall not guarantee that future markets will perform in a similar manner. No examples or instructions in this manual or instructions from an employee, agent or dealer of Gannsoft Publishing Company shall be considered to be trading advise. The original purchaser shall be entitled to purchase any future revisions of Ganntrader at a nominal chart. The exact price of the revision will depend on the nature of the changes.

The user shall have the right to use the chart output of the program in any newsletter, book or other publication without explicate permission from Gannsoft Publishing Company provided that a statement 'Chart by Ganntrader 3.0 Copyright 1999 by Peter Pich 509-684-7637' appears on the chart.

Configuration

The first order of business is to install the program onto your hard disk system. The Ganntrader program is distributed on 2 floppy disks labeled Disk #1 and Disk #2.

The program permits two installations to be made. These copies are intended for the exclusive use of the purchaser or registered owner. Any other use is a violation of the license agreement and copyright laws. We are a small company attempting to provide good service and products at a fair price. Every free copy that is given away makes it more difficult to provide the level of support that the legitimate user deserves. Trading as you know is a zero sum game. Why make it possible for other traders to have the same tools you are using to beat them in the market?

The original program disks are used by Gannsoft Publishing Company as proof of ownership of the program. No updates or warranty replacements will be made without the return of the original disks. People change jobs, partnerships and marriages. The one retaining the original program disks will be considered the owner of the program. Please keep them in a safe place.

Make sure the disk's write protect slider is covering the hole in the corner of the disk
The disk must be unlocked and writ able for the installer to work properly.

Ganntrader is compatible with Win 95/98, NT and Windows 2000. The higher resolution modes work only with Windows 95/98. The program can also be run from DOS but it must be installed through the Windows environment.

To install the program simply insert the disk into the floppy drive and select the Add/Remove Programs icon from the Control Panel.

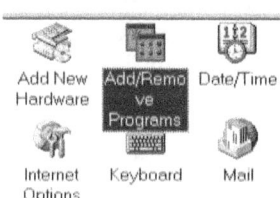

Install the Program

The installer's default values should work for most users and can be accepted simply by hitting the Next button in each dialog box.

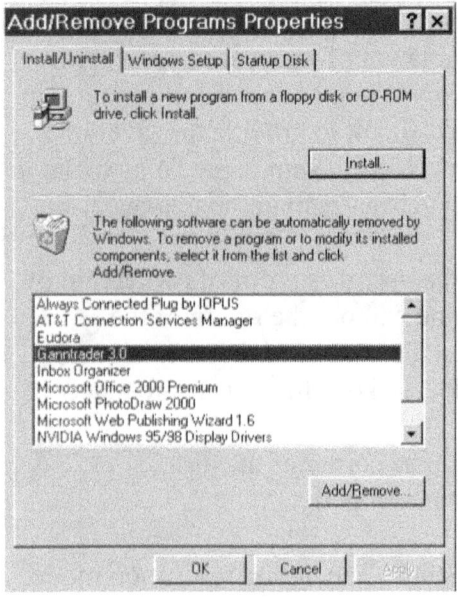

During the installation process you will eventually see this Authorization Manager dialog. This installs the program's authorization. The default settings should be correct for your installation. Notice that the authorization will be moved from the A: drive to the C: drive or whatever drive you selected for the installation. Simply click OK to continue.

You received 2 install authorizations on the your original Disk #1. Each time you install the count is reduced by 1. If you transfer the authorization back to the floppy the count is increased by 1. This way you will always have your authorized number of installations. In the unlikely event of a hard disk crash you may loose an installation count. Call or E-mail Gannsoft and we can restore your lost installation with a code number.

If all goes well you will see this dialog box. If an error occured please note the error number and call Gannsoft technical support.

The installer will next display the number of available installations on your original disk. The program is supplied with 2 installations on the original disk. If this is your first installation the remaining installations should be 1. Click OK and the remaining installations will be displayed.

The installer will next ask for Disk #2 and complete the installation. If Windows 95 or 98 is the operating system a utility program will run that checks the video card system and creates the correct video driver.

To avoid losing any installation counts when removing the program please refer to Appendix D for more information.

Starting Ganntrader
Once installed you can start up the program by using the shortcuts icons created on the desktop or in the Start menu.

If you will be running the program from DOS do the following:

1) Select the drive containing Ganntrader by typing C: <Enter>.

2) Change directories by typing CD\GANN30 <Enter>.

3) Type Gann to start the program.

After starting Ganntrader, the main program will be displayed on the screen...

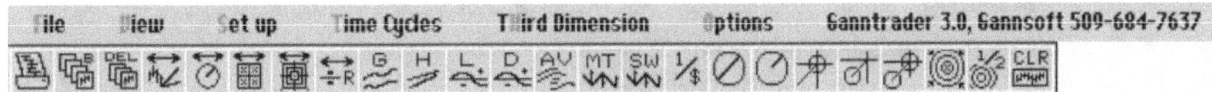

When the system is first loaded notice that most menu items are grayed out and can't be selected. These items will be turned on once a file is loaded.

The File menu is used primarily in the loading and printing of a data file or groups of files. The View menu is used to view angles, squares and planets. Some items under this menu are only available after being set up under the set up menu

The Set Up menu is used to enter the set up values for squares, angles and planets. The Time Cycles menu is used to display the planet aspects and the averages of the planets.

The Third Dimension menu controls the Arcs and Circles and their non-linear expansions.

The Options menu contains the system configuration functions and also contains the automatic screen scale and centering selections and other items that you may want to enable or disable as you use the program.

The Tool Bar icon strip offers a quick way to activate certain features of the program. the icons duplicate various menu and keyboard commands.

Selecting an Item

All menu items can be selected with a click on the Left mouse button. Click the mouse anywhere on the screen to close a menu. All menu items and buttons have a keyboard equivalent indicated in red. You can move through the menus with the up/down and left/right arrow keys. Type the hot key to select an item.

Type the <Esc> key to close a menu.

Help on Menu Items

A click on the Right mouse button displays a help window for each of the menu items. With the keyboard select the item and hit the <F1> function key.

A sample help box follows...

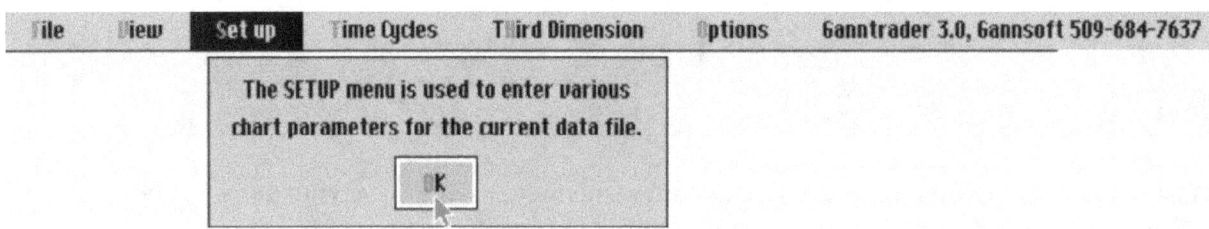

Configure System

Your first operation should be to configure the system and save the set up. With the mouse click on Options and then click on Configure System. With the keyboard type the letter <O> followed by a <C>.

After selecting Configure System the following box will appear...

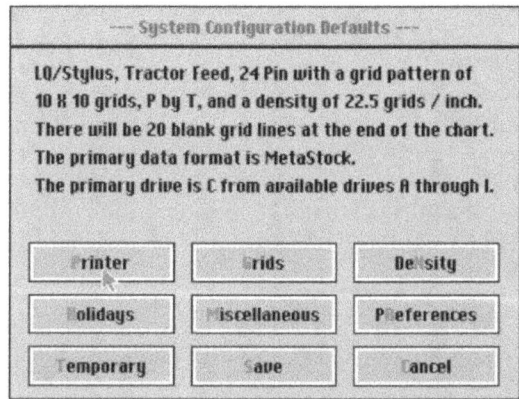

The text in the box describes the present configuration of the program. The text will be updated to reflect the new status as each box is selected. Click on any button that needs to be changed. A box will pop up and allow you to select an item After each button is selected one or more entry boxes will appear. They will each be described below.

Printer allows the selection of 9 pin or 24 pin printers. Letter sized 8 inch wide, 11 inch tabloid, A4 size and 14 inch wide Epson compatible printers are supported.

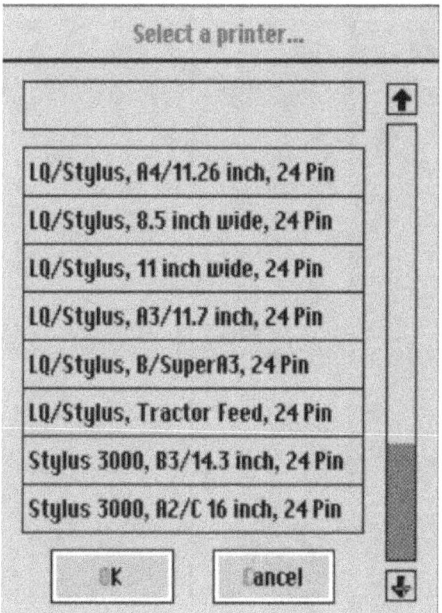

Grids

Grids refers to the dark grid line pattern (8X8, 8X10 or 1OX1O) or the line that is emphasized when printing. The 1X1 0 mode is useful for markets that trade in tenths and the 8X10 is better for markets such as Bonds that trade in multiples of 8. For example, a scale of .125 or 4-32 per grid line would create a full point difference at each emphasized grid line on the chart. The 8X8 pattern matches standard chart paper that you may be using.

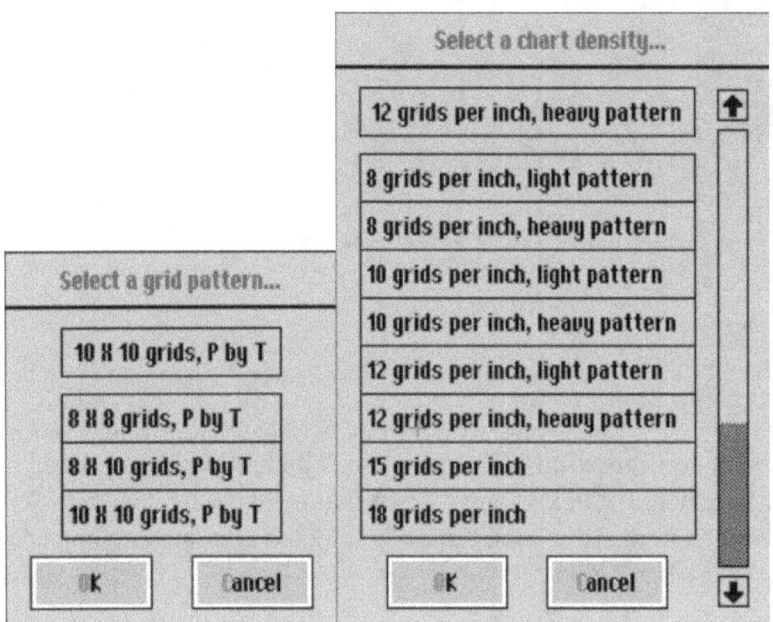

Density

Density refers to grids lines per inch. The LQ printers offer densities of 8, 10, 12, 15, 18, 20, 22 1/2, 30 and 36 grids per inch. Grid lines of 8, 12, 18 or 24 per inch are available on the 9 pin printers. Twelve per inch is a good place to start. The light or heavy pattern refers to the number of dots that are used to draw each grid line. The light pattern has a dot at the intersection of the vertical and horizontal lines. The heavy pattern has several dots instead. The light pattern is preferred by most users because it makes a chart that is less 'busy' looking and is thus easier to see the other lines that are being plotted. The smaller the grids the more grids you can have on a chart but at the expense of readability. The smaller grids print more than one grid each time the print head moves across the page so the denser grids will print faster. Use the chart below to decide the best trade-offs for your requirements.

Holiday Date List

On the second row of buttons there is Holidays which allows for the entry of those future holidays that fall on a weekday. When printing a trading day chart these days will not be printed in the extra blank grid lines at the end of the chart. It only effects trading day charts and only those holidays that occur on Monday through Friday that might otherwise be printed in the extra blank grids at the end of the chart.

For example, Independence Day 1999 falls on a Sunday but the following Monday, July 5 will be a trading holiday in most markets. If you were making a trading day chart that had extra blank grid lines that included July 5 no blank bar would be excluded in the chart. A calendar day chart includes weekends as well as holidays so this feature is not used for them. Once a holiday date is surrounded by valid data that holiday can be removed or replaced with a later holiday date. Holidays contained within the date range of the data file are marked as such and can easily be skipped by the program when necessary but there must be a way to tell the program about holidays out into the future.
Future year's holidays should be entered here as necessary. Your broker should be able to supply you with market holiday closing dates at least a year in advance.

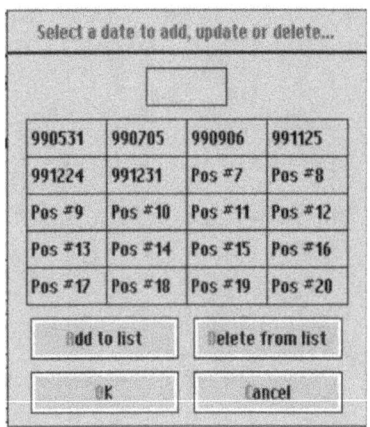

Date Entry, Y2K and Data Formats
When entering dates in the program there are several formats that are acceptable:

YYMMDD or YYYYMMDD
MM/DD/YY or MM/DD/YYYY
MM-DD-YY or MM-DD-YYYY

For example, the date of June 16, 1989 can be entered 890616, 6/16/89, 6-16-89, 19890616, 6/16/1989 or 6-16-1989. An illegal date such as 2-31-90 will produce an error box.

If you prefer to enter your dates as DD/MM/YY or DD/MM/YYYY activate the European or military style dates under the Preferences: General section described below. If this feature is active date entry as well as charts and screen displays will have the day and month reversed. With either style the date formats of YYMMDD and YYYYMMDD are also accepted.

Ganntrader from its original design in 1983 has always accepted Y2K dates correctly. Two digit dates are interpreted as 1900 + YY. If you want the program to treat a date entry as year 2000+ they must be entered with 4 digits for the year. If you would rather enter year 2000 dates with 2 digits see the Y2K changeover feature under the Preferences: General section described below.

Ganntrader supports the Y2K data formats offered by Commodity Systems Inc. commonly known as the CSI and CSI-M formats. The CSI-M format is the former Computrac format with CSI's Y2K extensions added. MetaStock format should be compatible after 1999 but Equis / Reuters refuses to supply Gannsoft with the technical specifications for their new Y2K format. We suggest you contact your data supplier and convert to the CSI or CSI-M format before 1999 ends.

Miscellaneous Button

The Miscellaneous button will produce the following box:

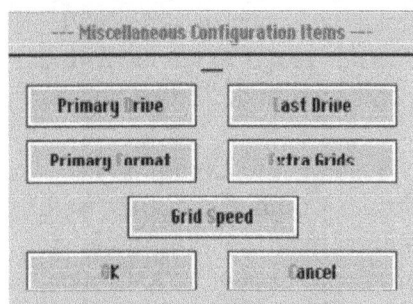

The Primary Drive is the first drive location that will be searched for data. When you load a file the program automatically searches this drive for any MASTER or QMASTER files. These files as you may know, contain the names of all your data files. The lists of files are displayed for easy selection. The Last Drive is the last drive letter in your system that might contain data. Its value is not critical and is already set to drive H. The Primary Format is the first data format that the program will attempt to find on the disk. The choices are CSI Quicktrieve or CSI-M formats.

The primary drive and data formats can be changed at any time while running the program. These settings are simply a starting point for the program.

The Extra Grids are the number of blank lines that will appear at the end of the charts and screen after the price bars. These lines will contain any angles, squares or planet lines out into the future. Twenty lines is a good starting point for this value but any number could be entered.

Grid Speed is used by the program to calculate and display the total printing time for a chart. The value entered is the time in seconds for your printer to print one grid line. Use a stop watch to measure yours or use 1 second which is close for most newer printers. Once these changes are made click OK and you will return to the previous box.

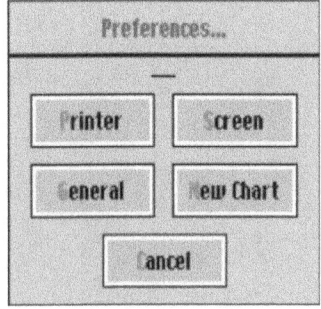

The Preferences button breaks down into four preferences and allows for more customizing. Move to the desired entry point using the <Tab>, <Shift><Tab> or <Enter> keys. Most items won't need to be changed but here is a description of each item. The entry spaces appear with the default values entered.

Printer Preferences

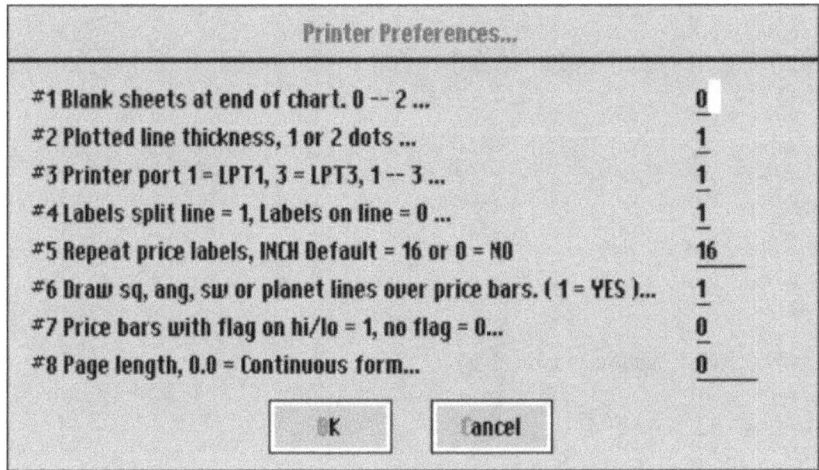

#1 Blank sheets at end of charts. 0 --2
Some printers need a blank sheet at the end of the chart in order to allow for easy tear off at the perforation.

#2 Plotted line thickness, 1 or 2 dots. This will darken some of the plotted lines. Try setting this to 2 dots if your printouts are too light for your tastes.

#3 Printer port 1 = LPT1, 3 = LPT3, 1 -- 3
This is the printer port that the program will use to print charts. The pre-set value is 1 and should only be changed if you have more than 1 printer port installed on your system.

#4 Labels split line = 1, Labels on line = 0
If you prefer the price labels on your charts to rest on top of the grid line enter a zero. The default is to have the chart labels centered in the middle of the grid line. The top line on the chart can be labeled only if the label splits the line. This has no effect on the screen display.

#5 Repeat Price Labels. The program will label the prices at the far left of the chart and again every 16 inches. This repeat rate can be changed to your liking. If set to zero only the first set of labels will print at the far left of the chart and none in the chart area itself.

#6 Draw lines over price bars determines whether the plotted lines print on top of the price bars or leave the price bars clear of any lines.

#7 Price bars with flag on hi/la gives you a choice of Gann's method of drawing a price bar or the more common method used by most chart services. This entry effects the chart printouts only, not the screen display.

Screen Preferences

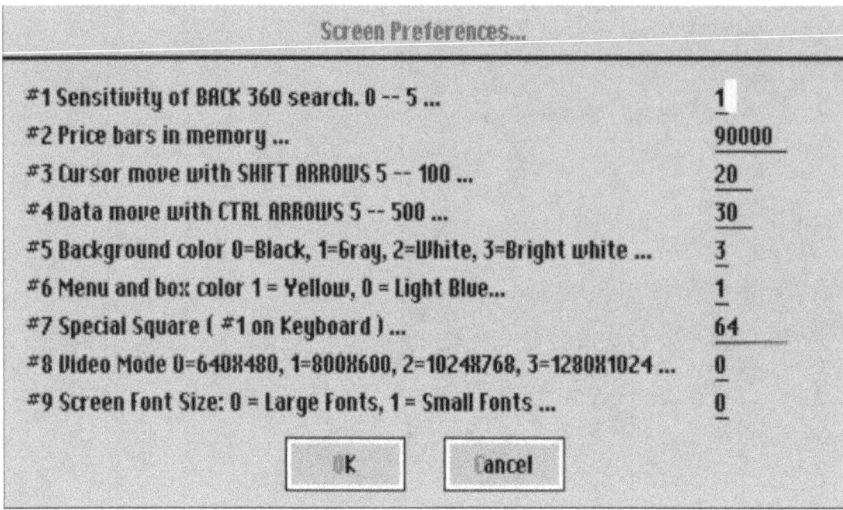

#1 Sensitivity of BACK 360 search 0 – 5 In the BACK 360 angle mode the program determines all highs and lows that are multiples of the circle back in time from the cursor position. Only those highs or lows that are 45, 60 or 72 time period multiples will be drawn. This number indicates the tolerance you are allowing for a hit. For example, if you set it to 1, a time period of 89, 90 and 91 days would be marked. Set it to O and only an exact hit of 90 days would be plotted. The pre-set value is 1.

#2 Price bars in memory... is set to 50000 bars. It should not need to be changed. This value corresponds to about 137 years of daily prices which is much more data than you are likely to have. Only a machine with very limited memory (< 4 Meg) would be effected.

#3 Cursor move with SHIFT ARROWS 5 -- 100 is set to 20 as a default. When you hold the <Shift> key and the left or right arrows the cursor will be moved this amount.

#4 Data move with CTRI ARROWS 5 -- 500 This number is set to 300 which corresponds to about 1/3 of the bars on the screen. It is only a relative value since the number of bars on the screen will vary depending on the spacing between the bars.

#5 Background color can be set to a value of 0 to 3 based on personal preferences. The bright white is best when printing screen dumps or pasting into other documents. A black background would print as black on a printer consuming large amounts of ink with poor results. The screen shots in this manual were created with the bright white background with the screen captures saved by hitting the <Print Screen> key. The results can be pasted into a paint program or word processor.

#6 Menu and box color permits you to set the box colors to your choice. This change won't take effect until the program is restarted.

#7 Special Square entry can be used to store a Gann square that is not one of the common sized squares. It is enabled with the #1 key on the keyboard. Its use will be described in the chapter tided Squares later in this manual. The value of 64 corresponds to the 'Murray Math Lines' value that was the rage a few years ago. It can be reset to any value you find useful.

#8 Video Mode lets you set your video mode to the SVGA or XVGA modes. A 17 inch monitor is best at 800X600, a 19 at 1024X768 and a 21 inch at 1280X1024 but you can try others on your system. The program must be restarted for these changes to take effect. This feature is not supported in NT3.51, 4.0 and 2000 at this time.

Once you have made any changes click OK and you will return to the previous box.

General Preferences

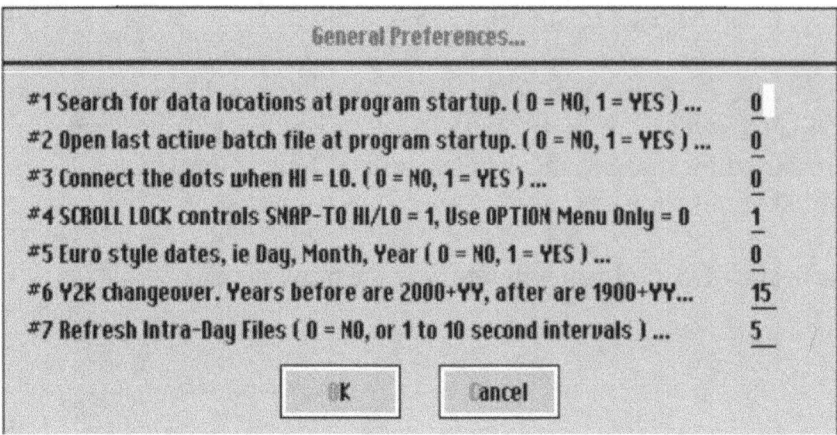

Item #1 enables the program to do its MASTER or QMASTER file search when the program is initially started. Once the list of files is build this way it will appear instantly when File: Load File is selected.

Item #2 will automatically open the last batch file used when the program is first started. You can immediately hit the <Tab> key to look through the batch entries. The use of Batch files is covered later in this manual.

Item #3 will make the program connect the 'dots' in the early part of a commodity contract when the high and low are the same price. With this feature disabled these prices would only appear as tiny, hard to see dots on the screen. This feature does not effect the printer output either way.

Item #4 effects the 'Snap-To' feature of the program. When you are moving the cursor with the mouse the 'Snap-To' will cause the cursor to snap to the high or low price of the price bar depending on which is closest. Normally the 'Snap-To' feature is enabled under the Option menu. If you normally use this feature you would need to disable it under the Option menu on those occasions when you didnk want the feature active. By enabling #5 the Scroll Lock key on the keyboard can also be used to change the status of the 'Snap-To' function.

Item #5 changes the program's date handling routines from the American method of MM/DD/YY to the military style of DD/MM/YY. The change effects date entry as well as output to the screen and printed charts.

Item #6 adds yet another way for the program to deal with the Y2K issue. In this default setting of 15, any year entered with 2 digits that is between 01 and 14 will be treated as YY + 2000. Any 2 digit year from 15-99 will be treated as 1900 + YY. Currently the dates in a data file are stored as YYMMDD. If your data vendor simply rolls over the date 991231 to 000101 this feature will treat those dates as 2000+ years and the program will run properly. With the current setting of 15 your data supplier has until 2014 to get their software truly Y2K compliant!

New Chart Preferences

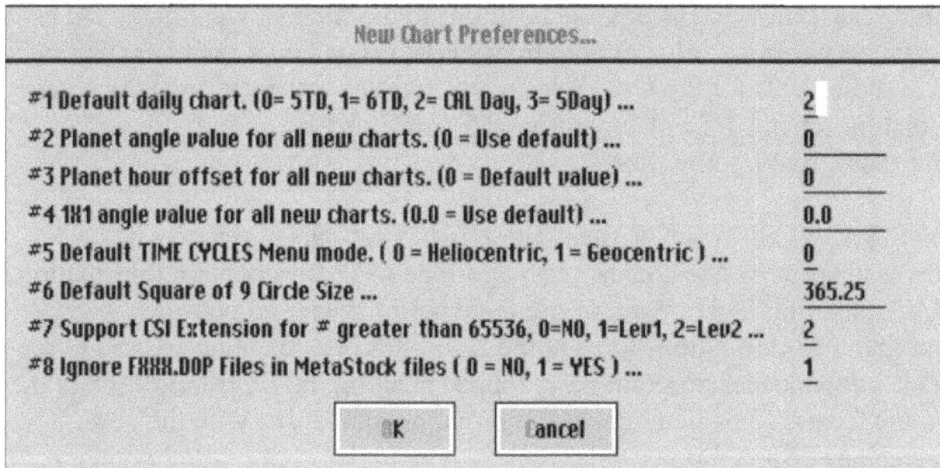

Chart effects how the program treats a chart that is loaded for the first time. These entries will be used unless there is a Default File Setup or a batch file entry associated with the file.

Item #1 determines the default style of daily chart such as 5 trading day, calendar day etc.

Item #2 can be used to set the planet angle multiplier to a default value. For example, some users may find themselves resetting the programs default value to their own preferred value such as 1.0. Entering the value here would saves the trouble of resetting the value with each new file.

Item #3 has a similar effect on the program's default planet hour value. The program uses 12 noon in Greenwich England as it's default value. This corresponds to 0° longitude at the Greenwich observatory. If you llo mostly at New York markets and would like the planet positions calculated for 9 AM New York time you woud enter a value of +2.0. New York is 5 times zones West so 12:00 noon Greenwich is 7:00 AM in NY setting the value to +2.0 would make it 9:00 AM in New York or 2:00 PM in Greenwich. Fractional hours may also be entered. To enter 15 minutes past the hour the value would be .25 or ¼ of 60 minutes.

Item#4 has the same effect on the 1x1 angle value for squares and angles.

Item#5 sets the defaults mode when any item under the Time Cycle menu is first selected.

Item #6 sets the default value for the circle size used in the Square of 9 portion of the program. Normally on a calendar day basis the circle of dates surrounding the Square of 9 would be equal to 365.25 days or one year. If you primarily use trading days this value could beset to 261 which is the number of trading days in a year assuming all holidays occur on the weekends. (365.25 x 5/7 = 261 or 261)

Item#7 activates CSI's new extended price specifications. Until recently no market prices exceeded 65536, the largest number usable with the original format. The S&P 500 at 655.36 and the DJIA at 6553.6 among others, have exceeded this limit. Extension level #1 expands the capacity to 262143 and extension level #2 is for future expansions. Extension #1 is recommended at this time. These new extensions use positions in the file that were marketed as 'reserved' and should have been set to a value of zero by your data supplier. If your supplier has not been putting a zero in these fields for the last 15 years you may see some spurious price bars on the screen with this feature activated. Contact your vendor, not Gannsoft for a fix or deactivate the feature for those troublesome files.

Item#8 ignores the MetaStock or CSI-M 'DOP' files. These files were part of the original Computrac format that was adopted by MetaStock years ago. The DOP files contain information about what is in the 'DAT' data files. After years of use the types of files used became standardized to the point that the information stores in the DOP files became unnecessary. IN a new release of MetaStock's downloader program they stopped creating the DOP fields unless the user explicitly activated the feature. This item makes the program compatible with the new downloader program but can be disabled if necessary.

Save Changes
You should save your changes to the System Configuration by clicking on the Save button or the Temporary button. The Temporary button will change the settings only until the program is restarted. The save button stores the changes on the disk so they will become the current default setting for the program.

Saving Default Values
Certain program settings can also be saved as defaults using this same Save button in System Configuration. Simply select Option: Configure System and click on the Save Button.

Discount Coupon for Purchase of Ganntrader 3.0 Software

The original purchaser of this book is entitled to take off the purchase price of this book or $100.00 to buy the software program Ganntrader 3.0 from Traders World. This book constitutes your manual.

Phone
You can do this by calling Traders World at 1-800-288-4266 or at 417-882-9697.

Fax
You can also fax this order to 1-417-886-5180

Mail
You can also mail this form to:
Traders World, 2508 W. Grayrock St., Springfield, MO 65810 (Shipping is free to anywhere.)

Ganntrader 3.0 Software……………………………………………………...……..$1695.00
Less Cost of Gann Masters II Book ……..…………………………………………..……100.00
Your Final Cost...………………………………………………………………….…..$1595.00

Method of Payment:
__ Check, __ MasterCard, __ Visa, __American Express

Number_____ Exp._____

Signature_____ Date_____

Ship To:

Name_____

Company_____

Address_____

City_____State_____Zip_____

Phone_____

Fax_____

E-Mail_____

www.ingramcontent.com/pod-product-compliance
Lightning Source LLC
Chambersburg PA
CBHW080240180526
45167CB00006B/2356